THE AGE OF CATACLYSM

THE AGE
OF CATACLYSM

By Alfred L. Webre

and Phillip H. Liss

Published by
BERKLEY PUBLISHING CORPORATION
Distributed by
G. P. PUTNAM'S SONS, NEW YORK

To our children, Erica, Freddie, and Miriam

Contents

PART III:
SURVIVAL AND REGENERATION

EPILOGUE:
THE FUTURE WORLD SOCIETY

APPENDIXES

Introduction

THERE have been two scientific revolutions of considerable dimension in the twentieth century, in nuclear energy and in the earth sciences.[1] The dimensions of the former are relatively well known: The holocausts of Hiroshima and Nagasaki, the preparations for global thermonuclear attack and retaliation during the postwar years, and the uncertain promise of nuclear energy to fuel the industrializing world. Much less appreciated—both in the policy councils of government and in the popular imagination—have been the implications of a profound revolution in the earth sciences, in the comprehension of the vast interior processes which govern the life of the planet mankind inhabits, and form its continents, mountain ranges, and ocean beds.

This revolution is occurring at the edge of a quarter century during which mankind will face its greatest collective challenge in recorded history: a rising pattern of dramatic and potentially catastrophic upheaval in the earth, the storm clouds of which are now unequivocally gathering. The period will bring with it massive earthquakes, tidal waves, floods, and droughts. It will witness the disappearance of vast stretches of existing land mass and the rising of new land masses. It may be accompanied by famine and the unprecedented disruption of the vulnerable civilization which has largely matured during the last half century.

It will involve the creation of new cities, the mass migration of populations across national borders, the cooperative production of food for the species in the few areas untouched by the upheavals, an explosion in science and in technology, logistical problems of a dimension beyond our wildest imaginings. It will bring perforce a return to wisdom and trust by man and be accompanied by a profound revolution in the human process and in the individual mind.

The period is a prelude to an era of world peace, and to

the unleashing of a level of creativity, cooperation, and happiness without precedent in human history. How man is to arrive at this era is largely within his hands. He is now coming into the knowledge which will potentially enable him to ride out the upheavals, and to resettle and reorganize in an intelligent fashion. This understanding—coming paradoxically in an age of rising emphasis on the limitations of reason—may, if heeded, become the new ark perching us securely on the dark waters of millennial flood.

Part I:

THE GATHERING STORM CLOUDS

We find in the records of the antiquities of man that the human race has progressed with a gradual growth of population . . . what most frequently meets our view is our teeming population; our numbers are burdensome to the world, which can hardly supply us from its natural elements; our wants grow more and more keen, and our complaints more bitter in all mouths, while nature fails in affording us her usual sustenance. In very deed, pestilence, and famine, and wars, and earthquakes have to be regarded as a remedy for nations, as a means of pruning the luxuriance of the human race.

—Tertullian, a Carthaginian writing in the third century A.D.[1]

Earthquake prediction, an old and elusive goal of seismologists and astrologers alike, appears to be on the verge of practical reality as a result of recent advances in the earth and material sciences.

—Christopher H. Scholz, Lamont-Doherty Geological Observatory, speaking before the American Geophysical Union, April 18, 1973, in Washington, D.C.[2]

Emergency situations such as earthquakes, famines, avalanches and wars force the development of a rational design for survival. At the moment these situations are undergoing particular scrutiny in schools of architecture around the world. It may be possible to use the world as a village—not only as an empty gesture, but by using the resources of one highly industrialized society to save the lives of another.

—Peter Cook, writing in EXPERIMENTAL ARCHITECTURE *(New York, Universe Books, 1970)*

1

1. Modern Earth Science

THE last decade has brought a revolution in the earth sciences comparable to the revolution in nuclear physics earlier in this century. The revolution has resulted not only in the development of radically revised theoretical models of the earth's behavior, but in a wide variety of analytical and predictive techniques and in a high technology with which to apply them. The techniques include the ability to analyze in detail trends and cycles in earth events over the course of millennia, and to predict with relative accuracy future trends of most natural disasters: earthquakes, hurricanes, floods, tidal waves, tornadoes, droughts, famine.

The revolution in the earth sciences has been dramatic and unexpected, and has afforded man an understanding of the dynamics of earth change, and the beginnings of an integrated view of the earth system. Importantly, it has made us realize that the apparently slow, normal rate of change in the earth to which we have all grown habituated does not occur independently from those changes conventionally termed catastrophic because of their suddenness and their unexpectedness. Both slow change and catastrophe function according to continuous, discoverable natural laws. Both can be measured and predicted. Both can, in principle, be anticipated and prepared for.

The single most dominant concept to recently emerge in the earth sciences is that of plate tectonics. The concept recognizes that the surface of the earth is composed of twenty or so large inverted curved plates in slow rolling motion, causing the continents to drift about the earth and the ocean floor to constantly renew itself.[1] Since its formulation in 1968, plate tectonics has permitted a rapid integration of findings in what the scientific world had habitually treated as independent disciplines: geophysics, geology, paleontology, geochemistry, hydrology, geodesy, oceanography, geography, and seismology.[2]

Plate tectonic theory has afforded strong evidence of a

3

single, relatively recent land mass composed of South America, Africa, India, Australia, and Antarctica.[3] It has reorganized many traditional views concerning the development of the earth's land masses and oceans, and the evolution and migration of its numerous forms of plant and animal life.[4] Importantly, for present purposes, plate tectonics has afforded a deeper understanding of the origins and mechanisms of what the United Nations has termed the most catastrophic of earth disturbances—the earthquake and its attendant phenomena: tsunamis (seismic tidal waves), volcanoes, landslides, fires, and floods.[5]

Much of this science is now in relative infancy. It appears to be maturing, however, at a time when man is undergoing a period of increased earth disturbance, and when he is grossly unprepared for an age of cataclysm.

There has been a dramatic increase in the rate and magnitude of certain types of natural catastrophe occurring about the earth during recent years, and especially during the years 1972 and 1973. These include:

1. Record flooding and inundation about the globe, especially in the United States, Central and South America, Australia, and the Indian subcontinent;

2. Record meteorological disturbance about the earth, including widespread and growing drought, and destructive and highly erratic storm weather such as tornado, hurricane, and unseasonal monsoons; and

3. Increased crop failure and consequent food shortage and famine in areas of the globe affected by natural catastrophe.

In addition, there have been unusual forms of seismic and volcanic disturbance occurring about the earth during recent years. These include:

1. Unusual levels and types of volcanic eruptions, especially in the South Pacific, the North Atlantic, the Caribbean, and the Sea of Japan;

2. Widespread seismic activity and earthquake about the earth, including shocks in areas such as Antarctica and the

eastern United States which have rarely felt earth disturbance;

3. The subsidence or rising of land masses about the earth,
especially along the Mid-Atlantic Ridge, in the northern
Pacific, and the eastern Mediterranean.

There has been an unprecedented increase in destruction
from natural catastrophe in the recent past in the United
States alone. In the twenty-four years since the passage of the
Disaster Assistance Act of 1950, there has been an average of
fourteen Presidential declarations of major disaster each
year. In recent years, the total of such declarations has
soared: twenty-nine in 1969, twenty-four in 1971, forty-eight
in 1972, thirty-five as of September, 1973.

The United States has in the past two years experienced
the most massive flooding in its recorded history. In June,
1972, torrential rains near Rapid City, South Dakota, took
237 lives and caused $150 million damage. In the same
month, tropical storm Agnes flooded over 5,000 square
miles of American land and caused $2 billion in damage. In
the spring of 1973, extensive flooding of the Mississippi
Valley left thirteen million acres of farm land under water,
causing $500 million in damage. The year 1973 brought a
record level of tornadoes in the United States, reaching 930
in the first eleven months of 1973.

The winter of 1972–1973 has been described as the worst
in living memory with "heavy snows in the Plains States,
unnaturally prolonged rains in the Midwest, freak spring
blizzards in the Upper-River States," over 600,000 livestock
animals destroyed, 50 percent of the Georgia peach crop
destroyed, and 30 to 45 percent of the California truck crop
destroyed.

A similar pattern has been experienced elsewhere about
the globe. Massive flooding along the Indus River in Pakistan
and northern India in August, 1973, was described as the
worst in memory and left five million persons homeless,
destroyed $250 million in rice, cotton, and sugar crops, and
seriously disrupted the Pakistani economy. Flooding along

the Ganges and the Brahmaputra rivers in November, 1970, resulted in the deaths of 500,000 persons and the destruction of one million acres of crops. A drought caused by the failure of the annual monsoon, in some cases for three successive years, has resulted in substantial crop failure —principally rice—along a belt encompassing nearly 800 million persons: the Philippines, Thailand, Bangladesh, and India. West Africa is in the throes of a six-year drought.

Major, and occasionally destructive, earthquakes have occurred over the past five years in Central and South America, California, Japan, the Soviet Union, the Middle East, and Southern Europe. Mexico, for example, experienced her most destructive earthquake in fifty years in August, 1973; Managua, Nicaragua, was largely destroyed in an earthquake in December, 1972. Unusual premonitory earthquakes have been felt in the American Northeast, the Georgia-South Carolina area, parts of the Midwest, and in the earthquake-prone West Coast.

The catastrophe-induced crop failure and resultant food shortage have the most disturbing present consequences. After a period of pessimism in the early 1960's about future world food stocks, the prevailing opinion among nutritionists was that "miracle grains" and agricultural technology would solve the world's food problems by the mid-1970's. The catastrophes of the early 1970's are bringing an abrupt and unexpected reversal of this judgment. In a real sense, the current world food shortage has caught the nutritional community by surprise. The shortage comes at a time when world food stores are, in absolute terms, at their lowest point in twenty years, and when world demand for food has increased 60 percent since 1950. There is substantial pressure on world wheat, corn, sorghum, and rice crops, and there has been an almost total and unprecedented failure of the Peruvian anchovy crop, traditionally a staple protein for world livestock. The shortage is to some extent reflected by the course of world commodity prices, which recently have achieved record levels. The closing price of wheat futures at the Chicago Board of Trade on February 14, 1974, was $6.115 per bushel, topping $6.00 a bushel for the first time in history. The record price follows eighteen months of trading during which a series of record prices for wheat were achieved. These milestone dates and prices are as follows:

August 31, 1972:	$2.00 a bushel
May 29, 1973:	$3.00 a bushel
August 6, 1973:	$4.00 a bushel
September 4, 1973:	$5.00 a bushel[6]

Similar increases were observed for the prices of corn, lard, and oats.

The shortage is placing substantial pressure on the populations of the Philippines, Bangladesh, Ceylon, Pakistan, India, and nine nations in drought-stricken West Africa. Food rationing of an extreme nature has been instituted in a number of the countries, and already serious food riots have erupted in India and the Philippines. During the last world food shortage of 1966–1967, famine was averted in India by the United States exporting one-fifth of its total wheat crop. The United States no longer has ample grain stocks and cannot be realistically counted on to help. The consensus of opinion among food experts is that the populations of these countries will be dependent on future local crops for survival. The success of these crops will largely be a function of the weather, and while one can make no hard predictions, there are no meteorological indications that the pattern of adverse weather which the earth has been recently experiencing will subside.

There is a divided but growing body of opinion that the high incidence of drought about the earth during recent years—and the disturbed meteorological patterns which accompany drought—are likely to continue for some time. Some of the more disturbing evidence in this regard is taken from an analysis of ice cores bored in the Greenland icecap by a geophysical team at Camp Century. The results of the effort indicated the occurrence of a period of abrupt climatic change at a time approximately 90,000 years before the present, including drastic changes in plant life along the Gulf of Mexico and rapid cooling of the Greenland icecap, from interglacial to glacial in character. The precise causes of the change and the specific earth events or catastrophes which may have accompanied them are not yet known. The findings detail, however, a number of present geologic trends which could signal a similar period of drastic earth disturbance, notably a general and rapid cooling of the ocean surface over the last thirty years.

The cooling has brought a marked decrease in precipitation about the earth and increased drought in many areas of the world: China, Southeast Asia, the Indian subcontinent, Africa, and parts of Eastern Europe. Moreover, what precipitation does occur tends to be erratic and often destructive in character. Thus, for example, the highly destructive monsoon which recently occurred in parts of the Philippines and Southeast Asia, and the period of extraordinarily erratic and inclement weather which plagued the North American continent over the past year.

Some opinion characterizes the global trend toward drought and meteorological disturbance as substantial and relatively long-termed. Professor Rhoades Fairbridge of Columbia University concludes, for example, that the general cooling which has characterized the earth for the last thirty years will continue and will result in a vast expansion of the arid zones of the earth. He notes that "the countries to be affected by increased desiccation with its associated scourges—droughts, soil erosion, starvation" include most of Asia, Australia, the Indian subcontinent, Africa, and South America. Another participant in the Camp Century ice core findings concludes that the conditions for a "catastrophic event"—presumably not unlike the earlier abrupt climatic change of 90,000 years ago—are present today.

Others have compared the general cooling and extraordinary weather of the past year to the "mini-ice age" which the earth suffered in the seventeenth century. One expert view of the climatological changes is described as follows:

> The World Meteorological Organisation is now considering a report which links the prolonged droughts in Africa and India with last year's poor harvests in Russia and China, and even the present dry summer in Britain, as symptoms of a major world-wide climatic change.
>
> Professor Lamb, who led the reporting team as director of the only climatology centre in Western Europe, at the University of East Anglia, is the foremost advocate of this theory. He argues that we are now experiencing what may be the greatest and most sustained shift in the world's climate since 1700. This shift, which began around 1950 and took definite shape in the 1960's, has not meant drier weather everywhere or all the time. In fact, the first sign of trouble was an excess of rainfall in equatorial Africa, where Lake Victoria started rising to dangerous heights. Climatologists, charting the patterns of rainfall and wind, discovered that the whole equatorial zone was perceptibly wetter than it had been in the first half of this century, while the arid and semi-arid zones north and south of the equator were correspondingly drier.
>
> Changes also occurred in the temperate zones, but these were patchier and less constant than in the lower latitudes, and resulted in alternating bouts of higher and lower rainfall. But still there was a pattern: in the United States, for example, rainfall along the East Coast was a significant 7–8 per cent down during the 1960's.
>
> Some meteorologists dismiss these phenomena as the normal and expected variations in weather from year to year. But climatologists of the Lamb school insist that they indicate a secular change which is likely to persist for the rest of the century unless man tilts the climatic balance, inadvertently or otherwise. This means that drought areas which have been marginally productive at the best of times may soon cease to support their present populations. One geographer has described this as desertification, or the southward movement of the Sahara. Another has called it a

new ice age, since the expansion of polar ice is one of the symptoms of the recent change. Mr. Lamb jibes at an ice age, but he believes we are on a downhill slope, heading toward conditions as cold as the coldest period in the past few hundred years.

The climatic shift was probably set off by fluctuations in the sun's heat. These fluctuations, possibly linked with sunspot activity, produced an expansion of the polar cap which in turn pushed circulating winds down toward the equator. The winds also grew weaker, so that instead of blowing out over the semi-arid areas and carrying equatorial rains with them they left clouds hanging over the equator which dropped the rain there. Weaker winds have similarly prevented rain from reaching areas far from oceans, such as Central Asia. Another aspect of the shifting winds is an increase in their variability. So while the general trend is towards colder, drier times, the changes from year to year may be even sharper than before.[7]

A more conservative opinion, notably the U.S. Environmental Data Service, rates as possible, but not probable, that the freakish weather of 1972–73, together with the general cooling of the past thirty years, represent a return to the mini-ice age of the seventeenth century. It does concede that the worldwide trend toward drought and disturbed climatic patterns is apt to continue for some time. The United States, for example, has been visited every twenty years this century by a drought as regular as clockwork. In 1973 there was a disturbingly persistent deficiency of rainfall in the Dakotas and Minnesota which may be the beginning of the drought. There is, moreover, no reliable basis on which to judge whether the trend toward drought in the Asia-India-Africa belt and in Eastern Europe will break in the near future.

2. Earthquake

ALTHOUGH the popular memory has generally retained only a dim outline of the destructive reality of earthquakes, they have in history been among the most devastating levelers of man and his works. The losses of the Asian earthquakes, coming even long before the advent of an industrial—and more fragile—society, are legendary: 830,000 dead in Shensi, China, in 1556; 300,000 in Calcutta in 1737; 180,000 in Kansu, China, in 1920; 143,000 dead in Tokyo and Yokohama in 1923. Other familiar places have suffered: Lisbon, Portugal, with 60,000 dead in 1755; Messina, Italy, with 75,000 dead in 1908; Huaraz, Peru, with 66,794 in 1970.[1] These deaths must be seen in the accompanying context of massive numbers of maimed or wounded, the destruction of wide portions of urban centers, and serious disruptions of local societies and economies.[2]

Earthquakes of serious dimensions have occurred in the past with relatively little loss of life, but in areas which are now populated and industrially developed. Although it is not generally appreciated, the United States has experienced a number of serious earthquakes in the course of the past three hundred years. Many of the earthquakes have occurred in the Northeast, in the Southeast, and in parts of the Midwest, all geographical areas not normally associated in the popular imagination with earthquake activity. Earthquakes of the highest intensity, in some cases felt over an area of more than 2,000,000 square miles, occurred in the New York State-St. Lawrence area in 1663; in Boston, Massachusetts, in 1755; along the Mississippi Valley in 1811 and 1812; at Charleston, South Carolina, in 1886; and in Central and Southern California in 1857, 1872, and 1906.[3]

Yet with the exception of the 1906 San Francisco earthquake, the United States has fortunately escaped any major damage to populations and to cities. The large earthquakes of the country's history have taken place in the sparsely

11

settled areas or unhurried cities of the past two centuries. Almost uniformly they occurred at times of day which minimized damage to human life. Were the same geographical areas to experience similar earthquakes today, the results would probably be catastrophic.

Although its dominant theories trace their origins to classical Greece, seismology—the study of earthquakes and their attendant phenomena—is a young science. Since the introduction of systematic quantitative methods in the late nineteenth century, the science has concentrated on two central points: an understanding of the genesis of earthquakes and of their mechanisms and an explication of the earth waves which are continuously being recorded at seismographic observatories.

It is now generally agreed that most natural earthquakes find their source in the accumulation of strain in the earth's interior resulting from the slow convective movement of the massive tectonic plates covering its surface.[4] The immediate cause of earthquake is persuasively argued to be dilatancy —massive cracking of interior rock in response to the accumulation of tectonic strain. The release of energy at the time of a quake reflects a failure in the weakened rock and an abrupt easing of the accumulated strain.[5] It is, moreover, accompanied by earth waves which propagate both through the interior of the earth (shear waves) and along its surface (compressional waves).

The entire process may take centuries. It is, however, accompanied by certain identifiable precursors. The behavior of these precursors forms the basis of recent and dramatic breakthroughs in the ability to predict earthquakes with scientific accuracy, and thus relieve man of the uncertainty with which he has been forced in the past to confront them.[6]

The breakthrough is not uncontroversial. The venerable C. F. Richter, credited with developing the most widely used scale of earthquake magnitude, has observed:

I don't define [earthquake prediction]. I think that harping on prediction is something between a will-of-the-wisp and a red herring.[7]

As recently as mid-1971, senior U.S. scientists were openly pessimistic to a Senate committee about the possibility of developing reliable earthquake prediction techniques, despite earlier reports of reliable predictions of large quakes by both Japanese and Soviet scientists.[8] An editorial in *Nature* magazine in January, 1973, suggested, in a burst of modern fatalism, that earthquake prediction was useless if the evacuated inhabitants of a destroyed city had no homes to return to. Better they should perish with the act was the clear implication.[9]

Yet, in a paper delivered to the American Geophysical Union in the spring of 1973, three young Columbia University seismologists reported that they had developed a simple, elegant, and reliable model for predicting earthquakes. The model can, in many cases, predict the location, magnitude, and time of occurrence of an earthquake years in advance.[10] The method centers on dilatancy—the network of cracking that appears in subterranean rock well before the triggering of a quake—and on six measurable phenomena which not only accompany dilatancy, but give a precise indication of the time and the intensity of the coming shock.

In brief, the precursory period before an earthquake is accompanied by a number of observable changes in these commonly known phenomena. There are specific deformations in the tilt of the earth's surface which follow regular laws. There are increases in the electrical conductivity of the ground and marked changes in the chemical composition of groundwater in the quake area. Other traditional seismological indicators—the velocity of local earth waves; the level of subliminal trembling of the earth; the configuration of interior earth stresses—all follow uniform and measurable patterns during the period preceding the release of a quake.

The calculation of the intensity and time of occurrence of a future quake results from the rather simple application of certain extrapolating techniques to readings obtained from observation of the one or more of the precursory phenomena. The nature of the physical relationships between the precursory phenomena and the triggering of the quake is such that an earthquake of high intensity will afford proportionally longer warning times than one of lower intensity. Thus the time of occurrence of a minor earthquake may be known days or weeks in advance. The time of occurrence of a major shock may be known years in advance.

The reliability of the prediction technique is uncanny. The developers of the technique report that they applied it to data obtained in thirty major and intermediate earthquakes of the recent past. They were successful in retroactively calculating the location, time of occurrence, and magnitude of each of the quakes.[11] They found, for example, that had the technique been fully applied in the 1971 San Fernando earthquake, it would have successfully indicated the certainty of a coming quake nearly three and a half years prior to the event. It would have indicated the location, magnitude, and time of occurrence of the earthquake approximately six months in advance of the event. The sole prerequisite for obtaining this remarkable information for future quakes would have been an adequate monitoring system.

Although the technique is far from perfected, the promise is that it can be widely operational in the short-term future, given adequate funding of the science. Before this scientific revolution, man had to accept earthquake as an unpredictable Act of God. Now, man has before him the possibility of knowing where and when disaster could strike. The implications of this knowledge are vast and difficult to absorb. Can man act rationally and effectively to minimize loss of life and general suffering?

There are gathering signs that this question is not without consequence. Clear and incontrovertible evidence exists that large and densely populated areas of the globe face destruction from natural disaster: from earthquake, tidal wave, flood, and drought. There is evidence of a growing pattern in nature which is fundamentally hostile to man and which will persist through the next generation. While science does not yet know the exact intensity of these disasters, and their precise times of occurrence, it does know for a fair certainty that they are coming. While scientists still disagree on how widespread the pattern of natural hostility will be, it is known that at least a sixth of mankind, 500 million persons, will be affected by earthquake alone. Moreover, the coming disasters are in large measure likely to occur in areas of the globe which have no recent memory of natural catastrophe, and where a modern civilization has grown up largely ignorant of and, in many cases, openly scoffing at nature.

Science has established that the rate and magnitude and location of earthquakes, droughts, floods, and tidal waves varies considerably over time, from century to century and from epoch to epoch. The pattern of natural disaster which the earth experiences is thus far from random. It is likely, though not yet completely provable, a pattern which increases and decreases according to fixed laws over long periods of time.

Most of the quakes which the earth experiences are concentrated along a small number of belts corresponding roughly to the boundaries between the huge plates forming the surface of the earth. (See Map I, page 79.) It is the collisions and convective motions of these plates which are credited with giving rise to the stresses producing earthquakes. The largest of the belts, the Circum-Pacific Belt, includes the entire rim of the Pacific Ocean: Central and South America, and the Pacific Coast of the United States up through Alaska, Japan, and the Philippine Islands. Two other major belts cut through the Himalayas and the Mediterranean to the Azores in the Atlantic; from the Arctic Ocean through the Mid-Atlantic ridge to the Antarctic, and around the southern tip of Africa into the Indian Ocean.[12]

Many of the countries bordering the belts exhibit all the

structural characteristics of high vulnerability to earth-quakes. Japan lies at the boundary of two massive tectonic plates, one of which is being thrust under the other. The entire country is crisscrossed with active faults. A similar condition obtains both along the coast of Central and South America and along the Pacific Coast of the United States. Although none of the most recent prediction techniques have yet been applied in these areas, the general opinion among the earth science community is that these areas may experience major earthquakes within the foreseeable future.

In its 1972 Report to the Congress, the President's Office of Emergency Preparedness (OEP)—now known as the Federal Disaster Assistance Administration and administratively part of the Department of Housing and Urban Development—starkly concluded that a half billion people—a sixth of the human race—were directly vulnerable to the destruction of earthquakes occurring in the foreseeable future:

> Earthquake-prone areas include some of the most densely populated regions in the world, such as Japan, Western United States, and the shores of the Mediterranean Sea. It is estimated that over 500 million persons could well suffer damage to their property, while a significant proportion of them are in danger of losing their lives in severe earthquakes.[13]

There is a growing though still divided opinion among earth scientists that the earth is entering a period of increased seismic disturbance. The implications of the trend are serious and disturbing. Many areas of high seismic risk—earthquake-proneness—about the earth have in recent years developed into populated and vulnerable metropolitan areas. Thus the potential consequences of earthquake have radically increased from the recent past.

The consensus of opinion among seismologists is that large portions of Central California are vulnerable to major earthquake. California is along a juncture point of the massive tectonic plates on which the Pacific Ocean, North America, and South America rest. Large destructive earthquakes have in the recent past occurred in Chile, Nicaragua, and Mexico and are thought to be an indication of the buildup of enormous tectonic strain along the Pacific coasts of North and South America. Most seismologists agree that the moderate-sized earthquake which struck the San Fernando Valley in February, 1971, probably aggravated and increased the accumulated strain in the area, and make a massive earthquake there more likely.

There is some division of opinion as to when the California earthquake might occur. Most U.S. seismologists tend to conservatively place the event at between one and three decades away. A group of Soviet seismologists is less conservative and has suggested that Central California might expect massive shocks and associated tidal waves "sometime between 1973 and 1975."[14] The recent Central and South American quakes tend to make the Soviet viewpoint more compelling.

Interestingly, the most significant factor in determining division of opinion among seismologists as to the likelihood of an earthquake appears to be nationality. Seismologists of one country tend to be more pronouncedly conservative in their predictions of earthquakes within their nation than elsewhere. The total pattern indicates that the more realistic (consensual) predictions about the possibility of earthquake in a particular nation tend to come from foreign seismologists.

The predictive techniques which will permit the calculation of the exact intensity, duration, and time of occurrence of a major California earthquake are still in their infancy. A number of seismological groups at the Lamont-Doherty Geological Observatory in New York and at various research facilities in California are experimenting with techniques which give a remarkably accurate prediction of minor earthquakes. It is likely that these techniques will soon be refined to a point where they can be employed on large earthquakes of the size of the expected California quake. This would permit a fair prediction of the probable intensity, location, and time of occurrence of the quake.

There exist widely varying opinions as to the precise extent of the damage of the coming California earthquake. In a general assessment, the California legislature's Joint Committee on Seismic Safety concluded as early as September, 1971, that "the present risk of life from earthquakes in California is at an unacceptable level."[15] The data upon which to base a precise estimate of damage has not as yet been fully developed. There is a relatively wide range of opinion as to the potential for destruction of a major quake in California. Even the most conservative estimates, however, foresee widespread and sizable destruction.

The range varies widely with the predicted time of day, location, and intensity of the quake. The variables considered include the number of deaths, injury, the physical devastation of dams, power plants, highways, and buildings. It includes, moreover, an assessment of the serious blow to the nation's economy, productive capacity, and morale which a major California quake would produce.

The estimates of potential damage are in some cases staggering. Professor Peter A. Franken, former acting director of the Pentagon's Advanced Projects Research Agency, estimates 1,000,000 dead in the coming California earthquake.[16] He further postulates that since the quake would probably originate between San Francisco and Los Angeles, the resulting shock waves could very well devastate both cities. The details of Professor Franken's estimate would do justice to any epic of cataclysm. He calculates the destruction of both the Golden Gate and Bay bridges, thus isolating San Francisco from evacuation and outside help, and effectively trapping the city's population to face the certainty of widespread fire and seismic tidal wave. Professor Franken foresees the widespread collapse of freeway systems in Los Angeles, severely hampering evacuation and regrouping. Needless to say, the effect of this level of devastation both on the local society and economy, and on that of the nation at large, would be traumatic and cruel. Other estimates of destruction in the San Francisco Bay Area alone place the total potential loss at up to $1.4 billion, depending on the magnitude, location, and time of occurrence of the quake, and foresee the loss of between 10,360 and 100,000 lives.[17]

Compounding the certainty of damage from quakes originating in California's fault system are scientific predictions as to the probability of destruction to the California coast from seismic tidal waves generated by undersea earthquakes occurring in the Pacific. The Soviet prediction alluded to earlier postulates three or four seismic tidal waves which would threaten the West Coast of North America before 1976. The tidal waves would occur, according to this view, along a Taiwan-Alaskan axis, thus presumably threatening the coast of Japan as well.

There is no strong reason for discounting these predictions. The National Oceanographic and Atmospheric Administration (NOAA) compilation of earthquake-generated Pacific tsunamis occurring in the period 1900–1970 lists nine seismic tidal waves of major destructive impact, and thirty-four of intermediate intensity.[18] Although Canada and the western U.S. coast have suffered only four tsunamis of minor intensity in the period, Alaska experienced three tidal waves, in 1946, 1957, and 1964. South America experienced two such waves, in 1922 and 1960; Japan, one in 1923, as a result of the Tokyo-Yokohama quake. Destructive tidal waves in the Pacific are thus not uncommon events. Unfortunately, their effects can be of serious magnitude. The OEP report notes:

> In disasters caused by earthquakes that generate tsunamis, landslides and other serious secondary effects, the tsunami can be the greatest hazard to human life. Tsunamis, major and local, took the most lives in the Alaskan earthquake of 1964. . . .In 1960, the people of Hilo, Hawaii, suffered 61 dead and 282 injured from a tsunami of distant origin, an earthquake in Chile.[19]

There is a growing likelihood that parts of the northeastern and southeastern United States may experience moderate to large earthquakes in the near future. Again, there is no very clear notion of the exact location, probable intensity, or time of occurrence of the shocks, and that will have to wait the development of these new predictive techniques. Although not as much is known about the typically deep-focus earthquakes that characterize the eastern part of the nation, it is generally accepted that they are in some measure caused by strain accumulated along the juncture of the Pacific Ocean plate and the North American plate. Thus, increased strain along the California coast in turn tends to aggravate inner earth strains in the eastern part of the nation.

The standard seismic risk map of the United States has divided the country into a series of zones ranked on a scale from 0 to 3, corresponding to the local area's vulnerability to earthquake damage.[20] (See Map II, page 80.) Areas falling in zone 3 are considered areas of maximum seismic risk and vulnerable to "major damage" from earthquakes. The map is based on the known distribution and intensity of earthquakes and on evidence of strain release and consideration of major geologic structures believed to be associated with earthquake activity. Apart from the states of California and Nevada, the following areas of the country are classified in zone 3: northwest Washington State; two continuous areas composed of portions of Montana, Wyoming, Idaho, and Utah, and of Missouri, Tennessee, Illinois, and Kentucky; Charleston, South Carolina; Boston, Massachusetts; and the St. Lawrence area.

Approximately one-third of the nation is classified in zone 2, areas subject to "moderate" earthquake damage and correspond to quakes of VII intensity on the MM (Modified Mercalli—see Appendix III) scale. These areas include most of the land mass west of New Mexico and substantial portions of the Northeast, Southeast, and Midwest.

It is true, as the Office of Science and Technology has pointed out, that great, potentially destructive earthquakes have not been frequent events in the United States during the past half-century.[21] Yet it is quite probable that this geologically short period of earthquake quiescence has functioned to permit the development of potentially catastrophic subsurface stresses in the earth, thus increasing the probability of massive quake. Moreover, the vulnerability of the United States—and the rest of the developed world—to earthquake has exponentially increased with the growth and complexity of industrialized society. Professor Clarence R. Allen of the California Institute of Technology points out:

> . . . the pressures of population growth are causing expansion into areas that are more difficult to develop safely than those of past decades—often into mountainous areas, active fault zones, or areas of artificial fill that necessarily have earthquake related problems associated with them.
>
> Society is rapidly becoming more complex and interdependent; so that we are becoming increasingly reliant on critical facilities whose loss can create major disasters.
>
> The increasing population density in some of our cities creates problems such as a very localized earthquake causing a major catastrophe, such as was not possible some years ago.[22]

This certainty of major earthquake in the foreseeable future is not limited in the United States to areas—such as California—which have traditionally been associated with earthquake hazard in the popular mind. The National Academy of Science Task Force on the Alaskan earthquake of 1964 concludes that: "Before the end of this century, it is virtually certain that one or more major earthquakes will occur on the North American Continent."[23] Areas of high seismic risk on this continent include, you will recall, portions of the Midwest, the northeastern and southeastern United States, and Canada.

Other scholars, such as Professor Carl Kisslinger of the University of Colorado (one of the only U.S. institutions with an ongoing program of research on the social effects of earthquakes), agree with this assessment. In a review of seismological developments during 1972 published in the January, 1973, issue of *Geotimes*, Dr. Kisslinger concludes:

> Although the number of large earthquakes east of the Rocky Mountains is much smaller than to the west, the much larger areas of high intensity for a given magnitude in the east makes the longterm risk, in terms of potential damage to property and loss of lives, roughly as great as in the west.[24]

This conclusion is based on a number of factors: the long absence of large earthquakes in the eastern United States, a pattern of premonitory earthquakes which is now appearing in the Northeast, the Southeast, and parts of the Midwest, and the occurrence of earthquakes along the Pacific juncture.

The properties of the earth's crust in the eastern part of the United States substantially compound the risk of massive damage resulting from a major earthquake. The land mass in the East is characterized by a relatively rigid crust, thus permitting the destructive energy released in a quake to be transmitted and felt in much wider areas surrounding the epicenter of the quake. This contrasts to the crust in the western part of the country, whose heavily fractured structure permits the attenuation of destructive shocks caused by earthquakes, and their confinement to a much smaller area of land around the quake's center.

The variation is dramatically demonstrated by the large differences in the total felt area of past major earthquakes occurring in the eastern and western parts of the continental land mass. In the eastern land mass, for example, the Canadian earthquake of 1870 (Mercalli intensity 8) was felt over an area of 1,000,000 square miles; the Missouri earthquake of 1811 (Mercalli intensity 12) was felt over an area of 2,000,000 square miles; the Charleston, South Carolina, earthquake of 1886 (Mercalli intensity 10) was felt over an area of 2,000,000 square miles. By contrast, the largest quake to occur on the western land mass, the San Francisco quake of 1906 (Mercalli intensity 11), was felt in an area of 375,000 miles, considerably less than the figures in the eastern quakes.[25]

The precursory signals of a period of major earthquake hazard are gathering in the eastern United States. Most recently, a minor earthquake (Richter magnitude 4.5) on June 15, 1973, reportedly "rattled windows and doors in much of the northeast U.S. and eastern Canada." Dr. Benjamin Howel of Pennsylvania State University indicated that the shock may very well have been a precursor of a much more intensive series of earthquakes centered in the St. Lawrence Valley.[26] The last major quake in this area, in 1663 (Mercalli intensity 11 to 12 at the epicenter), was felt in all of eastern Canada and the northeastern United States.[27] Although the damage in that quake was relatively limited because of the sparse settlement of the area, the same would not be true today, when 24 percent of the United States population is concentrated in the Northeast.

A pattern of felt intrusion into the routine of daily life in the East by small and precursory earthquakes appears to be emerging. For example, New York State officials were forced to halt mining operations by the Texas Brine Company in upper New York because of the high level of seismicity—earth rumbling—that the operations were causing, and because of the known seismic risk in the area.[28] Relatively rare and perhaps premonitory earthquakes have begun to occur in areas of known high seismicity in the United States: New Jersey, New York, Illinois, Wisconsin, Iowa, Indiana, Michigan, Missouri, Pennsylvania, South Carolina, and Georgia.[29] In the Southeast, relatively unusual and perhaps premonitory earthquakes have occurred in South Carolina and in Georgia (the last major earthquake in the area was in 1886). Significant and perhaps premonitory earthquakes have been taking place in the Mississippi Valley area, notably a shock which occurred several years ago and was widely felt in southern Illinois and

southeastern Missouri, the location of the single most powerful earthquake in the country's history in 1811. Robert M.
Hamilton, of the U.S. Geological Survey, a seismologist of
relatively conservative judgment, indicated he "would not be
surprised if there were a destructive earthquake in that area
[the Mississippi Valley]."

Although no precursor monitoring system exists in the
East, and consequently no precise prediction of the time of
occurrence, location, and magnitude of earthquakes in the
area is available, the above data strongly suggest the potential
for occurrence of intermediate and major quakes in areas
east of the Rocky Mountains within the foreseeable future.

It is difficult to arrive at a reliable assessment of potential
damage. What is known is that the vast majority of U.S. cities
vulnerable to earthquake are badly designed to resist seismic
shock and badly prepared to respond to earthquake. No
systematic estimates of potential damage have apparently yet
been drawn for cities in the northeastern, southeastern, and
midwestern portions of the nation, and the most notable
opinion in this regard thus far is that of Dr. Kisslinger, who
concludes that whatever actual level of long-term damage
from earthquakes may be, it is likely to be as high in the East
as in the West.

It is likely that major destruction from earthquake in other
parts of the globe will increase. Japan is a prime example.
The country has had a long history of earthquakes—the last
major quake killed 143,000 persons in the Tokyo-Yokohama
area in 1923—and the country is crisscrossed by major active
fault systems. There recently has been an increased incidence of unusually powerful (though luckily not destructive)
premonitory earthquakes in Japan. The nearly unanimous
opinion among seismologists is that what is now the most
urbanized portion of Japan is soon due for a major, perhaps
cataclysmic earthquake.

This assessment flows from the incidence of major and
premonitory tremors along the western side of the Circum-
Pacific Belt, often referred to as "the rim of fire."[30] Major
earthquakes have been recorded since 1968 in the Philip-

pines, Australia, China, the U.S.S.R., New Guinea, the Solomon Islands, New Zealand, and Japan. A number of the earthquakes were above 8.0 intensity on the Richter scale and in the range of the highest intensity known to man. Japan has probably seen the most dangerous and intensive quakes, and the earthquake of May 16, 1968, for example, registered 8.25 on the Richter scale, ranking it among the world's most powerful. The total solar eclipse in July, 1973, was accompanied by four sizable earthquakes. Three of these occurred on the northern portion of the Circum-Pacific Belt, and the last of these occurred in Iran. Extremely rare earthquakes have occurred as recently as February 8, 1971, in Antarctica.

In July, 1973, Japanese seismologists reported the detection of unusual earth movements and faults in the Tokyo area. These give signs of being the precursors of a major earthquake of the dimension of the 1923 Tokyo-Yokohama quake. Ominously, Japan has experienced serious quakes as recently as June 17, 1973, when a quake of Richter magnitude 7.9 struck northern Japan.

Again, there is some division of opinion on the potential time of occurrence, intensity, and destructiveness of the expected quakes. Interestingly, the U.S. seismologists tend to be decidedly less conservative than the Japanese in this regard. One U.S. seismologist sees a relatively imminent major earthquake. Japanese seismologists tend to place the event in the somewhat longer-range future, involving a shock comparable to the 1923 Tokyo-Yokohama quake. An event of this magnitude would, in the absence of intense preparation, be cataclysmic and involve the loss of a substantial portion of the nation's population and productive capacity. Further study may yield a more refined estimate of the expected earthquake. In the meantime, Japanese officials actively conduct earthquake drills, and there is every indication—from best sellers on the topic to earthquake kits in the department stores—that the population has the possibility of earthquake in mind.

The eastern side of the Pacific rim has equally disquieting

signs. As mentioned earlier, there is a substantial concurrence of opinion on the imminence of an earthquake of major proportions in California, the magnitude of which has probably been increased by the 1971 San Fernando quake. Unusual earthquake activity—such as a June 16, 1973, quake in Portland, Oregon—has begun to occur along the North American edge. Evidence of substantial tectonic strains along this edge of the Circum-Pacific Belt are probably most evidenced by the major Alaska earthquake of 1964, the Managua, Nicaragua earthquake of December 23, 1972, and the Mexican earthquake of August, 1973.

The condition appears the same in the Central American-Caribbean area and on the South American continent. Since 1968, major earthquakes have occurred along the Pacific coast of Central and South America in Mexico, Nicaragua, Ecuador, Peru, and Chile, including a major quake in northern Peru in 1970 which killed 66,794. Along the Caribbean, there have been recent signs of increased seismic strain, as in 1968 when the Leeward Islands experienced the largest earthquake ever recorded in the eastern Caribbean. Both Venezuela, which suffered a major earthquake in Caracas in 1967, and Colombia have recently experienced moderate and perhaps premonitory earthquakes, as has the greater Antilles area, particularly Cuba.

The same pattern is emerging along the Himalayan-Mediterranean belt. Major and perhaps premonitory earthquakes have occurred in the last five years in Turkey, Iran, Ethiopia, the Red Sea area, Yugoslavia, Sicily, Central Italy, and Portugal. For some of the areas this represents the highest level of seismic activity in 500 years. The Portuguese earthquake of February, 1969, registered 8.0 on the Richter scale, which was its largest since the devastating Lisbon earthquake of 1755 which traumatized the whole of Western Europe. Iran, for example, experienced major earthquakes on June 30, 1973, and April 11, 1972, and two others of similar dimension in 1962 and 1968.

Turkey experienced substantial earthquakes in 1970 and 1966. In the most recent episode, Ancona, Italy, was struck in late June, 1972, by the largest series of earthquakes in 500 years. At the end of the series, only 10,000 of the original 110,000 of the city's inhabitants had chosen to remain within the city.[31] An earthquake hit Tuscania, Italy, in February, 1973, bringing with it a destruction of art works as large as that caused by the flood which ravaged Florence in 1966.

The pattern extends to the Mid-Atlantic Ridge area, in a line running down the Atlantic Ocean from Iceland to Antarctica. Iceland has recently experienced a series of dramatic seismic events, including considerable volcanic activity, and the subsidence of large land masses. Farther down along the ridge there has been considerable underwater earthquake activity, including a strong shock on August 28, 1973.

This litany of seismic dramas has not been compiled from a single source, nor from sources that are not readily available to the public at large. Our major sources have been the Smithsonian Institution's Center for Short-Lived Phenomena, the U.S. Geological Survey's Preliminary Determination of Epicenters, and the country's leading newspapers and scientific journals. To our surprise we have encountered no single article which attempts to inform the public of the total of this threatening pattern of natural hostility.

Absent in the foregoing data has been a feeling for the trauma and horror that an earthquake inflicts on the city it strikes. The Managua, Nicaragua, earthquake of December 23, 1972 (Richter magnitude 5.6), provides a good inkling of the scenarios we might expect should densely populated metropolitan areas be hit by great earthquakes in the near future. The Managua earthquake was studied by at least thirty-nine groups of geologists, seismologists, and engineers from seven different countries in the weeks following the disaster. Thus, much information has been marshaled on the human impact of the earthquake. (For a fuller discussion of the implications of Managua, see Appendix II, Robert W. Kates, et al., "Human Impact of the Managua Earthquake.")

Although the magnitude of the Managuan quake was

moderate rather than severe, its effect on the physical structure of the city, its economy, and its population was devastating. The above-noted American investigators point out that:

> When the sun rose over the city of Managua on Sunday, 23 December, out of an estimated population of 420,000 at least 1 percent were dead, 4 percent injured, 50 percent (of the employed) jobless, 60 percent fleeing the city, and 70 percent temporarily homeless. In this nation of 2 million people, at least 10 percent of the industrial capacity, 50 percent of the commercial property, and 70 percent of the governmental facilities were inoperative. To restore the city would require an expenditure equal to the entire annual value of Nicaraguan goods and services. In a country where the per capita gross national product is about $350 per year, the 75 percent of Managua's population affected by the earthquake had, on the average, a loss of property and income equivalent to three times that amount.[32]

One journalist's account of the period immediately following the quake paints in vivid detail some of the more brutalizing aspects of the experience:

> *Shroud of Dust.* The first awful shock came at 12:28 A.M. in two jolts lasting only a few seconds. "It was a muffled, continuous explosion," says John Barton, a U.S. Information Service official. "It hurt your ears, teeth and bones." Nicaraguan businessman Jürgen Sengelmann found his house shaking so violently that he could not get out of bed at first. He finally managed to reach a balcony. "I saw dust rise like a blanket being lifted all across the city," says Sengelmann. "The dust rose to about 1000 feet, until I saw nothing but dust and fires."
>
> Santos Jiménez, a physician who was the volunteer chief of the Managua fire department, ran into the street with his family, then realized that a 14-year-old son had been left behind. Darting back into the house, Jiménez dug the boy from the rubble and carried him out just as the building collapsed. The youngster had stopped breathing, but

Jiménez was able to revive him with artificial respiration. Then Jiménez thought of his other responsibility and set off for fire headquarters.

He was stunned by what he saw: Managua was burning, and most of its fire-fighting equipment lay crushed almost flat beneath hundreds of tons of masonry. It made little difference: most streets were blocked by rubble, and there was no water in hydrants. Jiménez and his firemen sat down on a curb, dazed into momentary helplessness.

Two hundred people had been attending office Christmas parties that evening in La Plaza nightclub on the city's main square. The orchestra was playing a bolero when, suddenly, the roof collapsed on the dance floor, killing many couples. Survivors leaped in panic through plate-glass windows. One man was trapped by a beam that fell on his ankle. Rescue teams tried for the rest of the night to free him. Finally, they put a tourniquet on his leg and chopped his foot off with a machete.

The next day, Saturday, would have been payday in Managua, with Christmas bonuses also being distributed. Hundreds of sidewalk peddlers, counting on their best sales of the year, had gone to sleep with their families around the block-square Central Market building so as to get an early start in the morning. With the first shock of the earthquake, the masonry structure had collapsed. Sparking electric wires touched off a conflagration. Unknown numbers of people perished.

Fifty men and women were locked in cells in an ancient downtown jail called El Hormiguero (The Ant Heap). The men who survived seized the opportunity to escape through gaps in the walls. Women prisoners, confined in another section, were unable to get out and screamed for help. A guard ran back into the crumbling building, unlocked the doors and freed them.

Dr. Augustín Cedeño, chief of the emergency room at the 800-bed General Hospital, Managua's largest, had had a quiet evening, without a single emergency case. When the quake hit, however, the building cracked apart, killing perhaps 75 patients, including 17 babies in the nursery ward. Despite the danger, nurses ran into the hospital time and again to get patients out. One nurse scooped up eight premature babies, put them in a cardboard box, and rode with them in a car to the city of Léon, 50 miles away. Whenever an infant turned blue, she applied a portable respirator. All eight survived.

Within an hour, there were 500 new patients at General Hospital, brought by automobiles. Cedeño asked the drivers to keep their headlights on so that doctors and nurses could see. They strung bottles of intravenous fluids from bushes and, kneeling in the dust, stopped hemorrhages and set fractures. Cedeño himself performed three emergency amputations by flashlight. Eventually, 5000 casualties were processed on the ground in front of the wrecked hospital.

Ground Zero. When dawn came, a fire engine arrived from Costa Rica, the firemen having driven hellbent for six hours. They looked around and gave up. Fires burned everywhere. The devastation in down-town Managua resembled Hiroshima's Ground Zero. Twelve hundred acres there —nearly two square miles—were totally destroyed. An estimated 90 percent of the buildings elsewhere in the city were either demolished or badly damaged. Approximately 300,000 persons—75 percent of Managua's population of 400,000—were made instantly homeless. Thousands of corpses lay in the ruins; relatives clawed at the debris, seeking them.

Not only had there been a terrible catastrophe, but the very means for responding to it had been destroyed. The government had vanished. Civil servants and soldiers were either dead or had scattered, and almost every government office was reduced to rubble. Water, electricity and all communication service had ceased to exist, and normal food-distribution channels had broken down.

As if by instinct, tens of thousands of people, carrying what possessions they could salvage, began to flee Managua. One refugee was a thin, pale man with a little goatee who had been living since last August in the Intercontinental Hotel. Flushed into the open for the first time in years, billionaire recluse Howard Hughes sent out a private SOS. Not long after sun-up, a private jet whisked Hughes and his aides—but no one else—to safety.

Soon every road leading out of Managua was filled. Aftershocks were still continuing, and Managuans were desperate to get out before another shattering quake came. Mobs began looting, first from stores, then from private homes, stripping the city virtually bare.

If Managua were left to its own devices, disease, thirst and starvation would surely complete what the earthquake had started.

Care Amid Chaos. Vultures cartwheeled over Managua, attracted by the dead. So many people had been killed that bodies had to be dumped, layer upon layer, in deep pits and covered with earth by bulldozers. Many bodies remained in the rubble, however, and soon the stench of death permeated Ground Zero, particularly around the Central Market, where the peddler families had been sleeping. No one will ever know how many people perished in the quake. The government estimated the range to be between 11,000 and 12,000.

The rescuers' first priority was medical assistance for the survivors. At Fort Hood, Texas, 1800 miles away, a 100-bed hospital was loaded onto 12 huge jet aircraft. Included were eight ambulances, incubators, X-ray equipment, a field kitchen, 18 trucks to haul supplies—and 45 doctors and nurses. Landing in Managua on Sunday afternoon, the Americans set up the hospital in a pasture near the devastated General Hospital. (It came to be called Camp Christina, after the first baby born there, on Christmas Day.) Mexico, France and many other countries also sent medical teams. Even Fidel Castro, one of Somoza's deadliest enemies, sent an emergency hospital staffed by 59 doctors and other personnel. Nicaraguan and foreign doctors treated an estimated 20,000 persons for their injuries.[33]

The Managuan experience is especially relevant to any future scenario of devastation along the western coast of the United States, one of the most imminently threatened of the world's great developed regions and situated along the same tectonic rim as Managua. The American investigators continue:

. . . Managua reminds us in North America of our own vulnerability. While we can be encouraged somewhat by the comparative experience of the San Fernando earthquake, there is much in the Managua experience that is sobering. The Managua earthquake was a low-energy, short-duration earthquake, and another, perhaps 1000 times greater, can be expected to occur on the West Coast of the United States within the lifetime of most readers of this article. One set of scenarios for the San Francisco Bay area envisages between 10,360 and 100,000 deaths and property damage of up to $1.4 billion. The realism of such scenarios is underscored by three relevant aspects of the Managuan experience.

First, while the experience in Managua is reassuring as to the ability of construction built to current standards of seismic resistance to avoid structural failure, it is not reassuring with respect to functional failure. A building may be safe—that is, no one is killed or even injured by its collapse —but it may also be useless, unable to effectively house the functional activity contained therein. Managua provides a grim lesson as to what occurs when all the major hospitals that do not collapse become nonfunctional. Recent legislation in California now calls for hospital buildings to be not only safe but functional. Literal enforcement of such an act should require drastic changes in design practice.

Second, a center city disaster of the type envisaged in the scenarios, with a major fire, will necessitate massive evacuation of the surviving population. Three elements made the transport logistics in Managua possible: a simplified, one-level road transport system, a large pool of public transport equipment and a minimum of private automobiles, and the fortuitous survival of the oil refinery and its initiative in distributing gasoline to suburban stations. None of these elements would necessarily be present in California —indeed, the contrary could be expected. The freeway system can be fail-safe structurally but be rendered inoperative by unavoidable minor breaks and off-sets. The everyday operation of private automobiles under normal circumstances can result in massive traffic jams, and gasoline, while ample in the area, might be unattainable where and when needed.

Third, if a breakdown of public order takes place during such a major disaster and if extended aid, while forthcoming, is unable to penetrate effectively into the stricken area, a large West Coast urban center might suffer much of the social dislocation and none of the compensatory supports found in Managua. Already a norm similar to that of Managua prevails in many of our central cities—what is not watched is likely to be stolen. But the compensating norm of broad familial responsibility is missing. Thus, while 200,000 Managuans moved in with their kin and lived there for months, will 4 million Californians be able to double up with kin and strangers for an extended period?

These questions are perhaps the most one can derive from transferring the results of an unplanned experiment. In any event, the experiment of major earthquake disaster will be repeated somewhere else, possibly in similar fashion. If there is any conclusion to be reached, it is that the Managua-type experiment need not recur, but it probably will.[34]

3. Volcanic Activity

CHARLES Richter has pointed out the close correlation of volcanic lines with the epicenters of intermediate earthquakes, and it is possible that massive subsidence and volcanic activity of the sort experienced off Iceland is a manifestation of tectonic forces that may sooner or later generate earthquakes.[1] In this connection there is a further, and worldwide sign of disturbing seismicity: a spate of unusual volcanic eruptions about the globe.

Donald A. Swanson, of the U.S. Geological Survey, summarized the developments of 1972 in vulcanology in the January, 1973, *Geotimes* as follows: "Worldwide eruptive activity and growing concern about volcanic hazards characterized the year [1972]." Swanson went on to list twelve major volcanoes that had erupted during the year. The earth appears to be in a period of increased volcanic activity which started in 1955, and which shows no sign of lessening. During the earlier parts of the century, volcanoes were relatively quiescent. Since 1955, monitoring stations in various parts of the earth have recorded measurable increases in volcanic dustfalls.

Major eruptions have been reported in the past five years in Antarctica, Chile, Peru, the Galapagos Islands, El Salvador, Costa Rica, Nicaragua, Guatemala, St. Vincent, the West Indies, Alaska, Greenland, Iceland, the Canary Islands, Hawaii, New Zealand, the South Pacific, the Philippines, Indonesia, Japan, the U.S.S.R., Sicily, and Ethiopia.[2] There is every indication that the trend of increased earth disturbance will continue. Some of the eruptions are highly unusual in character. For example, the eruption of Tiatia, one of the largest volcanoes in the Kurile Islands along the eastern edges of the Soviet Union, in July, 1973, was its first activity since 1812, and was preceded by a series of earthquakes of considerable magnitude. The eruption of Mount Langila in New Guinea on July 20, 1973, was its first large eruption in this century.

Major volcanic eruptions, many of them highly unusual and the first volcanic activity in the area in this century, have begun to occur in the past five years in Antarctica, Chile, the Galapagos Islands, and Peru. In Central America, major eruptions have occurred in El Salvador, Costa Rica, Nicaragua, Guatemala, and Mexico. The eruptions are generally unusual in character. For example, the Santiaguito volcano in Guatemala erupted on September 16, 1973, in a series of ash clouds, an event which had not occurred there since 1934. Mt. Soufrière, on the island of St. Vincent, B.W.I., which erupted in March, 1972, had last erupted in 1902 in a similar fashion.

Quite apart from its potential implications with regard to earthquake risk, this increase is in itself cause for considerable concern. Though relatively rare, volcanic eruptions "have on occasion been enormously destructive."[3] Mont Pelée on Martinique, which erupted in 1902, killing all but two of the capital city's 30,000 inhabitants; Skaptar Jokull, Iceland, 1783, which killed 10,000; Tamboro, Indonesia, 1815, in which 12,000 died directly and 70,000 as the result of massive crop failure. More recently, Mt. Agung, Bali, with 1,500 dead in 1963; Taal, in the Philippines, 1965, with 500 dead. The Office of Emergency Preparedness has concluded:

> The people, property, economy and ecology of the area surrounding the active volcanoes in Hawaii, the Pacific Northwest, and Alaska are endangered by the threat of future volcanic activity.[4]

4. Meteorological Disturbance: Flood and Drought

There is general scientific agreement that the earth's climate during the period from the early years of this century through 1955 was extraordinarily benign and balmy. The earth's population more than doubled, industrial development flourished in areas which for a few centuries earlier were climatically harsh, and the productivity of world food crops was extraordinarily high. Although the present generation of humanity may have acclimated itself to the view that the earth's climate is relatively stable over time and will continue to be as benign as it has been over their lifetimes, recent scientific data shows otherwise:

> One of climatology's more surprising recent conclusions, derived from investigations of sea-floor sediments, is that

for at least the past 700,000 years, global mean temperatures have been as high as they are now only about 5 percent of the time. Says Cesare Emiliani, who has been plotting the long-term cycles at the University of Miami, "We used to think intervals as warm as the present lasted 100,000 years or so. Instead, they appear to be short, infrequent episodes." Another surprising finding is that sometimes transitions from one major temperature regime to another have taken place with astounding rapidity, often within a century or so.[1]

The past 6000 years of civilization have coincided with the warmest period in earth climate in 100,000 years, and the rise and fall of individual civilizations within this period are now being traced to radical and unexpected changes in climate. Major and minor global cool periods that brought sustained drought to formerly rich agricultural lands have been tied to the fall of such powerful civilizations as the Indus, the Hittite, the Mycenaean, and the Mali empire in Africa.[2] The growth of our civilization has occurred under conditions of extreme climatic benignity, and it is not unreasonable to assume that a deterioration in the earth's climate could have severe and widely damaging repercussions.

There are clear signs that this short balmy period is coming to a rapid and unforeseen end. The causes are complex and not fully understood. They involve a general decline in the earth's temperature, a larger differential between temperatures at the equator and temperatures at the poles, a shifting southward of the vital monsoon-bearing winds, and turbulent behavior among the wind patterns that bring either balmy weather or storm. The resulting symptoms are widespread, and include growing drought in a belt extending from Africa through Pakistan and India down through Southeast Asia and up into parts of China. They also include record flooding and destructive storm weather in many parts of the world. It is a trend which is apt to increase.

Although many conflicting theories about the causes and nature of the period of earth disturbance we are now entering exist, one plausible view is that the cooling of the earth is caused by increased reflectance of sunlight from the earth by dust in the atmosphere. Under this theory, though man-made dust may play some role, volcanic dust in the atmosphere is the major culprit:

> Scientists who have drilled through many layers of the Greenland and Antarctic ice sheets report evidence of lower temperatures in the same layers in which a lot of volcanic dust is deposited. And most climatologists agree that a diminution of the sunlight as small as 1 percent would suffice to initiate a cold period and perhaps even major glaciation.
>
> During the early parts of the century, when the climate began warming, volcanoes were unusually quiescent. They've been acting up again since 1955, and monitoring stations in places as scattered as the Caucasus Mountains, Mongolia, and Greenland have recorded measurable increases in dust fall, as well as decreases in the transparency of the atmosphere, and in the amount of direct sunlight reaching the earth.[3]

There are alternative, though not contradictory, theories which hold that the incidence of meteorological disturbances such as drought varies with large-scale astronomical disturbances such as sunspot cycles. For example, Professor Walter Orr Roberts of the National Center for Atmospheric Research in Boulder, Colorado, has uncovered a high correlation between the twenty-two-year sunspot cycle and the occurrence of serious drought in an 800 mile by 1,500 mile corridor from Canada to Texas. This is a geographic area which normally produces a substantial portion of the nation's food. According to Dr. Roberts' projections, this area should begin experiencing serious drought in the spring of 1975.

Although the trend has been evident to the earth science community for some time, it is only recently being reported in the popular press. Witness this account, dated November 25, 1973:

Drastic changes in the earth's climate are now under way—changes that can kill millions and threaten America with glacial conditions—warn alarmed scientists.

The earth is cooling off, they report—and effects of the shift in temperatures have already left millions starving, caused disastrous floods throughout the world, and disrupted the economy of nations.

"It appears that we are headed back toward the bitter-cold conditions of the 18th century," says Dr. Reid A. Bryson, professor of meteorology and director of the Institute for Environmental Studies at the University of Wisconsin.

"It is possible that there will be glacial conditions in America within the next 100 years. Winters in the South will continue to get colder. Heavy snow will be common in the once-sunny South. Northern Florida might be snowbound by the turn of the century.

"Generally, our weather will become similar to that of the 18th Century, when bitter-cold winters extended as far south as the Gulf Coast.

"The main feature of our weather, however, will be the way it jumps around crazily. New Orleans, for example, might be bitterly cold one year and mild the next."

Lower temperatures and "crazy weather" were also predicted by Dr. Murray Mitchell, Jr., project scientist at the National Oceanic and Atmospheric Administration. Speaking to *The Enquirer* at Silver Spring, Md., he said:

"It is quite possible that we are headed for a more severe climate than any in recent history.

"The most consistent feature of the U.S. climate in recent years has been its coolness. Except for the West Coast, the whole country has been a lot cooler for the last 10 years than for the previous 30 years.

"We seem to be heading back toward 18th Century

weather, when it was very cold all around the world—the mountain glaciers were advancing, Europe was cold and wet and stormy, and winters in the U.S. were bitterly cold.

"Then it began to warm up, peaking in 1940, when the Arctic ice cap was threatening to disappear completely.

"But for the last 10 years we have been cooling off again."

Dr. Bryson called the change in climate "the most significant environmental threat the world faces in this decade. There is a strong school of thought among scientists that we are headed back toward the Ice Age.

"Half a billion people in Asia are now facing food shortages because of the failure of the monsoon rains on which their crops depend.

"A 6-year drought is starving the six million people who live in the Sahelian region south of the Sahara in Africa. Exceptionally severe winters have almost destroyed the economy of Iceland, wiping out their sheep and cattle herds. A shift in high-pressure areas threatens Australia's future as a wheat producer. We have seen terrible floods during the past year in Mexico, Bangladesh, Tunisia, and Korea."

Dr. Robley Matthews, head of the Dept. of Geology at Brown University in Providence, R.I., said: "If the temperature keeps dropping at the present rate, we are heading quickly toward glacial conditions—perhaps in as little as 100 years."

Dr. Bryson said: "We cannot afford to sit back and ignore possible catastrophic conditions. The time to act is now."[4]

There has been an alarming increase in the number of floods and droughts of unprecedented dimension throughout the earth in the last several years. Aside from the immediate destruction these disasters bring, they often result in widespread food shortage, and even now, tens of millions of persons are in immediate danger of death by famine. The evidence suggests, moreover, that these phenomena are apt to increase in the future.

The evidence of flooding is great in the United States. As previously mentioned, in the spring of 1973, the Mississippi

River system produced the most devastating floods in recorded history. The Susquehanna River flooded in June, 1972, causing what the New York *Times* described as "one of the worst natural disasters in this nation's history, killing 118 persons . . . forcing a quarter of a million people from their homes . . . destroying $4 billion in property . . . and damaging or destroying more than 100,000 homes, businesses, schools, churches, hospitals and public buildings."[5] In that same year, massive flooding hit Rapid City, South Dakota, causing extensive damage which still immobilizes the region today. Vermont was struck in June, 1973, by the second-largest flood in its recorded history. In January, 1974, parts of the Northwest, including Oregon, experienced their worst floods in ten years.

Many other areas of the world have experienced floods of similar magnitude and trauma in recent years.[6] The greatest were the floods and tidal waves which hit Bangladesh on November 13, 1970. The floods extended along the delta of the Ganges and Brahmaputra and were responsible for the deaths of 500,000 people. Total destruction amounted to more than 1,000,000 acres of crops, 235,000 houses, and 265,000 head of cattle. The resentment created by governmental indifference to the catastrophe was largely responsible for the social turmoil which eventually led to the India-Pakistan war and the formation of Bangladesh. In May, 1969, southern China experienced a flooding of the Yangtze and Pearl Rivers that was described as the highest in the history of the area. Large floodings occurred in sections of the Philippines, Malaysia, and Brazil in 1970. Europe suffered from a series of devastating floods in 1966, and in the spring of 1970. In January, 1974, Australia experienced what were described as her worst floods in a century.

More disturbing than the evidence of dramatic increase in worldwide floods is that of the steady and widespread growth of drought in many of the lower latitudes of the globe. There are growing signs of a rapid melting of the polar icecaps, increasing the surface temperature of the oceans and greatly diminishing the moisture which enters the atmosphere and is precipitated back onto the earth in the equatorial latitudes. Portions of West Africa, Ethiopia and India are now experiencing widespread drought, and the resulting deaths from famine are projected to be in the tens of millions.[7] A prominent geologist has concluded that the present arid zones of the earth, north and south, will see a vast expansion in area. The countries most affected "by increased desiccation with its scourges—droughts, soil erosion, starvation"—include numerous countries in South and Central America, Africa, Asia, including India and China, and Australia.[8] Parts of China and Russia are now in the throes of drought. There is no immediate prospect that this will decrease; and there is considerable evidence that it will, in fact, extend itself in the coming years.

Moreover, the effects of food shortage are often exacerbated by pervasive policy confusion among the governments of hard-hit nations. India is a prime example in this regard:

Scarcity conditions always give the farmers a strong incentive to hoard their produce in the hopes of making a killing later on. But this year the government made matters considerably worse, first by setting unrealistically low purchase prices, and then by taking over the wholesale grain trade. In the absence of adequate preparation for this difficult and controversial manoeuvre, the trade has gone underground, leaving the official markets bare. Another side effect has been the inflation of prices of coarse grains like millet and gram, which has enraged wheat farmers and hit the poorest people very hard.

The government's only recourse now is imports. The food minister announced this week [June 23, 1973] that India will be seeking 2m [million] tons on the international wheat market, but the finance minister suggested earlier that it may need as much as 6m tons. This imported wheat will have to start filtering through to the fair price shops by

October unless a good monsoon persuades farmers to sell. In drought stricken Maharashtra rations have been cut from the subsistence level of 13 kilograms of cereal per person to five, but even this starvation diet is not always available. The state government has attempted to bolster its supplies by openly evading the central government's ban on inter-state dealings.

A good monsoon may fend off the onset of a real famine. But the rehabilitation of the drought victims will take time and money; they will need to replace the draft animals and farm tools they have been forced to sell, and they will need an assured food supply to rebuild their strength. A year from now India will still be suffering the effects of the drought.[9]

There is some danger that powerful nations may accelerate the deterioration of the climate through large-scale but short-sighted engineering projects of their own:

In the U.S.S.R., for example, a third of the grain crop comes from the drought-prone virgin lands of Siberia, and there has been talk of diverting some of the great Siberian rivers into vast irrigation projects. These rivers empty into the Arctic Ocean, where the light, fresh water spreads out atop the salt water and permits the arctic seas to freeze over. According to some experiments by a Russian scientist, O. A. Drozdov, and by British meteorologist R. I. Newson, who constructed a mathematical model of winds in the Northern Hemisphere, the paradoxical consequence of preventing the freezing of the Arctic Ocean is likely to be that winters would become colder and drier over many continental areas in middle latitudes. Even some prominent Soviet meteorologists have spoken out against the proposal. But if disastrous, prolonged droughts were to overtake the Siberian wheatlands, Soviet authorities might conclude that there is little to lose in going ahead with the projects.[10]

5. Public Policy and Unpreparedness

THERE exists a shocking lack of policy coherence and preparedness for natural catastrophe in the United States and in most other countries. The lack of preparation takes on many forms. One certain conclusion is that many of the major metropolitan areas threatened by earthquake are poorly designed to absorb a large seismic shock and poorly prepared to cope with the aftermath. Land use patterns in many populated areas of the globe are largely irrational and have resulted from inadequate enforcement of legal standards, where these are available, and from the pressures of urbanization. Emergency measures in most parts of the world, with the possible exception of Japan, are skimpy and inadequate.

There exist few mechanisms for equitably apportioning the losses caused by earthquake among the stricken population. At least one government, that of the United States, is moving to restrict the total amount of funds available for disaster relief in a time of rising natural disaster. (See Appendix III for a discussion of disaster relief funding.) The earth science community about the globe is not receiving a level of funding adequate to its task. In the United States, there has been a recent and disturbing trend of maladaption among populations hit by natural catastrophe, with the incidence of suicides, depression, mental disturbance, and alcoholism rising in the period following a catastrophic event. Clearly, the globe is in no present position to respond even to a moderate continuation of the present trend of catastrophe. The evidence is ample and readily available.

Land use planning is perhaps the best example. The literature on earthquake damage indicates that losses due to earthquake in crowded metropolitan areas are largely unnecessary and as much as 90 percent of the destruction to life

43

and property can be avoided by the firm and judicious application of modern land use techniques and improved structural design. Yet, even in California, the most immediately threatened area of the United States, there has been little rigorous development and application of legal standards in this regard. John J. Fried, in *Life Along the San Andreas Fault* (New York, Saturday Review Press, 1973), details the systematic undermining of standards intended to limit new construction to stable areas by influential real estate interests and by the pressures on local government to increase tax rolls through land development. Much of the potential benefit of a 1933 statute requiring the demolition and reconstruction of unsafe school buildings has been blunted by a failure to approve funds for the effort.

Schools, power plants, dams, hospitals, and other public facilities have been clustered along the active fault lines which run the course of the state. Elsewhere in the nation, little if no attention has been placed on rational and safe land development, and the National Commission on Urban Problems has estimated that 60 percent of U.S. localities have no full-time planning staff.

The single most potentially devastating consequence of this lack of coherent policy is probably the construction of nuclear power plants in areas which are susceptible to earthquake. In 1973 alone, major plants were to have been constructed in California, Virginia, and Puerto Rico on or adjacent to active faults, after an only cursory review of the seismic risk by the designers responsible for the projects. An Atomic Energy Commission document released on December 31, 1969, indicated that there were at that time sixteen operable nuclear power plants, forty-eight under construction, and thirty-four in the advanced planning stages. An unusually high proportion of these—forty-four—were located either in the Northeast or Southeast, both areas of known high seismic risk. Although we do not know if proper precautions against seismicity were undertaken at these plants, the experience in California, Virginia, and Puerto Rico suggests that there is some basis to doubt it.

In the only report on the potential destructiveness of a malfunctioning nuclear power plant, the AEC in 1957 indicated that serious malfunction at a 100,000 to 200,000 kilowatt plant located within thirty miles of a hypothetical city of one million persons would result in 3,400 dead, 43,000 injured, and $7 billion worth of property damage. The hypothetical plant, moreover, is only approximately 10 percent as large as major plants being constructed today.

There is a similar irrationality in most emergency planning, be it at the state or local level. The Los Angeles County Earthquake Commission found an "almost total lack of communication among the agencies" responsible for disaster measures during the 1971 San Fernando earthquake. A federal commission concluded that had the same lack of coordination which prevailed then been coupled with a similar earthquake occurring at a less-fortunate time of day, "utter disaster would have been the result."

We have seen no convincing evidence that authorities in California are substantially better prepared to respond to what is likely to be a much more destructive event. The Hayward, California, Planning Commission notes, for example, that in the case of one California city which had supposedly developed an adequate earthquake response plan, only one person was familiar with the details of the plan. Our latest information indicates that the emergency response plan developed by San Francisco is a classified document, thus preventing its review by a wide body of opinion and its wide circulation and absorption. San Francisco, by our latest report, has only one fireboat—it had two in the 1906 quake—and one helicopter available to municipal employees. A national board of fire underwriters has rated the probability of fire in San Francisco to be as high now as during the time of the 1906 quake.

In the eastern portion of the nation, many of the large metropolitan areas are substantially ill-prepared for earthquake. In Boston, a city of known earthquake hazard, the

Office of Emergency Preparedness was abolished by the local administration late in 1972 for reasons of economy. The former director, Walter Cameron, was transferred to the Fire Department, which had assumed the functions of the emergency preparedness office. One wonders at the adequacy of Boston's response to an unexpected earthquake.

A more general difficulty of most emergency response plans in the United States is that natural disaster plans are patterned after the civilian defense plans for recovery after nuclear attack. The assumption of the nuclear attack plans is that outside help to a community would not be available (because the whole country would be stricken) and evacuation of the population would not be feasible (because of nuclear damage and fallout). In the case of natural disaster, the opposite assumptions apply: Outside help could, if planned for, be available and there would be time for evacuation and resettlement if proper prediction techniques were employed.

Public policy and governmental measures to meet the mounting global level of natural disasters remain in general fragmented, ill-defined, and at times almost fatalistic. This is not to say that the beginnings of an intelligent world system for response to earthquake do not exist. There is, in many countries, a small and dedicated professional core of disaster relief workers, and not a few countries have a record of dedication and service to others in time of natural catastrophe.

Yet, the world is not capable of adequately responding to the upheavals the earth can expect for the coming quarter century. In most of the industrialized countries, funds have only recently been allocated to natural disaster research and to the social and public policy consequences of the research. No effective international system for disaster relief and planning exists, and the United Nations only in late 1971 began to formulate a global system for intelligent disaster relief. Much of the general population of both the industrialized and less developed worlds are ignorant of the causes and nature of natural disaster, thus making them the more prey to nature's ravages, and incapable of intelligently responding to even the minimal plans which now exist.

Most important, there is a curious lack of communication which until recently has pervaded the worlds of the earth sciences, governmental authorities, and the populace at large. If the revolution in science of the last few years has taught us anything it is that the earth and its behavior and man and his process must be looked at as a single integrated system. Natural catastrophes—earthquakes, floods, droughts, meteorological changes—are not isolated events occurring randomly in time. They are predictable, interconnected phenomena occurring according to uniform natural laws, and in principle at least, no part of the earth is immune from their ravages.

Yet with a few enlightened exceptions, governmental authorities and general populations about the globe continue their daily routine as though natural disasters were random and rare events which need not affect the structure and design of society. Natural disasters have predictable and devastating consequences on human settlements, housing, industrial facilities, transportation facilities, agricultural areas, and local economies. Reason dictates that zoning and building standards governing these would reflect an area's vulnerability. Reason also dictates that local populations, especially in the densely populated centers of the industrialized world, would be educated in the mechanisms and nature of disasters, and well instructed in coping with impending disaster. This is not, however, the case. By and large the civilization of the industrial and postindustrial age has ignored its presence on a volatile and often dangerous planet, and has built itself a house of cards vulnerable even to the ordinary course of natural disaster.

The susceptibility is most visible in the lack of comprehensive preparedness for earthquakes, even in areas which are imminently threatened. The United States is a case in point. A recent issue of *Science* reports that despite the general optimism among university scientists about the prospect of earthquake prediction, "many geophysicists are concerned over the lack of any national plan for reducing earthquake hazards and they question the strategy of research now being pursued by the Geophysical Survey."[1] At the federal level, university research and development on societal response to earthquake is limited to a few National Science Foundation grants and to occasional conferences for professionals in the field. Until recently, a dozen federal agencies maintained an ongoing interest in earthquakes, but their efforts were often uncoordinated and for divergent ends.[2]

The visible lack of policy coherence among state and local governments on whom the carrying out of any effective earthquake disaster plans would ultimately depend is ominous. The OEP reports that fewer than one-third of the states have even applied for matching federal funds for the development of disaster plans, despite their availability since 1969.[3] The disaster laws of states have been changed in relatively few instances over the past two decades, despite the extraordinary growth in the complexity and vulnerability of metropolitan areas. Even in localities of highly visible seismic risk, local governments appear almost immobilized. Only a handful of cities have adopted building codes or zoning laws explicitly intended to reduce earthquake hazard, and even in these there has often been a systematic failure to seek compliance.[4]

A striking example of the present lack of capacity for effective public measures in response to an earthquake can be found in the San Fernando Valley earthquake of February 9, 1971. The quake was of an intermediate nature (magnitude 6.3 on the Richter scale) and occurred at 6:00 A.M. in a largely suburban area. It was responsible for sixty-five deaths and $553 million in property damage, the highest earthquake damage in the history of the United States. Importantly, it occurred in an area of known earthquake hazard, and with ample opportunity of over more than four decades for the development of intelligent response plans.

In a detailed evaluation of government response to the quake, the Los Angeles County Earthquake Commission found "an almost total lack of communication among the agencies."[5] A federal evaluation team, composed of representatives of the Department of Health, Education and Welfare and the Veteran's Administration concluded starkly:

> Had the lack of (1) emergency medical communications in the public sector, (2) predisaster planning, (3) organizations, and (4) definition of lines of medical authority and responsibility, which prevailed in this quake, been coupled with the circumstances of a similar quake occurring at a more vulnerable hour and with an epicenter closer to the densely developed center of Los Angeles, utter disaster would have very probably been the result.[6]

It is true that a number of single operations, such as the evacuation of 80,000 persons from the area of the threatened Van Norman dam, were carried out with remarkable efficiency and lack of incident under the circumstances. These single incidents stand out, however, in the context of a general confusion and lack of clear direction.

Indeed, perhaps the most compelling evidence of the state of policy confusion in the face of earthquake disaster lies in a conclusion buried in a massive ten-volume study of the 1964 Alaska earthquake (magnitude 8.3 on the Richter scale) published in 1969 by the National Academy of Sciences. After surveying the probable consequences of the occurrence of a similar earthquake in a more densely populated area, the authors conclude phlegmatically:

> Under urban conditions in the United States, it is not clear what constitutes a proper evacuation strategy.[7]

Nor does a brief survey of the literature disclose a high level of preparedness among other societies of the world. In South America, earthquakes have historically devastated many of the larger settlements of the Pacific coast. Yet research and planning for earthquake disaster is largely limited to the academic world, and regional colloquia on the subject are only now being held. There are indications that Japan may be developing the beginnings of an adequate earthquake response plan. There is no indication of a developed public policy in other areas of high seismic risk: Central America, the Mediterranean, and the eastern coast of the Soviet Union. The United Nations' development of a global disaster relief plan is only now getting underway.

The evidence suggests a widespread reluctance to plan and organize for earthquake disaster which is neither justified nor rational. It is not as though society were unaware of a series of measures which could potentially greatly reduce the coming devastation. These exist in the lexicon of any competent public planner and are not beyond the reach of most present governmental authorities. One can point to at least a half-dozen general categories of public measures in this regard: development of a general understanding of the nature of earthquake both among the public and the professionals who manage the details of society; application of techniques to determine which specific areas are vulnerable to earthquake and to predict an approaching quake; development of effective land use policies to minimize the destruction in time of earthquake; development of adequate emergency evacuation and shelter plans; development of an equitable way of sharing the cost resulting from the destruction, and of rebuilding; agreements for the orderly cooperation among the many levels of governmental authority that inevitably bear responsibility even in a single disaster. Yet there are unmistakable signs of policy neglect and incoherence in each of these areas.

Since the occurrence of the 1971 San Fernando earthquake, there have been the beginnings of rigorous basic research into core questions of disaster preparedness. The Environmental Research Laboratories have completed two detailed studies of potential earthquake losses in San Francisco and Los Angeles, respectively. Further studies are planned for Salt Lake City, situated on an active fault system, and the Memphis, Tennessee, area. (None are planned for seismically vulnerable areas of the northeastern and southeastern United States, however.) The Earthquake Engineering Research Institute, under Professor C. Martin Duke of UCLA, will report in the near future on a project designed to develop an effective information-gathering methodology applicable during the often confusing postearthquake period.

A highly professional and thorough appraisal of public policy issues underlying fifteen categories of natural catastrophe is being prepared at the Institute for Behavioral Sciences, University of Colorado, under Gilbert F. White and J. Eugene Haas, both eminent men in their field. The study systematically outlines major research questions in alternative relief systems, integrated catastrophe warning systems, catastrophe insurance, general governmental planning, and the practical limitations on the ability of local governments to respond to natural catastrophe. A further study on the policy implications of the new earthquake prediction models is planned for the near future.

These studies show a farsightedness and high sense of professional responsibility among that segment of the earth science community concerned with formulation of the broadest questions of disaster preparedness. And they do indicate that the federal government, and at least one state government—California—are beginning to act responsibly in funding basic research. There remains much to be done, however, in further developing basic research and in effectively transmitting this information throughout disaster prevention systems within the nation and about the globe.

6. Public Attitude and Natural Disaster

THE available experience in prior disasters makes it clear that the level of awareness and mental state of the stricken population is the key to the success of any societal measures to minimize destruction and quickly resume normal life. There is much to suggest, however, that the general level of awareness of the nature of earthquake and its causes and mechanisms is abysmally low in our society, even in areas of high and well-established seismic risk. Moreover, there is disturbing evidence during recent disasters in the United States of a growing inability to face the necessary hardships of a natural disaster with equanimity, optimism, and tolerance. Even in areas which have experienced relatively limited floods there persists an extraordinarily high incidence of mental disease, depression, and loss of will.

One cannot underestimate the effect of an educated and tolerant populace on the mitigation of destruction during an earthquate and the recovery after. Haroun Tazieff, a French commentator, noted the deep terror which has historically been engendered by tremors in the earth:

> An earthquake is by its very essence terrifying, more terrifying than nature's other dreadful outbreaks, since more than any other it sets the stability of the underlying basis of human life itself in question.[1]

That earthquake may evoke deep-seated fears is confirmed by the widespread cults that have grown up over the centuries in societies in which earthquakes have frequently and devastatingly struck. In Peru, a country long exposed to intermittent destruction by earthquakes, there is an annual weeklong festival of worship and prayer to Christ, Lord of the Earthquakes, deriving from the miraculous survival of a Christ statue in an early earthquake that otherwise razed a large Peruvian town. It is a time of public procession in purple robes, and prayer for protection against any coming upheavals. In the sense that it serves to foster a deep sense of community and interdependence in time of earthquake, it is probably highly functional and a strong reinforcer of an underlying adaptability that permits the population of the area to build and rebuild over time.

And adaptability appears to be a key trait to healthy survival of a disaster. R. W. Kates notes in the lengthy National Academy of Sciences analysis of the 1964 Alaska earthquake: "Human adjustment to earthquake hazard thus requires adaptation to phenomena that confuse man's senses and confound his beliefs." Other commentators compare the trauma of earthquake to the sense of shock and confusion that often besets the individual caught in the nightmare of combat:

> In disaster, therefore, exactly as in certain combat situations, individuals can be psychologically overwhelmed. Once again the source may be traced to a high level of environmental stimulation. The disaster victim finds himself suddenly caught in a situation in which familiar objects and relationships are transformed. Where once his house stood, there may be nothing more than smoking rubble. He may encounter a cabin floating on the floodtide or a row boat sailing through the air. The environment is filled with change and novelty. And once again the response is marked by confusion, anxiety, irritability and withdrawal into apathy.[2]

The same commentator notes in a study of the public response to tornado that, "the first reaction . . . may be one of dazed bewilderment, sometimes one of disbelief, or at least of refusal to accept the fact. This, it seems to us, is the essential explanation of the behavior of persons and groups in Waco when it was devastated in 1953. . . . On the personal level, it explains why a girl climbed into a music store through a broken display window, calmly purchased a record, and walked out again, even though the plate glass in front of the building had blown out and articles were flying through the air inside the building."[3]

The recent governmental studies on disaster planning stress the need for an informed and patient public, both in the period of emergency during the actual disaster and during the tedious time of reorientation and rebuilding in the aftermath. The Office of Emergency Preparedness noted that there was a direct correlation between public understanding of the nature of a natural disaster—in this case Hurricane Camille, which brought property losses of nearly $1.5 billion to the Gulf Coast in 1969—and the effectiveness of measures to mitigate death and devastation. Its recent report notes:

> Persons who have experienced severe hurricanes have greater respect for the threat, and generally more comply with warnings and evacuation advisories. . . . A survey immediately following Hurricane Camille found that those who evacuated comprehended the danger of a storm surge much better than did those who stayed behind.[4]

The brunt of available data indicates, however, that the public is largely unaware not only of the high certainty of coming earthquakes, but of the nature of the community response necessary to avoid large-scale devastation. In certain high-risk areas of the country, this unawareness is almost schizophrenic, suggesting a strong irrational desire to repress the facts of coming catastrophe. Charles Richter notes in one of the few commentaries available on the proper steps to take in earthquake: "Lately, a serious problem has been created by the arrival in California of many persons who have no experience of earthquake. . . . Panicky and thoughtless actions by frightened persons may add to the disaster and may interfere with relief work."[5]

The tendency toward repression of the certainty of earthquake is especially disturbing in California. Responsible dispatches report the puzzling apathy among residents of San Francisco to what is certain to be a series of earthquakes in the approaching years. The last few years have seen the erection of high-rise office buildings which are highly subject to collapse in a future quake. A book * detailing the myriad examples of irrationality notes the recent celebration in San Francisco of the anniversary of the 1906 earthquake. The account mentions that the affair was attended by civic leaders in the area and systematically sought to make light of the probability of the coming disaster. The bar was labeled "Emergency Disaster Relief" and the place mats were set on a seismic risk map of the area setting out the network of faults that surrounds the San Francisco area.[6] A BBC film, *The City That Waits To Die*, amply documents the sense of apathy and withdrawal that is prevalent among large sectors of the threatened population.

These examples are not listed to denigrate the people of the area or to suggest that lighthearted fun is not a healthy human response to an impossible situation. Far from it; humor has long served as man's chief ally in the face of demoralizing odds. Yet the evident lack of preparation in San Francisco appears to betray a deep sense of unreality both among the leaders of the community and among the population which depends on them, and it is in this context that this insouciance is described for the reader's benefit.

These examples bear on the level of awareness of the population as to the nature of earthquake and on the adequacy of this consciousness to cope with the immediate trauma of the coming calamities. Even more disturbing is the emerging pattern of evidence which suggests that our society is fast losing its resilience and ability to deal with the long-term dislocations and frustrations of a natural catastrophe. This pattern, which is becoming more evident in the reactions of certain communities to a series of floods and landslides that has recently affected parts of the nation, is a

*Peter Briggs, *Will California Fall into the Sea?* New York: David McKay & Co., 1972.

source of considerable disquiet to the professionals who deal in disaster relief and preparation. A recent and unusual federal conference on the psychological effects of disaster concluded:

> Recent disasters that have occurred in the United States have understandably produced mental stress among survivors. While there has been no systematic observation, documentation, and evaluation of the nature, scope, and duration of the stress syndrome, there is abundant evidence in reports from various health agencies and disaster relief organizations that a problem exists.[7]

What is emerging is a pattern of deep phobias, nightmares and sleep disturbances, depressions, withdrawal, despair, alcoholism, and general loss of will accompanying natural disaster which cuts across class and age lines in a number of affected communities throughout the United States and in other areas of the world.

A singular example is provided by the Rapid City, South Dakota, flood of 1972. The flood left 237 dead in its aftermath, along with the destruction of 770 houses and 565 mobile homes, and more than $100 million in property damage. In a survey of the area more than a year after the flood, the *Wall Street Journal* noted: ". . . serious problems remain in Rapid City. Health officials say mental disorders have increased sharply. Hundreds of people still live in the shattered flood plain, where ruined houses and dead trees still serve as a grim reminder of last year's disaster and where, Mayor Donald Barnett points out, 'There's nothing to guarantee there won't be another flood.' "[8] The survey goes on to note: "A study prepared for the National Institute of Mental Health notes sharp increases in alcoholism, anxiety, depression and other emotional problems since last June (the date of the flood). The city, the study said, is 'facing a mental health crisis.' "[9] The cited report goes on to point out that "the Outreach workers encountered numerous individuals with maladaptive behavior patterns, suicidal tendencies and severe depressional states."[10]

Moreover, the pattern has repeated itself at the site of other disasters. Much of the same behavior was exhibited at the site of a landslide in West Virginia in 1972. The report on the federal conference notes that "among the aged in the Wyoming Valley in Pennsylvania, the emotional response was one of depression and despair from having lost homes and being uprooted from familiar surroundings,"[11] as the result of massive flooding in June, 1972. In the 1971 San Fernando earthquake, many children reportedly suffered in the aftermath from "fears, phobias, sleep disturbances, and nightmares long after the incident." Children in the Rapid City area reportedly still play "flood" together, establishing rules as to who will die and who won't.

Nor is the phenomenon limited to the United States. A noted example in this regard is perhaps that of Managua, Nicaragua, in the aftermath of the December, 1972, earthquake. News reports indicate the presence of much dissatisfaction with the existing established order, an attitude which cuts across all social and economic lines in that city, and which is in many cases accompanied by a profound sense of despair about the future.

One cannot draw any definite conclusions as to the nature and dimensions of this spreading pattern of maladaption to disaster, for no systematic studies as to its causes and cures have yet been done. There have been more optimistic findings on behavior during natural catastrophe, notably those made by the Disaster Research Center of Ohio State University. It is unnerving, however, to extrapolate these tendencies to despair to a pattern of widespread destruction that seems a certainty in the foreseeable future. Such an extrapolation suggests that a policy of maximal information and responsible and visible community leadership in the preparation for the coming calamities is of the first order.

7. Earthquake Prediction

SOCIETY is at present in a condition of uncertainty with respect to earthquake prediction. The degree of certainty as to earthquake is likely to be much larger in California, with a relatively active scientific establishment, than it is in Nicaragua, which possesses considerably less information as to the certainty of a coming earthquake and the probable details of its occurrence. Yet even in the areas of the earth with the highest degree of scientific observation, our present condition of knowledge is uncertain. Our best evidence with regard to the areas of highest seismic risk is limited to a series of vague generalizations which speak of a large quake taking place sometime within the next five to ten years somewhere along the California coast. Predictions with regard to other areas of high seismic risk—for example, the Northeast—are based on an even greater degree of uncertainty and ignorance. By and large no systematic monitoring of seismic movements exists for areas east of the Rocky Mountains, and the official establishment—the state and local governments to whom falls the responsibility for protecting and guiding society through a disturbance—are largely ignorant of the area's tendency to earthquake.

The measures for bringing society into a condition of certainty, with relatively detailed ongoing knowledge regarding future earthquakes, are well within reach of present technology and can be undertaken with a modest expenditure of public funds. These measures would generate reliable and complete data on the probability of future earthquake—at least in areas of known high seismic risk —and would ensure that these facts are filtered down to governmental authorities and the general public in an orderly and complete fashion. It is difficult to isolate any reason other than governmental inertia for the present paucity of earthquake monitoring and for the present sketchy distribution of the data.

The elements of a rational and effective earthquake

monitoring system have been detailed by a number of expert panels, most recently by the Ad Hoc Task Force on Earthquake Hazard Reduction, whose report in August, 1970, set out the essentials of a "national program for the reduction of human suffering and property damage" attendant to earthquake. The elements include the development of seismic risk and earthquake geologic hazard maps for the United States; the institution of local seismic monitoring networks; research in earthquake prediction, earthquake control, and tsunami hazard; geodetic research; basic research in seismology and in the causes and mechanisms of crustal failure; and continuation and expansion of the worldwide seismic monitoring system.

To a large extent these recommendations are being implemented in a piecemeal and unhurried fashion, in studied ignorance of the apparent certainty of coming earthquake. The Office of Emergency Planning notes in this regard: "There has been insufficient attention to systematic analysis of the vulnerability of communities or larger jurisdictions to natural disasters. As a consequence, state and local governments are often not as well prepared to cope with natural disasters as they could be."[1] There is an evident lack of effective translation between the data collected by the scientific community and what eventually is fed to the governmental authorities. The OEP report notes:

> The risk maps prepared, moreover, often have not been of a sufficiently small geographic area or have not included adequate detail to be useful as a basis for promulgating local regulations that contain strong hazard reduction features.
>
> The results of risk mapping, often couched in scientific terms, need to be translated into terms more readily useful to local planners, engineers, architects, and builders. Seismicity data on earthquake-prone areas, for example, should be reduced to extreme dynamic load factors and disaster mitigation criteria in the land-use and construction activities. A wider dissemination of easily understood risk-mapping data is required to facilitate the efforts of local planners.[2]

Although there has been a recent upward swing in the level of research funds made available in the earthquake area, these remain a dismally low percentage of our national research funds and in no way do their present levels reflect the potential cost of destruction in the coming series of quakes. The research recommendations of at least four national scientific bodies in 1965, 1968, 1969, and 1970 have been to a great extent ignored, even though the relative amounts of public expenditures involved in each of these recommendations were low. The result, as alluded to earlier, is that earthquake risk research is limited in the United States to a small number of universities. Monitoring for the precursory signals of coming earthquake is practically nonexistent, except for limited areas in Central California and upstate New York. Moreover, with the notable exception of Japan, there exists no widespread monitoring for precursory earthquake signals in areas of known seismicity elsewhere in the globe. The present extensive monitoring and research system in Japan began in earnest in 1962 in the context of a clear statement of national research priorities:

> All through her history, Japan has suffered frequent great earthquakes, and each of these has caused a large number of casualties and an enormous amount of damage. It is certain that earthquakes will occur in the future in a similar way as in the past and disasters as caused by them must be prevented as far as possible by ourselves. Prediction of earthquakes is an urgent necessity of the nation and is also the final aim of scientific endeavors in the field of seismology in this country. Seismological studies up to the present do suggest possibilities of realising this aim of earthquake prediction. In order to make such possibilities a practical reality, deep understanding and ample financial support by the government is indispensable, in addition to the constant and conscientious endeavours of all the researchers concerned.[3]

Except for a limited monitoring system in the Tashkent region of the Soviet Union, seismological monitoring in the remainder of the globe is limited to the recording of earthquakes that have occurred and is grossly inadequate in terms of the present state of the art of earthquake prediction. As detailed earlier, the costs of installing a reliable earthquake prediction system in areas of known seismicity is small, and the installation well within either present technological capacity or capacity within the near-term future.

This is not to say that the state of the art is at present in a position to fully monitor areas of moderate or high seismic risk about the earth, in order to have available timely and accurate information with regard to earthquake hazard. A number of commentators have noted the refinements in instrumentation, and the deployment of information-gathering systems necessary to achieve even a minimal degree of accurate and widespread prediction. At present, monitoring for precursory signals in the United States is limited to an area of high seismic risk in central California, and to occasional limited experimental deployments, such as a recent one in the Blue Mountain Lake area of upper New York. Other networks are planned for Southern California, Oregon, Utah, Nevada, and Missouri. The Japanese maintain what appears to be a more extensive monitoring system, as does the U.S.S.R in the Tashkent region.

Yet from all indications, the full deployment of an adequate monitoring system in the short-term future appears to be technologically feasible and in the context of existing levels of public expenditures, relatively minor. Under any rational cost-benefit analysis the potential advantages of having access to clear information as to the certainty of earthquakes clearly outweigh the level of cost that is generally considered minor even by moderate-sized public bodies. Fortunately, the drift of current public policy appears to have intuited this, and funds for earthquake research are increasing, although they remain far below levels recommended by a number of expert Presidential Task Forces, and by the National Academy of Science.

The details of an adequate earthquake research and information distribution system have been amply laid out by at least four expert bodies during the past eight years, and one can only again reiterate the urgency with which our government should address these needs.

8. Emergency Planning

WITH few exceptions, there is much to suggest that communities both in the United States and in other parts of the globe are inadequately prepared to oversee and execute effective and orderly plans for evacuation in the face of earthquake or tidal wave, and to offer a minimum of emergency shelter, food, and medical care. This conclusion is based on the evident lack of coherent emergency plans for all but a handful of heavily settled areas which can expect calamity in the future, and on the low level of real assimilation of plans by those jurisdictions that have concerned themselves with developing them.

There appears, again with certain notable exceptions, a high degree of ambivalence toward the proper steps to take in the wake of a disaster warning in areas which are subject to earthquake emergency. The ambivalence has been in part traced to the infrequent occurrence of destructive earthquakes in the near past, and the paucity of knowledge with regard to the causes of earthquakes. There have been two decades of intensive development in the understanding of earthquakes and in the refinement of social planning within such areas as mass communication, evacuation, and re-settlement of endangered populations. Yet, the community of scholars and officials within whose jurisdiction responsibility for developing adequate evacuation plans falls remains curiously paralyzed.

The apparent confusion at the policy-planning level of our institutions is compounded quite ironically by a set of evacuation plans at the local level whose underlying premises and method of operation are diametrically opposed to the assumptions underlying an earthquake emergency plan. These conflicting plans are a nationwide set of civil defense plans, designed to evacuate cities faced with the certainty of nuclear attack and destruction, a set of plans which grew out of the excesses of the Cold War. The Office of Emergency Preparedness has dryly noted the conflicting objectives and strategies of the two plans:

> . . . natural disaster plans are patterned after civil defense plans for recovery from nuclear attack—plans that assume that outside help would not be available (because the whole country would be stricken) and evacuation would not be feasible (because of the lack of mobility due to nuclear damage and radioactive fallout). In natural disaster planning, the opposite assumptions apply: outside help could be made available immediately; there would be time to evacuate, if necessary, and a place to go; and movement would not be impeded (as by nuclear damage and radioactivity).[1]

Notable and long needed planning at the federal level is finally underway in the United States and we refer the reader to the National Science Foundation testimony in Appendix III for a summary. However, effective institution of emergency planning may be a good time off in the future. For example, the Los Angeles Earthquake Commission, set up in the wake of the general ill coordination in the aftermath of the 1971 San Fernando earthquake, found a shocking and total lack of communication among the various governmental agencies charged with responsibility at the time, and issued a set of recommendations for local governmental agencies:

> —Local governments should establish emergency operating centers in the event of a serious disaster.
> —Local governments should ensure the existence of emergency communications for any foreseeable emergency.
> —Local governments should evaluate and update plans, procedures and preparedness measures.

—Provisions should be made to improve interjurisdictional coordination in future disasters.

—Officials should develop a countywide emergency transportation plan.

—A study should be undertaken to ascertain the best disaster communication system.[2]

The recommendation, however commendable, is a startling document. It is primarily addressed to agencies within Los Angeles County, but may be more generally considered to apply to local governments within the area of high seismicity of Southern and Central California—not to mention other areas of high seismic risk throughout the country. It suggests implicitly that many of the local governments have not accomplished even the steps mentioned in the recommendations, which taken together can be considered the bare bones of an adequate emergency plan.

Nor do cities on the eastern coast of the United States with a high degree of exposure to seismic risk appear to have developed a coherent set of response plans. Officials at the New York City Emergency Control Board, for example, revealed only a dim awareness of any disaster relief plans specifically designed for earthquake or tidal wave hazard. The authors did not have the resources to personally conduct a thorough and systematic survey of the states of disaster relief plans in the nation's large cities. Our judgment is that such a survey would reveal serious deficiencies.

9. Land Use Planning

AS much as 90 percent of the devastation and death following earthquakes can be avoided by the judicious and firm application of modern land use and engineering techniques. C. F. Richter noted before a 1971 NATO conference on earthquakes that:

It should be generally understood that earthquake losses are largely unnecessary and preventable. In the whole of past history, something like 90 percent of the loss of life in earthquakes, and a major fraction of the destruction and economic loss, has been due to the failure of weak structures, such as would never be erected under any modern system of building regulation and inspection. This is particularly evident in the Mediterranean region and in the Near East; but the condition exists in many countries, even to a considerable extent right here in California.[1]

One might add that this injunction applies equally to the adequate enforcement of laws designed to make rational use of land space: the intelligent placement of cities, factories, aqueducts, dams, hospitals, schools, public buildings, power plants, residential areas, airports, and open space, in patterns that reflect the seismic risk of the land mass on which they are built.

The best example of land use planning in this regard is probably in the city of Long Beach, California, which has incorporated a concept of "balanced risk" into its building and zoning codes. Both the placement and the structural design of existing and new buildings are determined by an assessment of the seismic and geologic hazards of the land mass on which the building is located, the required structural resistance adequate for the location, and of the intended occupants and use of the building. The approach is novel and makes full use of available information on seismic risk. The example unfortunately is limited, and the balanced risk approach has to this date been adopted by only two localities—Las Vegas, Nevada, and Santa Rosa, California.[2]

Much more prevalent is the pattern of crazy-quilt, unfettered, and often irrational land development in areas that are of known tendency to earthquake. Existing land use laws are often enforced by a fragmented array of jurisdiction, with little coordination in substantive regulation and enforcement, and often by officials who divide their time among various duties. Thus the National Commission on

Urban Problems estimated that 60 percent of the local jurisdictions located in metropolitan areas had no full-time planning staff.[3] Even where the local zoning law has provisions which limit the uses of land mass of high seismicity, enforcement has been spotty and often prey to the financial and political pressures which vested interests can muster. The Presidential Task Force on Earthquake Hazard Reduction thus concluded: "Moreover, the police power in the hands of small communities has not always been effectively used in zoning problems involving earthquake geologic hazards. This has been true for a variety of reasons, not the least of which are political influences by those having large monetary stakes in the outcome."[4] Startling examples of this slow corruption of the planning process abound.

The single most disturbing of these has been the construction of nuclear power plants in areas which are susceptible to earthquake, thus exposing a population which is already endangered by the threat of collapsing buildings to the risk of nuclear explosion. This threat is not to be taken lightly. The only public study of the possible effects of explosion or serious malfunction of a nuclear power plant was a relatively brief report released by the Atomic Energy Commission in March, 1957, and titled, "Theoretical Possibilities and Consequences of Major Accidents in Large Nuclear Power Plants." The report engendered a bitter controversy and has never been updated by the agency, despite the wide proliferation of nuclear power plants and the enormous increase in the size of present plants. The report focused on a 100,000 to 200,000 kilowatt capacity plant (only 10 to 20 percent of the size of current plants) located near a large body of water about thirty miles from a city of a population of one million. It concluded that the worst possible accident considered, the release of 50 percent of all fission products into the atmosphere, would result in 3,400 killed, 43,000 injured and property damage of $7 billion, killing people in a radius of fifteen miles, injuring within a radius of forty-five miles, and contaminating an area of up to 150,000 miles. The report continues:

> In addition, there could be weather conditions which, when combined with other imaginable extremely adverse conditions, could result in damage greater than the maximum considered in the study.[5]

The implications of the report are quite serious when considered in the context of the massive and destructive release of energy that occurs in earthquake. The evidence suggests that nuclear plants may not be designed to withstand the seismic risks to which they are exposed. The New York *Times* of August 13, 1972, reported that the AEC was forced to call a halt in the construction of a 1,200,000 kilowatt plant in Aguirre, Puerto Rico, after it was discovered that the plant would be located over the Esmeralda Fault, one of the branch faults of the Anegada and Puerto Rico Trench fault system. The contracting designer of the plan—Westinghouse—had dismissed the seismic risk factor in several paragraphs of a $500,000 consulting and design report. On December 27, 1972, the *Times* reported that the U.S. Geological Survey had strongly recommended against the Pacific Gas and Electricity's plans to construct a 2,230,000 kilowatt atomic power plant at Point Arena, California, within 10,000 feet of an active fault.

These developments shock the sensible observer. The energy released in a severe earthquake (8.5 on the Richter scale) is the equivalent of one hundred underground 100 megaton nuclear explosions on a single line. The destructive radius of such an earthquake can be as wide as 2,000,000 square miles in the East Coast, and 325,000 square miles along the California coast. The susceptibility of nuclear power plants to destruction in a major quake is beyond doubt. Moreover, quakes are often accompanied by adverse weather conditions which can multiply the damage. The

Puerto Rico and Point Arena plants are, respectively, between five and ten times the capacity of the theoretical reactor studied in the 1957 AEC report on accidental hazards of nuclear plants. They are being designed and constructed by the largest and most eminent of our technological giants, who should be well aware of the seismic risk factors in nuclear power plant design. Yet both plants were located either on or in close proximity to earthquake fault systems, and to large centers of population in what one can only explain as a mad game of dice with humanity.

One shudders to wonder what the risk of exposure is in the remaining 100 or so nuclear plants which will dot the countryside by the end of the decade. To what extent were seismic risk factors taken into account in the design of the thirty-four-odd plants that lie in the Northeast, along the St. Lawrence Seaway, and the Great Lakes, which in 1663 experienced earthquake? In the location of the sixteen-odd nuclear plants in the Southeast of the United States which in 1883 experienced an earthquake of the highest magnitude? In the design and location of the six present or planned nuclear plants which are constructed along the heavily populated coast of California? Perhaps there are satisfactory answers to these questions. The Puerto Rican and Point Arena experience suggests the contrary. The design and construction of our nuclear plants has proceeded in an atmosphere of secrecy, irrationality, and utter disregard of the facts of nature and the protection of our populations.

Nor does the threat to the populace of nuclear destruction unleashed by the forces of earthquake end with nuclear power plants. Scientists attending the annual Pugwash Conference in Oxford, England, in a statement dated September 13, 1972, formally expressed their fear at the potential devastation that the growing stockpiles of nuclear weapons throughout the world would pose in the event of major earthquake.[6] Their reference was the first to relate the growing arsenals of defensive and offensive warheads and stockpiled weapons to earthquake.

Still another major irrationality in land use planning has been the construction of dams and reservoirs of insufficient structural integrity in areas of high seismic risk. The risk of structural failure of the dam—and consequent catastrophic flooding of the low-lying areas before it—is compounded by the tendency of the weight of water in reservoirs to increase the seismicity in the local area. These effects build on themselves: The risk of failure of a dam which was not in the first place designed with sufficient structural resistance to earthquake is in itself increased by the crushing effect of the reservoir on the local land mass. The weight of the trapped water in effect makes the local area more susceptible to earthquake, creating a vicious circle that in turn increases the risk of dam failure.

Again, the evidence strongly suggests that one cannot assume that existing dams, many of them close upon heavily populated areas, have been adequately designed for seismic risk. A notable example is that of the Van Norman Dam, which very nearly collapsed in the San Fernando Valley earthquake of 1971, and forced the evacuation of 80,000 persons in the threatened areas surrounding the dam. The near failure of the dam was ominous in view of the relatively limited size of the earthquake itself. A slightly more intense quake would have sent thousands of tons of water rushing into a densely populated residential area. A more recent example of this lack of adequate design is that of the $428 million Libby Dam in Montana, an area of moderate seismicity. Dr. Richard L. Konizeski, a hydrologist at the University of Montana, in a detailed position paper released in April, 1972, accused the U.S. Army Corps of Engineers of designing and building the dam without having completed seismology studies recommended by the National Oceanographic Survey, the federal agency charged with jurisdiction in the area.[7] Konizeski noted that the underlying land mass was heavily fractured and faulted, and that the region was tectonically active. He made reference to experimental results obtained in the oil fields of Colorado, which suggest that the injection or seepage of water into underlying rock strata results in an increase in the frequency and magnitude of local earthquakes, and surmised that the dam would be inadequately designed to resist the new loads.

There is nothing to indicate that the Libby Dam was constructed with any less care and attention in design and construction by the U.S. Army Corps of Engineers than is normally devoted in these cases. A statement by corps officials suggests much to the contrary, and indicates that the corps was aware of seismic risk factors in the design of the dams, despite their having ignored the recommendations of another federal agency which indicated a need for further seismic studies. This raises a legitimate and important question with regard to the safety and reliability of the myriad of dams that have been designed and built throughout the country. The Libby Dam was allegedly designed with seismic risk factors explicitly in mind, and yet is thought to be sorely deficient by a professional hydrologist and by the National Oceanographic survey. One wonders about the structural adequacy of other dams throughout the country that may not have even received the minimum of attention to seismic design that is evident at Libby. Should their structural integrity be marginal—and the experience with the Van Norman Dam suggests that this may indeed be the case—one can expect an added dimension to the catastrophe that the coming earthquakes may rain upon the countryside.

The most pervasive irrationality in land use planning derives from the pattern of sprawling and unfettered development that has marked the countryside since the end of World War II, and that has seen its counterpart in many other countries of the industrialized world. The resultant "unrestrained, piecemeal urbanization"—a term coined by the federal Task Force on Land Use and Urban Growth —has the consequence of vast residential subdivision areas being located along active fault areas, and in soft plateaus of artificial fill. The creation of vast urban housing on manmade fill is probably most acute in cities of the West Coast, where the relative scarcity of land and the pressures of urbanization have caused a large expansion of the city into the surrounding waters. C. F. Richter noted this danger in a pamphlet issued on earthquake hazard in California.

> The risk of strong shaking, whether close to the fault or far from it, depends mainly on the character of the ground. Only large earthquakes reach damaging intensity on solid rock; but many moderate or even small earthquakes cause damage, more or less serious and widespread, to weak structures on alluvium (near the coast) or in valleys, beach sands, artificial fill, loose grading material and the surfaces of old land slides.[8]

Mexico City stands out as an example in a foreign country of a city whose location makes it highly vulnerable to seismic destruction. This city of nine million people is built in a seismically active zone, on fill in what was a few centuries ago a large lake.

A recent report by the urban Growth Task Force indicates that even under normal conditions the pressure for urbanization is likely to continue into the mid-1980's, with the anticipated creation of 27,000 new households in the United States—equal to the size of Green Bay, Wisconsin—each week by 1985.[9] This expansion very much suggests the continuation of pressures to develop land whose safety in time of earthquake is at best marginal. There is room for limited optimism that some of the more irrational practices in development may be curbed in the future, at least along the California coast. Much of the development along the urban bays in the state has been stayed by the operation of laws restricting new artificial fill on environmental protection grounds. However commendable this legislation, there still remains the potential for destruction of structures built during past booms on areas which are highly subject to earthquake tremor.

In a related area—building construction—there is much to suggest that a widespread pattern of inadequate local building codes and erratic enforcement practices have resulted in vast areas of structures which are unsound and incapable of withstanding the forces of local earthquake. The OEP report noted a startling lack of building codes in over 20 percent of municipalities in the United States, and a lack of uniformity among those jurisdictions which do have codes. The report also noted the uniform delays in updating many codes—with the result that advances in building technology are only belatedly reflected in current legal requirements—and a general pattern of laxity and inefficiency in enforcement of existing codes.[10]

The recent proliferation of high-rise concrete buildings in many urban areas of the West Coast is cause for concern. A recent report of the National Earthquake Information Center in Menlo Park, California, noted that after the 1969 Santa Rosa quake, "practically every reinforced concrete column was cracked and several exterior beams were cracked [on reinforced concrete buildings]. This . . . is not at all reassuring when extrapolated to reinforced concrete high-rise frame construction."[11] The report continued, "there is an increasing number of high-rise reinforced frame structures being built throughout the metropolitan San Francisco, Los Angeles and other western cities," and the collapse of one or more of them in earthquake "would not be a surprise." Indeed, an official of the center noted that the Veteran's Administration hospital which had collapsed in the 1971 San Fernando quake, causing the death of thirty-nine persons, was a reinforced concrete structure.

Some measures have been taken, at least in California, to insure the structural soundness of buildings of high public use. The most notable of these, the Field Act, passed in 1933 in the aftermath of the Long Beach earthquake, requires earthquake resistant design of school buildings, and has resulted in the demolishing of a considerable number of unsafe structures. Yet the state's voters have yet to approve bond issues designed to adequately fund the Act. This limited degree of success in the state has not been carried over into public measures which attempt to upgrade the structural soundness of old and vulnerable buildings and the notoriously dangerous proliferation of overhanging parapets. Los Angeles did not start requiring earthquake resistant structures in its buildings until 1933, and San Francisco until 1947. At last report, neither Los Angeles nor San Francisco have the funds available to require the anchoring of overhanging parapets.[12] A Presidential report noted that the legacy of old and vulnerable buildings in West Coast urban areas was particularly troublesome:

> . . . certainly thousands of buildings with bearing (sup-porting) walls of nonreinforced bricks, held together by sand lime mortar, are extremely vulnerable to earthquake damage. . . . A great earthquake will cause many of these to collapse either partially or totally. . . . The safety of many multi-storied buildings, speculatively constructed during the boom years of the 1920's is also questionable.[13]

Elsewhere in the world one jurisdiction of note to institute rigid building requirements has been Japan, due perhaps to its long and frequent history of earthquake and its generally enlightened tradition of architectural planning. Interest-ingly, the Imperial Hotel, designed by Frank Lloyd Wright—the only structure to survive the 1923 Tokyo earthquake intact —was razed in recent years to make way for a new high-rise construction. Most of the urban areas along the seismic belts of South America, the Mediterranean, India, and the Middle East are characterized by struc-turally unsound construction, easily subject to devastation by major earthquake.[14]

10. Sharing the Costs Resulting from Destruction and Rebuilding

ALTHOUGH the certainty of future earthquake is likely to bring with it a wide-scale destruction of property: housing, industrial and agricultural facilities, transportation and water, energy and sewerage systems, the means for equitably distributing the financial burden of this destruction and sensibly sharing the cost of rebuilding are primitive and inadequate. Moreover, many anomalies within the local tax structure tend to inhibit effective measures which property owners might otherwise take to reduce the potential for earthquake damage.

Except for a minimum of emergency aid and shelter provided by a variety of governmental agencies and private organizations, it is the property owner who is expected to bear the brunt of earthquake loss, either from savings or through earthquake insurance. Few households or property owners possess savings of a level adequate to cover the massive destruction of earthquake, and from an actuarial point of view a policy of relying on savings is highly inefficient and unreliable.

Yet earthquake insurance remains almost uniformly unavailable, and where available, often involves high premiums and requires a wide measure of noncovered losses. A recent study by the U.S. Department of Housing and Urban Development estimated that "the aggregate value of property exposed to earthquake damage is probably in the tens of hundreds of billions of dollars," yet only about $3 billion of this total potential loss is covered by earthquake insurance.[1] In analyzing this low level of coverage, the OEP report documents the pervasive public lack of knowledge about the need for earthquake insurance, reflective no doubt of the general level of ignorance with regard to risk in earthquake-prone areas and the unwillingness of governmental authorities in these areas to mount an effective information campaign. The report indicates that this ignorance is often compounded by "complacency—particularly in California—about the threat of serious earthquake," due probably to the relative infrequency of destructive quakes in the past. For example, the report indicates that "there is no evidence indicating a substantial increase in the purchase of earthquake insurance in the affected areas following the San Fernando quake." Moreover it is apparently difficult to purchase earthquake insurance. Most general property damage underwriters will not write earthquake policies, thus forcing the property owner to search among a limited number of underwriters who will issue them.

This inconvenience is itself accentuated by a general reluctance among insurance companies to write coverage in large amounts and to sell policies aggressively. The reluctance may be due to an understandable fear that companies could not meet the claims resulting from a single, highly destructive quake. The recent HUD study notes for example that "growing values of commercial and industrial properties have been concentrated in certain high risk areas and have increased to the extent that the potential liability on a single building may exceed the area-underwriting limits of a reasonably large insurance company."[2] Furthermore, rates for earthquake insurance vary widely and often involve a large deductible factor which is not subject to coverage under a policy. In the western part of the country, the losses not subject to coverage may run as high as 15 percent of the total coverage, thus rendering the policy ineffective for all but the largest earthquakes and making it considerably less attractive to prospective purchasers.

Nor does the current rate structure of earthquake insurance reflect any rationality with regard to the true underlying risks to which property is exposed, and with regard to any preventative measures which a property owner may have taken in an effort to reduce his losses. Thus a broad geographical area of the country will often be subject to the same premium level, despite the substantial difference in actual risk of earthquake within the area. And the premium levels do not reflect any measures which the property owner may have taken to reduce potential for damage to his property. These measures can include structural improvements such as the elimination of parapets, which would significantly reduce the potential for personal injury by the structure.

Many areas of high seismic risk contain property which is generally covered by insurance against fire, flood, or malfunction of a nuclear power plant. (In the case of the damage caused by malfunction of a nuclear power plant, the total damages for which the owner of a plant can be liable is limited to $560 million, thanks to a federal law passed in the 1950's largely at the insistence of insurance underwriters.) In the case of earthquakes, most of the damage to property and loss and injury to life is owing not to the tremor of earth itself, but to the consequences of tremor: large-scale fire, flood, and structural collapse. Yet many insurance policies designed to cover these calamities explicitly disclaim coverage if the loss was due to a calamity initially caused by earthquake.

This anomaly was most acutely made apparent in the wake of the 1923 Tokyo earthquake, in which large sections of Tokyo and Yokohama were destroyed by fire and flood caused in the first instance by earthquake. Nearly all the existing fire and flood insurance policies explicitly disclaimed coverage if the loss was in the first instance caused by earthquake, and argued that the entire loss was to be borne by individual property owners. The public indignation was such that it caused the resignation of the government and the passage of an act of parliament requiring insurance companies to pay 10 percent of the face value of premiums to policy holders. The brunt of the loss still fell, as it generally does, on the backs of the stricken population.

Certain anomalies in local tax structures tend to inhibit measures which property owners might otherwise take to reduce losses from earthquake.[3] The property tax often inhibits local government from enforcing seismic hazard restrictions when the enforcement might result in the condemnation and removal of a building which thus would reduce local tax base. Individual property owners are likewise reluctant to take measures which would otherwise reduce the potential for damage on their property, but result in an increase in the assessed valuation of their property.

These irrationalities indicate that the capacity of the nation to recover from the coming series of earthquakes is seriously in question. They indicate a strong need for clear and firm measures by governmental authorities charged with responsibility in the area. The results of these irrationalities could be disastrous to the intelligent and effective recovery of the nation from what appears to be a wide measure of destruction in the coming earthquakes. Indeed, the Presidential Task Force on earthquake hazards pointed out that major calamities "present a rare opportunity to reorganize urban structure." Our policies with regard to risk sharing should reflect this.

11. Intergovernmental Cooperation

COOPERATION among the governments of the earth in times of natural disaster has been largely limited to a series of unilateral actions by nations with a history of philanthropy, and by limited actions on the part of private, regional, or United Nations agencies. There was, and presently still is, no specific regional or global plan for confronting even those disasters with international implications. This deep lack of coordination has to some extent begun to change in the aftermath of the 1972 Stockholm Conference on the Human Environment.

The United Nations has now called for the development of a global master plan to deal with natural catastrophe, and has established a small permanent Office of Disaster Relief, located in Geneva.[1] If properly funded and encouraged by the member governments and the UN apparatus, these rather humble beginnings have the makings of an adequate global system.

A number of international agencies have taken intelligent, if small steps in the recent past. UNESCO, for example, has instituted regional monitoring and research facilities in various countries. A half-dozen UN affiliates or independent multinational organizations have a measure of relief they can offer, especially in the postdisaster period of resettlement and rebuilding. Many of these are hampered by poor habits of cooperation and restrictive charters, however, and cannot offer the full range of services and assistance required. The level of formal intergovernment relief commitments remains abysmally low, and a 1971 UN report indicated that only two governments, those of Sweden and Norway, had any standing commitment to help a country in the throes of natural disaster—in this case Peru.[2]

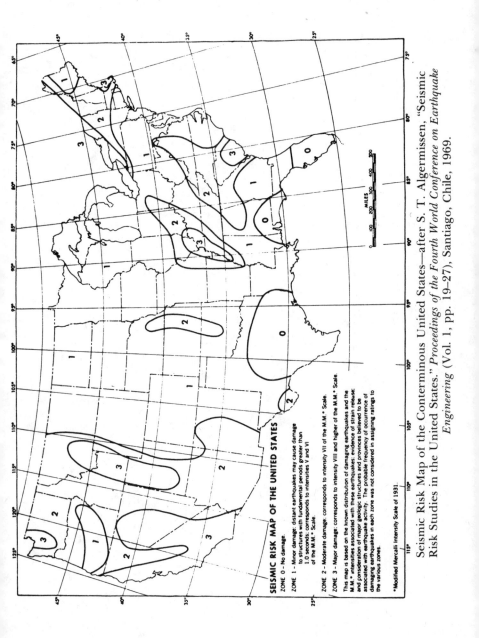

SEISMIC RISK MAP OF THE UNITED STATES

ZONE 0 – No damage.

ZONE 1 – Minor damage: distant earthquakes may cause damage to structures with fundamental periods greater than 1.0 seconds; corresponds to intensities V and VI of the M.M.* Scale.

ZONE 2 – Moderate damage: corresponds to intensity VII of the M.M.* Scale.

ZONE 3 – Major damage: corresponds to intensity VIII and higher of the M.M.* Scale.

This map is based on the known distribution of damaging earthquakes and the M.M.* intensities associated with these earthquakes; evidence of strain release; and consideration of major geologic structures and provinces believed to be associated with earthquake activity. The probable frequency of occurrence of damaging earthquakes in each zone was not considered in assigning ratings to the various zones.

*Modified Mercalli Intensity Scale of 1931.

Seismic Risk Map of the Conterminous United States—after S. T. Algermissen, "Seismic Risk Studies in the United States." *Proceedings of the Fourth World Conference on Earthquake Engineering* (Vol. 1, pp. 19–27), Santiago, Chile, 1969.

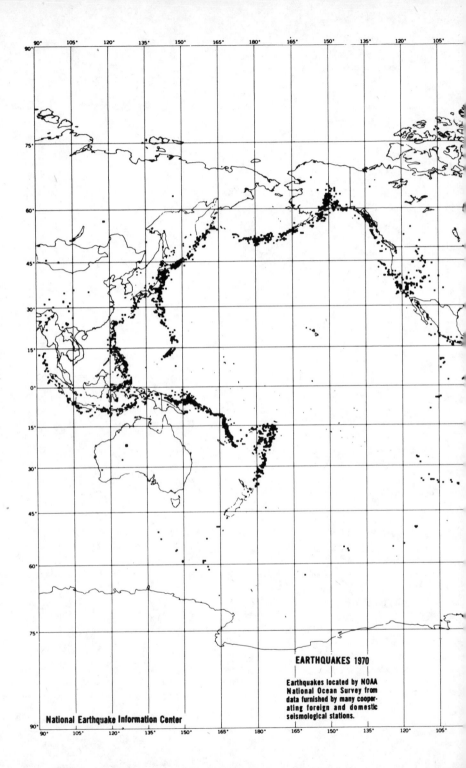

EARTHQUAKES 1970

Earthquakes located by NOAA
National Ocean Survey from
data furnished by many cooper-
ating foreign and domestic
seismological stations.

National Earthquake Information Center

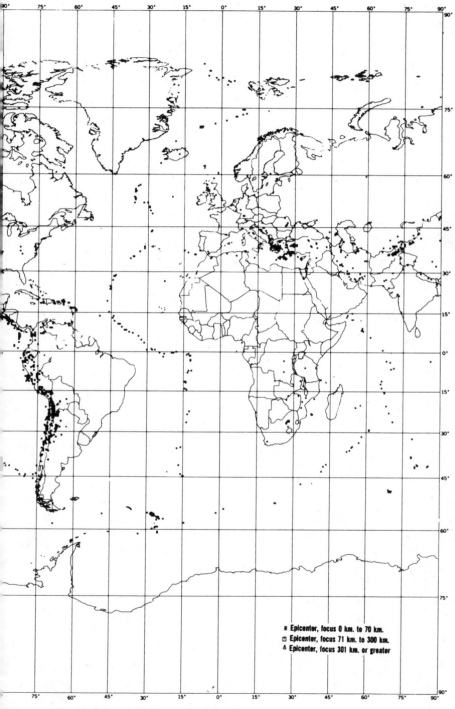

World Seismic Belts—NOAA map.

Part II:
THE EVIDENCE OF PRECOGNITION

For the windows on high will be
opened
and the foundations of the
earth will shake.
The earth will burst asunder,
the earth will be shaken apart,
the earth will be convulsed.
The earth will reel like a
drunkard,
and it will sway like a hut;
Its rebellion will weigh it down,
until it falls, never to rise
again.
   —Isaiah, Chapter 24, verses 18–20

There will be famine and
pestilence and earthquakes
in many places. These are
the early stages of the
birth pangs.
   —Matthew, Chapter 24, verses 7 and 8

1. The Scientific Basis

THERE appears to be a high degree of correspondence between the catastrophic events reported or predicted by earth scientists and sets of predictions concerning earth changes made by a number of "high psychics." It is possible that the trend of increased natural catastrophe is in fact confirmatory of these sets of psychic predictions. If valid on the whole, even if not in all detail, these psychic predictions may be of aid in forming fruitful hypotheses about the nature of our immediate future, and in suggesting neglected avenues of approach in the modern earth sciences and in the formulation of public policy.

Precognitive information regarding future earth changes —true information about the future given by individuals or high psychic ability other than through normal experience of reason—has traditionally been shunned in both modern public policy formulation and in the modern earth sciences. It seems that precognitive information is not taken into account as a factor in decision making about the future because policy makers or scientists are ignorant of its existence, because the information is assumed to be unreliable when tested scientifically, or because of numerous social prejudices against its serious consideration.

This oversight has followed, most probably, from a general and habitual antagonism both in the popular mind and among a substantial segment of the scientific world to considering precognitive information—valid information about future events by means other than inference from present and past events—as potentially true and valid data. The hostility has been particularly fierce within the community of earth scientists, to whom religious and psychic pronouncements have long been a *bête noire*. Richter probably reflects the majority opinion on the subject of precognitive earthquake prediction: "Claims to predict usually come from cranks, publicity seekers, or people who pretend to foresee the future in general."[1]

While one may question how much reliance should be placed on particular sets of precognitive information, the validity of certain forms of paranormal phenomena —precognition, psychokinesis, telepathy—is firmly established. In fact, there is much scientific evidence demonstrating that precognitive information is valid and true data about the future. Research in the field traces back to Sir Francis Bacon (1561–1626), who was the first in England to devise experimental methods of testing paranormal cognition, and has since included an impressive array of scientists: Charcot and Richet, William James, Henri Bergson, Sigmund Freud, William McDougall, Paul Kammerer, Wolfgang Pauli, Carl Jung.

Much of the most interesting recent research on precognition done in the United States has involved the application of rigorous experimental method by scientists with established reputations in more conventional fields.

Perhaps the most remarkable of the modern research in the field is that of Helmut Schmidt, a physicist formerly with the Boeing Scientific Research Laboratories and successor to Rhine at the Institute for Parapsychology. Professor Schmidt has experimented with a number of subjects' attempts to predict future events whose occurrence is determined by the theoretically unpredictable decay of a radioactive particle.

Schmidt's experimental method requires his subjects to predict which of four bulbs before them would next light. In order to assure randomness, he has devised a sophisticated and complex technology: The bulb to be lit is determined on the elementary quantum level by the radioactive decay of a strontium 90 particle, an event which according to the laws of physics is itself theoretically unpredictable. In a total of 63,066 trials, three subjects made correct predictive guesses of theoretically unpredictable subatomic processes with a probability of two billion to one against chance. In a second experiment of 20,000 trials, the subjects made correct predictive guesses at a level of odds against chance of ten billion to one.[2] Unlike many of the earlier results of Rhine and his colleagues, Schmidt's experiments have been reported in the most conservative scientific journals and have generally been accepted as valid.

Substantial psychical research has also been conducted in the Soviet Union, most notably in the field of telepathy, by Professor Leonid Vassiliev of the University of Leningrad. The number of scientific publications on parapsychology in the U.S.S.R., for example, grew from two in 1958 to thirty-five in 1967, and seventy in 1969.

H. J. Eysenck, who occupies the Chair in Psychology at the University of London, and is Director of the Psychology Department at the Maudsley and Bethlem Royal Hospitals in London, probably reflects the views of intelligent scientific observers:

> Unless there is a gigantic conspiracy involving some thirty University departments all over the world, and several hundred highly respected scientists in various fields, many of them originally hostile to the claims of the psychical researchers, the only conclusion the unbiased researcher can come to must be that there does exist a small number of people who obtain knowledge existing either in other people's minds, or in the outer world, by means as yet unknown to science.[3]

Other research has focused on those personality factors which correlate closely with the ability to accurately predict future events. In general, a high level of paranormal accuracy is exhibited by individuals who tend to be less defensive about the outputs of their deeper subconscious. They are usually capable of relaxing deeply and "stilling the mind."

Professor Gertrude Schmeidler of the Psychology Department of City University of New York, has demonstrated that the highest scores on tests of psychic capacity are obtained by subjects whose personality pattern most closely fits the ideal of the social group the subject most closely identifies with—student, businessman, or nurse.[4]

Recent data obtained by E. Douglas Dean of the Newark College of Engineering confirms these correlations. Dean has requested many hundreds of persons to predict a hundred-digit number that would be generated by a computer one hour after the time of their prediction. Dean found that the single group with the highest degree of precognitive accuracy was made up of over 100 corporation presidents. Within this group, those presidents whose companies have doubled profits over the five years prior to Dean's test performed most accurately.[5] Interestingly, precognitive ability does not appear to be a function of intelligence. In tests of members of Mensa, a group whose sole qualification for membership is an IQ within the top 2 percent of the population, researchers found ESP scores at the chance or less than chance level.[6]

Although the tasks performed in these experiments are as a general rule limited in scope, the experimental results suggest two principles which can be applied in determining the probable validity of predictions made by psychics under other than experimental conditions. First, if the individual's predictions have exhibited a high level of factual accuracy where verifiable, there is a higher probability that his predictions about events which have not yet occurred will be accurate. Secondly, if the psychic's personality structure tends to be receptive and nondefensive, the probability that his predictions about the future will be accurate increases. The experimental literature suggests, moreover, that there is a wide spectrum of psychic ability, and that individuals vary widely in the nature of events which they can accurately predict and the span of time over which they can accurately predict. This study limits itself to the predictions of psychics who have demonstrated a high level of factual accuracy where verified and whose predictions tend to span long periods of time. These are the "high psychics."

2. High Psychics

THE sets of predictions of future earth disturbances which we have examined vary in degree of specificity. They do contain, however, a number of common and mutually reinforcing elements. Taken together, the psychics generally agree that the last third or quarter of the twentieth century will be a period of destructive and rising natural catastrophe, principally marked by earthquake and famine, and culminating in a shift in the earth's axis. The predictions which contain specific dating agree that the period of earth disturbance will end sometime close to the year 2001, following the occurrence of significant and culminating earth disturbances in the years 1998 and 1999.

One set of predictions, which was made in the nineteen thirties and early forties by Edgar Cayce, suggests that the period of earth disturbances would definitively begin in the year 1958 and that a rising trend of earth disturbance would continue until the year 1998, with a shifting of the axis in 2001.

Predictions made by a Polish monk in the eighteenth century substantially agree with this view and add that the earth may be struck by a destructive comet in 1988 and devastated by earthquake in 1996. The monk also predicted that a world war would begin in 1938.[1] Count Louis Hamon, a British psychic known as Cheiro, predicted in the early twentieth century a destructive earthquake in the Atlantic and the Western Hemisphere for the latter quarter of this century.

We can only inferentially date the period of earth disturbance and famine which is stated in a famous set of predictions lacking specific dates. The high psychics involved in these latter predictions are a number of the Hebrew prophets whose predictions appear both in the Old and New Testaments —Isaiah, Ezekiel, Daniel, Jesus (as quoted in the Four Gospels), and John. These individuals predicted a

period of rising natural and social catastrophe, again principally marked by earthquake and famine. From what we can
gather of their biographies, each of them exhibited personality traits normally associated with a high degree of precognitive ability. Each predicted a large number of events concerning the near and long-term future, and where verifiable,
each has shown a relatively high degree of accuracy. None of
them attach specific dates to their predictions.

There is some external evidence to support a hypothesis
that the coming age of cataclysm represents a fulfillment of
Biblical prophecy. All of the later high psychics who converge on the latter portion of the twentieth century as a time
of catastrophe indicate that this period represents such a
fulfillment. There is, moreover, some degree of consensus
among the community of analysts or interpreters of Biblical
prophecy, who generally agree that we are now entering the
age of prophesized cataclysm and times of trouble.[2]

3. The Cayce Predictions

THE set of predictions with the highest degree of specificity concerning the expected earth disturbances of this period
is that of Edgar Cayce (1877–1945), an American and a
professional clairvoyant who completed his formal education
in the seventh grade, spent his young adulthood as a
salesman and photographer, and whose adult reading was
largely limited to daily passages from the Old and New
Testaments. During the last forty-three years of his life he
gave a prolific number of psychic "readings" which included,
besides predictions, extensive historical and scientific data
and medical diagnoses and treatment. By the time of his
death he had accumulated over 14,000 readings, approximately 9,000 of which consisted of medical diagnoses and
treatment of persons about the globe who had sought his aid
and most of whom he never met in person.[1]

Cayce's record of accuracy in these medical readings is, where verifiable, quite high, and the documented cases of inaccuracy on his part have been strongly correlated to occasions where he personally failed to maintain a positive and nondefensive attitude with regard to his subject. His readings of a scientific nature include descriptions of geological processes which were not in accord with the earth science of his day, but which in the opinion of at least one geologist have tended to be rendered more probable by the recent discoveries of geology. His readings of an historical nature are by and large highly unorthodox, but include for examble a discussion of the activities of Essene community along the shores of the Dead Sea in the few centuries immediately preceding Christ which was given ten years before the discovery of the Dead Sea Scrolls at Qumran in 1947.

By all accounts, Cayce was a gentle, selfless, and well-adjusted man, devoted to his family and to a life of quiet meditation, all traits which correlate positively with the literature on personality factors facilitating psychic or pre-cognitive ability.[2]

Cayce's method was dependent on his maintaining a deep meditative trance during which he would answer questions as to the health or personal history of the person requesting a diagnosis. Cayce's answer would often include detailed information regarding the personal characteristics of the subject, and would, at times, be delivered in the language of the subject, despite his never having met the subject and his personal ignorance of foreign languages.

Of overwhelming interest for purposes of this work are a series of approximately sixty-five psychic readings which Edgar Cayce gave describing past and future geologic events. Approximately fifty of these deal with past events in the earth's history, and cover events occurring as early as Pliocene times (10,000,000 B.C.). Fifteen readings concern predicted events for the period 1958–2001, and present a pattern of rising and widespread catastrophe on the earth, a pattern which is in deep contradiction with the standard Darwinian concept of gradual evolutionary change.

As early as 1959, a professional geologist—at his own request anonymous—concluded that the pattern of past geologic events described in the Cayce material was rendered more probable by the then emerging revolution in the earth sciences:

> Most of the readings on prehistorical subjects were given in the 1920's and 1930's and all were on file before 1945. It is thus clear that the majority of the psychic statements antedate nearly all of the striking discoveries recently made by such youthful fields of scientific endeavor as deep-sea research, paleomagnetic research, and research on the absolute age of geologic materials. Whereas the results of recent research sometimes modify, or even overthrow, important concepts of geology, they often have the opposite effect, in relation to the psychic readings, in that they tend to render them the more probable.[3]

It is difficult for a mind habituated to a perceived reality of gradual earth change to comprehend rapid changes of the dimensions predicted by the Cayce material. All the more so when a pattern of cataclysmic evolution of the earth's structure is apparently deeply at odds with the prevailing scientific viewpoint. Yet it is submitted that there are persuasive and substantial grounds which do not permit the rejection of the Cayce material out of hand, and which require the intelligent observer to weigh this material carefully in any attempt to set a rational public policy for the coming quarter century. Cayce had a remarkably high rate of factual accuracy in other areas of psychic information which are subject to easy verification. The documented instances of substantial error in his medical readings, for example, can be generally correlated to a lapse of Cayce's usual high-spirited state of mind. Many of the Cayce predictions with regard to future earth changes are woven into more general health or personal history readings whose details have been verified as accurate. Given the nature of the intimate relationship between an open, meditative state of mind and highly accurate psychic ability, it seems improbable that Cayce could give either fraudulent or inaccurate predictions with regard to earth changes while at the same time preserving a high rate of accuracy on the accompanying medical or personal history material.

Secondly, it is not always altogether provable that the rising crescendo of cataclysm predicted by Cayce is at odds with modern science. The rate of theoretical change in the earth sciences is such that major geologic concepts such as that of continental drift, disputed within the scientific world as late as 1968, are now accepted as fact. Moreover, there is much to suggest that the doctrine of uniformity—a hypothesis that changes in the earth's features occur in a slow, gradual, continuous fashion over long periods of time—is no longer completely tenable. Even relatively minor catastrophes such as the 1964 Alaska earthquake were found to be accompanied by massive elevation and subsidence in ocean beds and adjacent land masses. The well-documented discoveries of frozen animals and tropical flora in the Arctic and the Antarctic, caught in poses of death agonies, is persuasive evidence that these areas were once temperate and were subjected to traumatic and instantaneous cataclysm.[4]

An examination of the history of the doctrine of uniformity—it was elevated to the position of a scientific law by Charles Lyell (1797–1875), a British lawyer and mentor of Charles Darwin—suggests that its success in the middle of the nineteenth century had more to do with an overwhelming desire in Western Europe for stability and order than with a search for scientific truth. Indeed, Charles Darwin, one of the pillars of the doctrine, and a scientist who denied the occurrence of continental catastrophes in the past, "in a letter to Sir Henry Howorth admitted that the extinction of mammoths in Siberia was for him an insoluble problem."[5]

Finally, and of significant interest, certain of the specific geologic events predicted by Cayce have in fact taken place and one can detect a pattern of factual confirmation of the general trends of long-term meteorological disturbance, increasing volcanic eruption, subsidence and elevation of large portions of existing land mass and ocean bed, and increasing worldwide food shortages, which are the subject of the Cayce predictions. This pattern of confirmation is so definite as to be beyond the bounds of coincidence. Under any rational application of the scientific method, one is forced to the serious consideration of the Cayce material as at least accurate hints and suggestions of the dimensions of a coming period of cataclysm.

This is not to say that the Cayce materials form by themselves an adequate basis for the formulation of public policy for the coming quarter century. The predictions themselves are, with limited exception, quite general, and give only a brief indication of the dimensions and of the time of occurrence of the earth events. A rational and responsible public policy would necessarily be based on the sound and thorough findings of the earth sciences. This is not at all in contradiction to a position which at least considered the Cayce prophecies as having a reasonable scientifically verifiable basis, and which considered them as general statements of the dimensions and location of future earth changes. It is important to note in this connection that Cayce himself admonished the reader to rely on his predictions only when science tended to confirm them and to discount them otherwise.

The Cayce readings on earth changes which are predicted to occur during the period 1958–2001 appear in approximately fifteen readings given toward the latter part of his career, in the 1930's and 1940's, and constitute a relatively minor segment of this total work of more than 14,000 readings. The specific earth changes information is in response to the standard question and answer format followed by Cayce when in a meditative trance. The entire proceedings were stenographically recorded, and as is the general case, the specific earth changes information appears interspersed with other material not explicitly related to predicted earth changes. As the reader will note, Cayce employed an unusual and often complex syntax in his answers which differed significantly from the not unusual Midwestern way of speaking he employed when not in a meditative trance. The phenomenon corresponds to many cases of other psychics, who tend to employ unusual vocabularies, dialect, poetry, and generally unfamiliar patterns of speech when in the psychic mode.

As noted, Cayce's predictions tended to be of a general nature, pointing to the dimensions and general location of the predicted changes, and with only three exceptions did not predict a specific event at a specific time. The exceptions were the prediction of the discovery in 1968 or 1969 of artifacts of an advanced civilization reputedly destroyed in a series of cataclysms culminating about 10,000 B.C.; the prediction of a shifting in the earth's axis in the year 2001; and the prediction of inundation of portions of California and Nevada by seismic tidal wave or flood within three months after volcanic eruptions had occurred in either Mont Pelée or Mt. Vesuvius. No date is given for these eruptions.

As will be detailed below, some evidence exists for the predicted archaeological discovery. Furthermore, sudden shifts in the earth's axis probably have occurred in prior geologic times. Although there is no way of presently verifying the relationship of the predicted California inundations to eruptions in Vesuvius or Pelée, evidence does exist that inundations of California are not improbable.

The reader is directed first, however, to a statement of Cayce's more general predictions, which detail a series of changes in the South Pacific, the Atlantic, Japan, Europe, North and South America, the Arctic, and the Antarctic. In order to give the reader who is unfamiliar with the Cayce material a better feel for his style and for the nature of the information presented, the readings are offered *seriatim*, and without an attempt to editorially reconstruct the predictions according to their geographic location, or relative time of occurrence.

1. QUESTION: How soon will the changes in the earth's activity begin to be apparent?

ANSWER: When there is the first breaking up of some conditions in the South Sea (that's South Pacific to be sure), and those as apparent in the sinking or rising of that that's almost opposite same, or in the Mediterranean, and the Aetna area, then we may know it has begun.

QUESTION: How long before this will begin?

ANSWER: The indications are that some of these have already begun, yet others would say these are only temporary. We would say they have begun. '36 will see the greater changes apparent, to be sure.

QUESTION: Will there be any physical changes in the earth's surface in North America? If so, what sections will be affected, and how?

ANSWER: All over the country we will find many physical changes of a minor or greater degree. The greater change, as we will find, in America, will be the North Atlantic Seaboard. Watch New York! Connecticut, and the like.

QUESTION: When will this be?

ANSWER: In this period. As to just when. . . .

QUESTION: What, if any changes will take place around Norfolk area, Va.?

ANSWER: No *material*, that would be effective to the area, other than would eventually become more beneficial —in a port, and the like.

—April 9, 1932[6]

2. ANSWER: The earth will be broken up in many places. The early portion will see a change in the physical aspect of the west coast of America. There will be open waters appear in the northern portions of Greenland. There will be new lands seen off the Caribbean Sea, and *dry* land will appear. . . . South America shall be shaken from the uppermost portion to the end, and in the Antarctic off of Tierra del Fuego, land, and a strait with rushing waters.

—January 19, 1934[7]

3. ANSWER: As to the changes physical again: The earth will be broken up in the western portion of America. The greater portion of Japan must go into the sea. The upper portion of Europe will be changed as in the twinkling of an eye. Land will appear off the east coast of America. There will be the upheavals in the Arctic and in the Antarctic that will make for the eruption of volcanoes in the Torrid areas, and there will be the shifting then of the poles—so that where there has been those of a frigid or the semitropical will become the more tropical and moss and fern will grow. And these will begin in those periods in '58 to '98. . . .

—January 19, 1934[8]

4. ANSWER: As to the conditions in the geography of the world, of the country—changes here are gradually coming about.

No wonder, then, that the entity feels the need, the necessity for change of central location. For many portions of the east coast will be disturbed, as well as many portions of the west coast, as well as the central portion of the U. S.

In the next few years lands will appear in the Atlantic as well as in the Pacific. And what is the coast line now of many a land will be the bed of the ocean. Even many of the battlefields of the present [August, 1941] will be ocean, will be the seas, the bays, the lands over which the *new* order will carry on their trade as one with another.

Portions of the now east coast of New York, or New York City itself, will in the main disappear. This will be another generation, though, here; while the southern portions of Carolina, Georgia—these will disappear. This will be much sooner. The waters of the [Great] Lakes will empty into the Gulf, rather than the waterway over which such discussions have been recently made. It would be well if the waterway were prepared, but not for that purpose for which it is at present being considered.

Then the area where the entity is now located [Virginia Beach, Virginia] will be among the safety lands, as will be portions of what is now Ohio, Indiana and Illinois, and much of the southern portion of Canada and the eastern portion of Canada; while the western land—much of that is to be disturbed—in this land—as, of course, much in other lands. Then, with the knowledge of these—first the principles, then the material changes. The choice should be made by the entity itself as to location, and especially as to the active work. . . .

QUESTION: I have for many months felt I should move away from New York City.

ANSWER: This is well, as indicated. There is too much unrest; there will continue to be the character of vibrations that to the body will be disturbing, and eventually those destructive forces there—though these will be in the next generation.

QUESTION: Will Los Angeles be safe?

ANSWER: Los Angeles, San Francisco, most all of these will be among those that will be destroyed before New York even.

—August 13, 1941[9]

* * *

In addition to these readings given in his trance mode, Cayce reports having had an apparently prophetic dream on March 3, 1936, while returning on a train from Detroit to Virginia Beach following the successful end of a court action concerning his arrest in November, 1935, for practicing medicine without a license.

> I had been born again in 2100 A.D. in Nebraska. The sea apparently covered all of the western part of the country, as the city where I lived was on the coast. The family name was a strange one. At an early age as a child I declared myself to be Edgar Cayce who had lived 200 years before.
>
> Scientists, men with long beards, little hair, and thick glasses, were called in to observe me. They decided to visit the places where I said I had been born, lived and worked, in Kentucky, Alabama, New York, Michigan, and Virginia. Taking me with them the group of scientists visited these places in a long, cigar-shaped, metal flying ship which moved at high speed.
>
> Water covered part of Alabama. Norfolk, Virginia, had become an immense seaport. New York had been destroyed either by war or an earthquake and was being rebuilt. Industries were scattered over the countryside. Most of the houses were of glass.
>
> Many records of my work as Edgar Cayce were discovered and collected. The group returned to Nebraska taking the records with them to study.[10]

In summary, the Cayce predictions postulate a period, from 1958 to 1998 or 2001, in which major earth changes would occur. These include:

1. Destructive earthquake activity along the western coast of the United States.

2. The disappearance of the southern portions of Carolina and Georgia.

3. The disappearance of the greater portion of Japan into the sea.

4. Rapid earth changes in the upper portion of Europe.

5. The emptying of the Great Lakes into the Gulf of Mexico.

6. The rising of new lands along the eastern coast of the United States.

7. Dramatic earth changes along the North Atlantic seaboard, including the destruction of New York City.

8. Upheavals of the earth in the Arctic and Antarctic.

9. Volcanic eruptions in the torrid zones.

10. A shift in the axis of the earth, with corresponding climatic changes.

There are a number of good reasons for some skepticism as to the accuracy of the Cayce predictions. First, the earth science community is not at present making as drastic predictions as Cayce. Second, Cayce has apparently made erroneous predictions of earth changes in the past. For example, in February, 1933, he gave the following inaccurate prediction with regard to earth changes in San Francisco:

QUESTION: Will the earth upheavals during 1936 affect San Francisco as it did in 1906?

ANSWER: This'll be a baby beside what it'll be in '36.[11]

In fact, no significant earth changes occurred in San Francisco in 1936. Finally, the earth is now, in 1974, sixteen years into the thirty-three-year period, 1958–2001, and none of the major devastations has yet occurred.

Despite these problems in the Cayce predictions, there is a good basis for considering their possible validity. Cayce was a man unschooled in the earth sciences, who limited his reading to the Bible. His psychic predictions uncannily select devastations that are well within the realm of probability. The earth science data indicate that we are entering a period of profound earth disturbance. There is nothing in the present data that makes any of Cayce's predictions grossly improbable. A number of them are highly probable. Moreover, the present period of sustained global flooding and drought appears related to another element of Cayce's predictions: food shortage and famine.

Professor Lamb's previously quoted climatological studies indicate that the present world climatic shift "began around 1950 and took shape in the 1960s" and that "a secular change . . . is likely to persist for the rest of the century. . . ." The timing of these drastic changes in the world's climate corresponds closely to the 1958–2001 time scale predicted by Cayce. The increase in global volcanic activity since 1955 may be taken as further confirmation.

In *Earth Changes*, the professional monograph alluded to earlier, the geologist author systematically compares the Cayce predictions with the contemporary (1959) seismological and geological information on patterns of change in the earth's structure and surface. His detailed analysis concludes that the substantive geologic trends predicted by the psychic material are in fact confirmed by information derived from the earth sciences. He notes, however:

> It is in the advocation of a very rapid acceleration of this trend that the psychic information departs from the standard geological concept of gradual change.[12]

A brief review of his conclusions underscores the likelihood of occurrence at some future date of the Cayce predictions:

● Japan: The psychic information predicts that a substantial section of Japan will become ocean floor. The geologist notes the rapid and remarkable subsidence of substantial portions of the Japanese land mass, leading in one case to the submergence of an entire forest due to instability of a block of the local earth crust. He further notes the high seismicity of Japan, and its location on a mass of highly active faults.

● Europe and the North Atlantic: The psychic information predicts rapid changes in the upper portion of Europe. The geologist notes evidence of significant uplifts in the land mass in Northern Europe and concludes that the appearance

of new land in the northern Atlantic, an event predicted by
Cayce, would produce a sudden blockage or diversion of the
Gulf Stream, thus cutting off Northern Europe from the
warming influence of these currents. Moreover, the
geologist indicates that recent measurements of crustal
unwarping in the Canadian Arctic, Spitsbergen, and Greenland show relatively rapid rates of uplift—believed due to
unloading by recently vanished or presently melting ice
masses.

• The South Pacific: Cayce indicates that seismic activity in
an area of the South Pacific diametrically opposite Mount
Aetna in the Mediterranean will signal the start of a
significant phase of the earth changes. The geologist notes
that this area of the South Pacific (longitude 175 degrees E
and latitude 20 degrees S) is an area of great seismicity, easily
susceptible to activation.

• The Mediterranean: The psychic information is of
sinking or rising of land in the Mediterranean. The geologist
noted the rapid and unexplained drop in the level of waters
along the eastern portion of the Mediterranean in the years
immediately preceding 1959.

• The Eastern U. S. Seaboard: The Cayce material predicts extensive submergence and change along both the
northeastern and southeastern seaboards of the United
States. The geologist notes the relatively high seismicity of
the Northeast and the Southeast, and the phenomenon of
massive sinking of large areas adjacent to major eastern
earthquakes of the past, the most remarkable in the case of
the New Madrid, Missouri, earthquake of 1811. The U.S.
Geological Survey's *National Atlas of the United States* (1970)
indicates that New York City and immediate environs suffered an earthquake of VII–VIII intensity on the Modified
Mercalli scale sometime during the period 1638–1864. According to the scale, such an earthquake would cause "moderate to considerable damage in well-built structures; walls
and chimneys collapsed. Felt area: 50,000 to 250,000 sq. mi."

• New Land Masses: Cayce predicts the rising of new land
masses in the Pacific, Atlantic, and Caribbean. The geologist

notes the not uncommon emergence of land masses as the result of earthquake, in many cases involving a subsidence or rising of several thousand feet. He cites the emergence of land masses off Ecuador in 1960 and the tremendous submarine upheaval off the coast of Morocco in the Agadir earthquake of 1960. One can add the emergence of land mass off the coast of Iceland as a recent example.

• The Great Lakes: The Cayce material predicts the emptying of the Great Lakes into the Gulf of Mexico. The geologist notes the rapid degree of tilting occurring in the land mass northeast of the Great Lakes, and the consequent southeastward tilting of the lake basins. Even at its current relatively small rate, the degree of tilt would cause the emptying of the Great Lakes into the Mississippi drainage system within 1,600 years.

• South America: Cayce predicts severe earthquake for South America. The geologist notes the historical high seismicity of South America and its location on the boundary lines of several tectonic plates.

• Antarctica and Tierra del Fuego: The Cayce data predicts upheavals in Antarctica, the Arctic, and land off Tierra del Fuego, South America. The geologist notes the occurrence of an extremely rare and large earthquake—the first such ever recorded—in the northern Magellan Straits in July, 1959. Other commentators have noted the occurrence of an extremely rare volcanic eruption off the Antarctic in December, 1967, and a second in 1969, the first eruption in the area in 120 years, and the rapid rise of volcanic eruptions in the tropical zones since 1947.

• Safety Lands: The Cayce predictions indicate that portions of Ohio, Illinois, Indiana, and southern Canada are safety land that will be relatively stable during the period of upheavals. The geologist notes that these fall in areas of low seismicity. No comment is made with regard to the eastern portion of Canada and to the Virginia Seaboard, both safety areas according to Cayce, and both areas of moderate seismicity.

Cayce's forecasts of earth change include three predictions

of specific geologic events. One of these, made in 1940, predicts the rising in 1968 or 1969 of a submerged land mass in the Atlantic, which Cayce identifies as Poseidia, a region of the continent of Atlantis. The other two deal with specific earth events in the future—the timing of a series of shocks and inundations in California and the shifting of the earth's axis in the year 2001. There is some doubt as to the fulfillment of the prediction concerning Poseidia. It is possible that the discovery off Bimini, Bahamas, in 1969 of many miles of massive sea wall, and the remnants of pillars apparently predating the earliest known civilization in the New World may constitute a fulfillment.

The second of the Cayce predictions treats the timing of massive earthquake and inundation in California and Nevada within three months after volcanic eruptions in either Mt. Vesuvius in Italy or Mont Pelée on Martinique. If correct, it suggests an underlying relationship between phenomena which the earth sciences now consider as not meaningfully related: the eruption of volcanoes and subsequent appearance of seismic tidal waves each in relatively distant parts of the globe. The Cayce juxtaposition of these two phenomena would seem a logical one, flowing naturally from the unitary nature of earth processes that underlies plate tectonic theory, and in this sense the prediction supplies an interesting and potentially fruitful course of inquiry for future earth science. Moreover, the Cayce prediction of inundation is theoretically scheduled to occur approximately "a generation" prior to the predicted destruction of New York City toward the end of the century. Should events prove out the California prediction, the probability of Cayce's accuracy in other areas would necessarily increase.

The last of the specific predictions—the shifting of the axis in 2001—is especially relevant in two respects. It provides a point of departure for general discussion on the validity of the doctrine of uniformity in geologic change. The doctrine is squarely at odds with the pattern and rate of change which the Cayce material implies. If there is sufficient present evidence from which it can be reasonably adduced that the earth's axis has in fact suffered instantaneous and catastrophic shifts in past geologic time, a substantial scientific hurdle to consideration of the Cayce material—the doctrine of uniformity—is rendered considerably less credible. Finally, the prediction of a shift in the earth's axis, and the consequent revolution in the geography of the earth, suggests that any attempt to devise an even minimally effective public policy for the coming times need of itself be comprehensive, imaginative, and not least of all, possessed of great courage. The reader is turned for the moment to a brief examination of the substance and probability of the specific Cayce predictions.

The 1969 Bimini Discoveries

The specific predictions of the "rising" in Poseidia in 1968 or 1969 of artifacts of an advanced civilization, allegedly destroyed in a final series of cataclysms occurring about 10,000 B.C., appears in a fragment of a psychic reading given by Cayce on June 28, 1940. In a series of earlier readings, Cayce had postulated the existence of a continental land mass—Atlantis—positioned between the Gulf of Mexico and the Mediterranean.[13] In a series of cataclysms occurring in 50,700 B.C., 28,000 B.C., and 10,000 B.C. respectively, this land mass was broken up into a series of loosely connected islands, the most westerly of which lay in the area now occupied by the Bahamas, and may have been known within the culture that populated it as Poseidia. Remnants of the civilization, according to Cayce, appear in British Honduras, Yucatan, and Bimini on the western side of the Atlantic, and in the Pyrenees and Morocco on the eastern border.[14] Cayce's prediction as to the Bimini artifacts is succinct:

> And Poseidia will be among the first portions of Atlantis to rise again. Expect it in sixty-eight and sixty-nine ('68 and '69). Not so far away.[15]

It would be fruitless to attempt at this juncture to enter the labyrinthine debate on the existence of Atlantis and its advanced civilization, a debate that has spanned at least twenty-four centuries, from Plato's *Critias* through the adamant scientific denials of the 1950's. For present purposes it is sufficient to note that the morphological structure of the earth's crust lying beneath the Bahamas, composed of surface accumulations of coralline structure, suggests with high probability that the area once supported continental land mass. At least one scientific observer, after examining the results of intensive aeromagnetic surveys of the Bahamas made in the late 1940's by several oil companies, has concluded:

> The implication of magnetic contours by Aero Services is that the crystalline or sedimentary rock basement beneath the northwest Bahama Bank is generally deep, exhibits broad compositional changes, and is more continental than oceanic in crustial characteristics.[16]

It is thus at least in theory not at all improbable that what is now the Bahama Bank once supported a land mass of continental proportions.

There was, in 1969, a series of archaelogical discoveries off the coast of Bimini, Bahamas, which could arguably represent at least a partial confirmation of the Cayce prediction. These began with the initial discovery in February, 1969, in relatively shallow waters off the northwest coast of North Bimini of a 700-yard section of what has eventually come to be a thirty-one-mile series of massive sea walls. The walls stretch in circular fashion around the islands of North and South Bimini. The find, which has been documented in a recent book,[17] but has received surprisingly little attention elsewhere, has profound implications for modern archaeology, let alone for the accuracy of the Cayce predictions. The massive stones making up the sea wall, some of which are twenty feet across, have been preliminarily though not rigorously dated at about 9500 B.C., the date supplied by both Cayce and Plato for the final destruction of Poseidia,[18] and are of a quality indigenous to the Andes Mountains in South America. The dominant school of thought in modern archaeology dates the Olmecs as the oldest major cultural group in Central America, at about 1250 B.C., and no early cultural group has yet been thought capable of a technology which could design and build structures of these proportions.[19]

The details of the finds are remarkably impressive. In a series of expeditions in 1969 following the initial find, a group of archaeologists, underwater photographers, and amateur divers found three further sections of wall, 80 yards, 350 yards and 50 yards long, respectively. In initial accounts the rocks appeared to be rectangular and of massive proportions, the largest being 20 feet long and 10 feet wide, and the smaller closer to 6 feet in length. All appeared to have a uniform thickness of 2½ feet.[20]

Count Pino Turolla, a professional underwater photographer and archaeologist, describes his first encounter with the structures as follows:

> On reaching it [the sea wall structure], I immediately put on my scuba diving gear and dove. The scene was overwhelming. When my feet reached the bottom I was standing over a rectangularly cut stone approximately ten feet by five feet and two and one half feet thick. The surrounding stones were perfectly matched, some smaller, some bigger, but connected to each other like a huge mosaic pavement. I calculated that the width of the site of these square and rectangularly cut stones was at least sixty-feet across. The scene was startling because this huge stone layout stuck out clearly from the monotonous flatness of the sand covered bottom. The depth varied from between fifteen and thirty-five feet.[21]

Successive expeditions in the period from July to November, 1969, uncovered a series of broken sections of pillars, each section perhaps 3 feet long and some as large as 5 feet in circumference, and hand-carved from stone indigenous to the Andes. The pillars, forty-four of which were uncovered in 1969, appeared at intervals and in groups along the western or seaward edge of the wall and are believed to have been the remains of either mooring places or temples.

The years since 1969 have yielded a remarkable series of further finds, and our most recent information is that Count Turolla intends to continue his explorations. A total of thirty-one miles of sea wall have been discovered, together with countless pillars and other artifacts, some of which have been reportedly dated at 12,000 B.C. Perhaps the most remarkable, and in ways most mysterious single find has been that of a large astrological symbol—the symbol of Mars—composed of a semicircular ring of stone pierced by a massive stone arrow, lying in relatively shallow waters and in clear view of the surface of the sea. The distance from the mouth of the semicircle to the tip of the arrow is 180 feet, and the arrow itself is pointing due west.[22]

What is of more than passing significance for the purposes of the Cayce predictions are the explicit motives of Ferro and Grumley, the two young writers who made the initial discovery, and the intricate drama of their search. The Bahama Bank and the area surrounding Bimini had been subjected to intensive borings by prospecting oil companies in the 1940's and 1950's. No evidence pointed to subsurface structures or to the previous existence of any land mass other than the coralline islands and seabed of the area. A rock-boring project off South Bimini in 1966, financed by the Edgar Cayce Foundation and led by the professional geologist familiar with the Cayce material, failed to turn up any definite evidence in this regard.

Ferro and Grumley both had a personal interest in the Cayce material and were familiar with his predictions. Although neither had any prior experience with undersea diving or archaeology, both decided largely on personal grounds to leave Rome in late 1968, where they were then living, and journey down the East Coast of the United States in the family cabin cruiser *Tana*. Their explicit intention was to discover Poseidia and thus fulfill the Cayce prophecy. In the course of the journey to Bimini, they joined forces with several other groups which had similar motives. When the initial discovery was made, substantially all the private groups searching for the structure were represented on the *Tana*. Moreover, it must be noted that the discovery was made by amateurs, without the systematic use of scientific method (professional archaeologists were called into the find two weeks after the discovery), and by and large following the suggestions of a local Bahamian fisherman. Such are the vagaries of fortune and coincidence.

The California Earthquakes and Inundations

Cayce's prediction with regard to future earthquakes and inundations in California and adjacent areas are unusual in that they are related in time to the occurrence of what is presently considered an unrelated event, the eruption of a far distant volcano. The specific prediction was made in January, 1936, and appears in the context of a more general question relating to the nature of earthquakes, permitting an interesting insight into the nature of Cayce's seismological views:

QUESTION: What is the primary cause of earthquakes? Will San Francisco suffer from such a catastrophe this year? If so, give date, time and information for the guidance of this body, who has personal property, records and a wife, all of which it wishes safety.

ANSWER: We do not find that this particular district (San Francisco) in the present year will suffer the great *material* damages that *have* been experienced heretofore. While portions of the country will be affected, we find these will be farther *east* than San Francisco—or those *south*, where there has *not* been heretofore the greater activity.

The causes of these, of course, are the movements about the earth; that is internally—and the cosmic activity or influence of other planetary forces and stars and their relationships produce or bring about the activities of the elementals of the earth; that is the earth, the air, the fire, the water—and those combinations make for the replacements in the various activities. If there are the greater activities in the Vesuvius, or Pelée, then the southern coast of California—and the areas between Salt Lake and the southern portions of Nevada—may expect, within the three months following same, an inundation by the earthquakes. But these, as we find, are to be more in the southern than in the northern hemisphere.[23]

The substantive portions of the prediction—earthquakes and inundations in California and Nevada and eruptions in Vesuvius or Pelée—are not of themselves at all improbable, and in fact are likely given the weight of current geological evidence. What is unusual about the prediction is the juxtaposition of the two events in time, a juxtaposition for which there is no clear current scientific basis. The vulnerability of the southern California coast to earthquake-generated tidal wave has been detailed earlier. A seismic risk map of Nevada and Utah indicates that between Salt Lake in Utah and Lake Mead in southern Nevada lies a belt of relatively high seismicity. It is not improbable that a major earthquake in the area would displace the waters of these lakes and result in flooding of the area.[24]

Moreover, the recent dramatic increase in the level of world volcanic activity makes it likely that eruptive activity will occur in the near future in either Mt. Vesuvius or Mont Pelée. Mont Pelée last erupted in 1902 and resulted in the deaths of all but two of the capital city's 30,000 inhabitants.

Quite ominously, a nearby volcano, Soufrière, on the island of St. Lucia, only fifty kilometers away, experienced a series of small eruptions which terminated for the present in March, 1972. Soufrière also last erupted in 1902, resulting in 1,565 deaths on the island.[25] It is not known what the nature might be of the relationship between eruptions on Soufrière and on nearby Pelée. It is likely, however, because of their close proximity to each other and to the south Caribbean fault area, that they are responsive to closely related inner earth processes in the area. One can surmise that this close relationship, taken in tandem with the visible increase in worldwide volcanic activity, makes it highly likely that Pelée might experience eruption in the not so distant future.

Vesuvius' major eruptions occurred in 79 A.D., 1906, and 1944. The first of these resulted in the destruction of Pompeii, buried until its rediscovery in 1595, and the death of 16,000 persons. Like Pelée, it is located in relative proximity to volcanoes which have had recent eruptive activity. Mount Etna and a volcano on Stromboli Island —both some 300 kilometers from Vesuvius—have erupted within the last ten years; Etna, violently in 1964 and in 1974, and the volcano on Stromboli in 1967. All three volcanoes are located along the same Mediterranean fault system and presumably are responsive to the same set of earth forces. It is thus not improbable that eruptive activity could soon develop at Vesuvius.

The Shifting of the Axis

Cayce's third specific prediction is one that culminates the period of rising earth catastrophe from 1958 to 1998 in a dramatic shifting of the earth's axis in the year 2001, and in a consequent realignment of the earth's position with regard to the sun. The prediction occurred on August 11, 1936, in response to a specific question:

QUESTION: What great change or the beginning of what change, if any, is to take place in the earth in the year 2000 to 2001 A.D.?

ANSWER: When there is a shifting of the poles. Or a new cycle begins.[26]

In a later reading Cayce gave an indication that the shift in the earth's axis would, as expected, result in climatic changes throughout the globe:

ANSWER: . . . so that where there [have] been those of a frigid or the semi-tropical will become the more tropical, and moss and fern will grow.[27]

Although the dimensions of the shift are not set out with any specificity, the reading implies that the shift is substantial, and would result in the conversion of areas of the globe which are presently frigid—artic or subarctic—to more tropical or temperate areas. Moss and fern are typically native to the forests of North America, implying that the nature of the change will be at least such as to provide a temperate climate for areas now adjacent to the 70 degree meridian at both the arctic and antarctic circles. This would include parts of northern Canada, the Soviet Union, Greenland, and Alaska in the northern, and the outlying parts of Antarctica in the southern hemisphere. The shift itself, as the professional geologist points out, is internally consistent with the Cayce predictions of massive earth disturbance in the period 1958–1998, and would be the logical consequence of large-scale crustal displacements during the period.

The doctrine of uniformity is a major scientific constraint on the likelihood of the Cayce prediction, and most of the scientific commentary on the probability of shifts in the earth's axis in past geologic time has postulated the rate of shift as gradual, corresponding in theory to an equally gradual rate of displacement in the earth's crust. T. Gold, in an article in *Nature* magazine in 1955, concluded in this vein:

> If a continent of the size of South America were suddenly raised by 30 meters, an angle of separation of the two axes of the order of one-hundredth of a degree would result. The plastic flow would then amount to a movement of one-thousandth of a degree per annum. The earth would hence topple over at a rate of one degree per thousand years or by a large angle in about 10^5 years. . . . It is thus tempting to suggest that there have been just a few occasions when the axis has been "free" and has swung around as rapidly as would be given by the stiffness of the earth and the rates of tectonic movement, leading to a time-scale of the order of 10^5 or 10^6 years, but scarcely longer.[28]

Although we are not earth scientists, it appears to us reasonable that a toppling over of the earth and a consequent shifting in its axis in response to crustal displacement is not at all improbable, and the rate of shift itself would be a function of the rate of change in the earth's crust. The dominant view postulates that free shifting in the earth's axis has occurred in earlier geologic times and did so in response to gradual changes in the earth's crust. The shift of the axis was itself gradual. The plausibility of the Cayce prediction of a sudden and large displacement in the earth's axis thus in turn depends on the likelihood that the causal crustal displacements would be as predicted: large and relatively sudden.

Like the debate on Atlantis, the controversy over whether the evolution of the earth's surface is solely determined by gradual change over long periods of time, or is largely a function of a series of intermittent cataclysmic events, has been bitter, angry, and in large part inconclusive. One view of evolution closely interrelated the development of new species with the occurrence of natural catastrophes, and is poetically expressed by Ovid:

> When, therefore, the earth, covered with mud from the recent flood, became heated up by the hot and genial rays of the sun, she brought forth innumerable forms of life, in part of ancient shapes, and in part creatures new and strange.

Darwin saw in this catastrophistic view a considerable adversary to his conviction that species evolved by competition in a context of gradual change. His deep emnity to a view of cataclysmic evolution—both of species and of the surface of the earth—found a strong ally in the intellectual establishment of Western Europe, whose interest lay in a strong popular perception of reality as highly structured and immune to sudden change. It was in this context that the great debates of the latter part of the nineteenth century on the nature of the evolution of life and of the planet were held.

While the array of intellectual and social forces was such that the hypothesis of uniformity was held to be fact by the turn of the century, the last thirty years have seen a growing awareness of the inability of a model of uniformity to account for much of the emerging data, both in the earth and biological sciences.

To some extent, the discontent of biologists with the adequacy of the Darwinian model is more articulate than that of the earth scientists, and Arthur Koestler has noted that the prevailing view of evolution maintains, in contradiction to the Darwinian view, "that the evolution of species is the combined result of a whole spectrum of causative factors, some known, most of them unknown."[29]

There are considerable grounds which cast doubt on the view that our planet evolved in a steady and uneventful march through time. Geology and archaeology provide some of the evidence. In 1963, two Cambridge geologists proposed the hypothesis that the long-noted alterations in the polarity of strips of lava found along the ocean floor were the result of eruptions that occurred in periods of reversed polarity of the earth's magnetic field: The North Pole alternately became the South and vice versa over intervals of geologic time. These reversals are not random and without reason. Another Cambridge scientist indicates that changes in the earth's magnetic field and in the polarity of the earth are in some way tied up with the rotation of the planet. He concludes:

> . . . this leads to a remarkable finding about the earth's rotation itself . . . . the earth's axis has changed also. In other words, the planet has rolled about, changing the location of its geographical poles.[30]

This tying of the earth's reversal of polarity with shifts in its axis is not without consequence for the view that the world has evolved through intermittent catastrophe. Some evidence—detailed dating and examination of the polarity of iron particles in the fired clay of Greek and Etruscan pottery of the eighth century B.C.—indicates that the earth's polarity last changed at about 800 B.C. This was itself a time of great cataclysmic upheaval in the earth, and included visible and recorded disturbances in terrestrial motion.[31] Moreover, even on a theoretical plane there is much to suggest that prior shifts in the earth's axis were of a magnitude considerably greater than one-thousandth of one degree. J. Evans, a British geologist of the latter part of the nineteenth century, "envisaged the possibility that, under a change of load in the crust, the crust would be forced to alter its position in relation to the axis by as much as twenty degrees."[32]

These conclusions are reinforced by much of the evidence of rapid climatological change and catastrophic destruction of flora and fauna that has grown out of research of the last 150 years. Under any rational application of the principle of parsimony—a principle which holds that the more valid scientific hypothesis is that which most simply and elegantly accounts for all relevant data—it is the hypothesis of change through intermittent catastrophe that appears the most valid. Julius Hann, an Austrian meteorologist who died in 1921, summarizes the case succinctly:

> The simple and most obvious explanation of great secular changes in climate, and of former prevalence of higher temperatures in northern circumpolar regions, would be found in the assumption that the earth's axis of rotation has not always been in the same position, but that it may have changed its position as a result of geological processes, such as extended rearrangement of land and water.[33]

Among the most notable of the examples of rapid geological change—an example, incidentally, known to Charles Darwin—is the evidence of extraordinarily rapid disappearance in sequence of the glacial cap covering North America, and of Lake Agassiz, the large glacial lake resulting from the melting of this cap. The duration of the process—less than one thousand years—and its relatively recent occurrence can only be explained under circumstances of rapid and catastrophic change. Other examples abound: the evidence of great areas of Western Europe being successively and in rapid sequence oceanbed and land mass; the appearance of great erratic stone masses from northern Canada and Labrador— some of them 13,500 tons and 144,000 cubic feet in volume—scattered around the Northeast and Midwest of the United States, often perched in precarious positions; the existence of similar "erratics" throughout the Alps and Scandinavia.

Evidence of the catastrophic and sudden death of all life in large areas of the earth is overwhelming. In northern Alaska, a section of frozen tundra contains the mangled remains of many thousands of mammoths, mastodons, superbison, and horses, frozen together in a common grave. Vast areas of the Arctic Ocean bed and the Siberian Peninsula have yielded similar and massive mounding of rhinoceros and elephants, prompting J. D. Dana, the leading American geologist of the second half of the nineteenth century, to write: "The encasing in ice of huge elephants, and the perfect preservation of the flesh, shows that the cold finally became suddenly extreme, as of a single winter's night, and knew of no relenting afterward."[34] In the stomachs and teeth of the mammoths were found plants and grasses that do not grow in northern Siberia, the site of the find, and an area generally desolate and barren of any vegetation. Medical examination of the skin of the animals indicated sudden death by suffocation from gases or water and not from long-term exposure to a slowly changing and hostile climate. Other finds in England and France indicated the contemporaneous grazing of hippopotamuses and other tropical animals with reindeer and bison, all destroyed in a vast mud deluge dated at no more than five or six thousand years ago. Vast areas of Britain and Western Europe show clear evidence of the agony and sudden death of entire marine populations.

A recent and remarkable set of evidence for catastrophic change is reported in a 1971 colloquium which examined the findings of Camp Century, a deep ice core in the Greenland ice sheet. The participants report a catastrophic climatic change occurring about 90,000 years ago, and strongly evidenced in transformations in the flora in certain parts of the Gulf of Mexico and in the structure of the Camp Century core. The participants report that "the conditions for a catastrophic event are present today." What is of interest is the deep recognition by these geologists of their present ignorance of the mechanisms and rate of geological change.

Indeed, what remains a curious and unexplained mystery to this day is Darwin's refusal to alter his adamant position against the existence of catastrophe as a significant force in the evolution of species and of the earth. He was aware of a good number of the finds of suddenly frozen animal populations and admitted that they posed an insoluble problem for him. Moreover, in *The Origin of Species*, he goes so far as to note that: "Scarcely any paleontological discovery is more striking than the fact that the forms of life change almost simultaneously throughout the world."[35] The finding is strange, and most emphatically confirmatory of a view that life has evolved in significant degree in response to widespread and general disturbances and destruction of the environment. It stands in square opposition to his closely held view that "the process of modification [of species] must be slow, and will generally affect only a few species at the same time."

All the evidence adduced suggests that a periodic shift in the earth's axis is far from implausible and is the logical result of rapid displacements among the tectonic plates composing the earth's surface. The responsible inference is that Cayce is describing for the last quarter of this century a course of geologic events not unsimilar to events which have shaped the face of the earth countless times in the forgotten past.

Food Shortage and Famine

Before leaving the discussion of the Cayce material, the reader is directed to a number of incidental predictions which he made. These are not without consequence for humanity during the coming period, and for which there is some gathering pattern of confirmatory evidence. Cayce predicted that the period 1958–1998 would be one of widespread food shortage and famine.

In a reading in 1943, Cayce was asked by a prospective farm purchaser whether the acquisition was a sound one. His response, pertaining to the period of earth changes in the last quarter of the century, was as follows:

> These conditions have not changed. For the hardships for this country have not begun yet, so far as the supply and demand for foods is concerned.[36]

Cayce reinforced this view in another reading on the coming period of world food shortage:

> Anyone who can buy a farm is fortunate; and buy it if you want to grow something and don't want to grow hungry in some days to come.[37]

The theme that the world's agricultural machinery would be insufficient to supply the nutritional requirements of mankind during the period of earth upheaval, requiring supplemental farming by a sizable number of persons presently outside the agricultural sector, appears in a number of places throughout the readings. One given in 1942 indicates:

> QUESTION: Should I hold the 25 acres of land near Oceana [Virginia]; also, two sites in Linkhorn Park and lots on 54th Street [Virginia Beach, Virginia]?

> ANSWER: Hold them until at least the early spring; that is, the lots. *Hold* the acreage; for that may be the basis for the extreme periods through which all portions of the country must pass—for production for self as well as those closer associated with the body.[38]

In one reading Cayce suggests that the world's food output may at one point during the period of upheaval be tied to a return to the soil by large sectors of the population:

> All that is for the sustenance of life *is* produced from the soil. Then there must be a return to the soil. Every man must be in that position that he at least creates, by his activities, that which will sustain the body—from the soil; or where he is supplying same to those activities that bring such experiences into the lives of all.[39]

At another point, Cayce appears to touch on the possibility of social upheaval resulting from the combined trauma of earth disturbance and food shortage. He advocates "a return to the land," and "not so much of the makeshift of labor in various field . . . for unless this comes, there must and will come disruption, turmoil and strife."[40]

It is true that these predictions are of a generally vague and indeterminate nature, leaving the reader to infer the timing and dimensions of food shortage, and the interrelationship of factors which may underlie the shortage: the destruction of the modern agricultural economy and its requirements of orderly transactions and readily available raw materials and machinery; the pattern of drought and climatological changes accompanying the period of earth upheaval. Importantly, in a reading in 1944—a year prior to his death—Cayce provides a suggestion of the future configuration of food-producing areas in the world at some point in the twenty-five-year period:

> Saskatchewan, the Pampas area of the Argentine. . . .
> portions of South Africa . . . these rich areas, with some
> portions of Montana and Nevada, must feed the world.[41]

These areas are generally ones of low seismicity, suggesting that the world regions of future food production will be largely determined by the nature and location of earth disturbances. The reading is largely puzzling in that it omits large present food-producing areas in Australia, China, and the Soviet Union, all of which exhibit a relatively low degree of seismic risk.

Much more specific, however, is the factual pattern of adverse meteorological change and consequent food shortage. These climatological factors have resulted in a world-wide food shortage, which gives every indication of becoming more acute in the next several years. Responsible dispatches have reported that many areas of India, West Africa, and Ethiopia are already experiencing widespread food shortage. In the United States, the unexpected development of a large protein shortage has already had wide ramifications both in terms of the price and supply of protein-dependent livestock.

The Peruvian anchovy crop, a staple source of nutrition for the world's livestock, has disappeared dramatically since 1972 and shows present signs of possible extinction. The fluctuations of ocean temperatures in the currents off the Peruvian coast—one major cause of the periodic changes in the level of the anchovy population—were, in the eyes of scientific observers, "one of the most severe ever observed." A recent commentator on the anchovy crisis indicates that the highly unusual combination of underlying earth forces which has caused the disappearance cannot be presently scientifically explained: ". . . some puzzling circumstances have made the scientists closest to the subject uncertain about the extent of the relation between the sea change and the reduction in the anchovy crop."[42] The brunt of the evidence indicates that the anchovy crop will probably no longer be available as a stable source of protein for the world's livestock:

> If things are as bad as the worst prognostications indicate, the anchovy fishery may, like the California sardine industry and the Hokkaido herring industry, collapse forever. Many aspects of the history of the Peru fishery bear a disturbing resemblance to the events that brought about these earlier disasters.[43]

Other potential sources of protein, such as wheat, corn, soybeans, and other grains are themselves in short supply.

The emerging world food shortage is all the more disturbing because it appears to be importantly affecting the United States, traditionally a supplier of excess food to places of famine throughout the world, and the country of highest agricultural productivity. This suggests that not only will the United States not be in a position to offset food shortages in other parts of the globe, but it may very well have to call on food supplies of other countries for its own needs.

4. Precognition, Public Policy, and Science

IT is difficult to evaluate the likelihood of any of the specific events predicted by the psychics in a manner sufficiently rigorous to support a substantial shift in public policy toward recognition of natural catastrophe. Such a shift could come only after thorough scientific study and debate. There is undeniably a high degree of correspondence, however, between the disturbances now occurring about the earth, those expected by the earth sciences, and the psychic forecasts, a correspondence which may be in fact confirmatory of the validity of the predictions in general if not in detail. Given this correspondence and the generally high rate of accuracy of the psychics in predictions of similar character, it would be irresponsible to dismiss the general framework provided by the psychics in developing hypotheses about the immediate future.

Their predictions may be of aid in the following specific respects:

1. *Time Horizon.* They provide an explicit time horizon for the duration of a period of extreme natural disturbance. Almost uniformly, the predictions converge on the years 1998 to 2001 as the end of the period of disturbance. Although there is much in the existing earth science literature to suggest that the planet is on the edge of a period of catastrophe, we have uncovered no single scientific statement which attempts to predict the timing and duration of the period. The psychic predictions provide a working hypothesis which has immediate and disturbing consequences.

2. *Specific Events.* The psychic material predicts a number of specific and potentially catastrophic events for the period, notably the destruction of a major portion of Japan, of major cities within the United States, and of large portions of Latin America. The earth sciences indicate that none of these

events is unlikely, and many of them are highly likely. The earth sciences have only a sketchy view of the specific nature of many of the events, notably destructive earthquake in the eastern portion of the United States. Moreover, there is a shocking lack of policy coherence and general preparation for catastrophe on the part of most governmental authorities about the globe. The specific events foretold by psychics provide at least an initial base upon which to concentrate efforts and resources.

3. *Scale of Destruction.* Although it is generally known that specific parts of the earth are presently prone to major earthquake, there is much division of opinion within the earth science community as to the specific scale of magnitude and destructiveness of the expected earthquakes. The psychics again provide an initial working measure of the potential destructiveness of expected disturbances, and a frame of reference within which to direct research and develop adequate response plans.

4. *Public Policy Measures.* If the scale of destruction predicted by the psychics is in fact valid, the response measures would probably include, for example, the construction of a number of new cities in relatively stable areas and the resettlement of large numbers of the human population. Barring the development of extensive prevention techniques, it probably includes the wholesale evacuation of the people of Japan and their resettlement throughout the world.

The social and logistical problems posed by the measure are immense and would require great study and debate. The present mechanism for global response to natural catastrophe is in its infancy. Many countries lack an adequate and functioning disaster response mechanism, and the United Nations has only recently established a disaster relief office. Widespread catastrophe is likely to involve serious questions of a national, regional, and international nature, and requires the development of adequate national and multinational disaster prevention and preparedness authorities.

122 THE AGE OF CATACLYSM

5. *Development of Science.* Much of the Cayce material on earth changes is devoted to new theoretical models and explanations of basic earth processes. Much of the material is highly unorthodox and delivered in obscure fashion. When it was first presented by Cayce in the 1930's and 1940's, the material was in conflict with then dominant scientific views on earth processes. The judgment of at least one geologist is that the recent revolution in the earth sciences has made Cayce's theories more rather than less probable. We have found Cayce's theoretical models useful in other fields, notably psychology and history, in integrating novel and often puzzling data. Our assumption is that the same may be the case in the earth sciences. It is the duty of an impartial scientist to scour all data that might be relevant to the development of his field.

Part III:
SURVIVAL AND REGENERATION

1. Man and the Earth

IT is clear that whatever measures mankind collectively decides to undertake during the quarter century of catastrophe must be taken from the perspective that the earth is an integral biosphere, and that the activities of man and his systems—societies, institutions, values, products—are part of a wholly integral earth process. The nature of this process is at once complex, subtle, interdependent, fragile, and resilient. One can strongly argue that successful measures to enable the human race to survive a period of intense catastrophe and to resettle and reintegrate himself in a progressive and wise fashion can only be taken from a perspective which fully appreciates the nature of our ecology.

In this sense, the rapidly growing literature on the state of the earth's ecology and the heightened public appreciation of the earth as a limited system, while not explicitly related to human needs in a time of sudden catastrophe, provide a strong frame of reference for the design and intelligent response to catastrophe. Caldwell, in *In Defense of the Earth*, has broadly characterized this growing body of knowledge and public action on the environment as a "movement to bring man's relationships with the planet Earth under some form of rational control."[1] The characterization clearly applies in spades to any program for rational adaptation by man to the coming catatrophes. Even the most cataclysmically oriented of the environmentalists—the Club of Rome—argue that complete breakdown of the world system and of world resources is about 130 years off, and that mankind's collective adaptive responses—the application of reason in his relationships to the earth—need be carried out in this relatively extended time frame. Any intelligent and effective response to the coming cataclysms—again, in principle, the application of reason in man's relationships to the earth—would have to be effected in a time frame of less than thirty years, and with a degree of change and disruption of the present arrangement of the human process far more vast than the restructuring argued for by the environmentalists.

In *An Endangered Planet*, Richard A. Falk argues persuasively for a new world-order based not on traditional concepts of power and division among nations, but on ecological urgencies and an explicit environmental perspective. He declares that "the first law of ecological politics [the new order] is that there exists an inverse relationship between the interval of time available for adaptive change and the likelihood and intensity of violence, trauma and coercion accompanying the process of adaption. Put in a less technical, but no less precise way: the sooner the better."[2] At another point, Falk assumes, however, "that no apocalyptic bridge to the future will or can be built in the decades ahead. That is, my reasoning supposes that there will be no nuclear war or equivalent ecological catastrophe (e.g., death of the oceans) and no sudden burst of enlightened cosmopolitanism such as would enable a world constitutional convention to produce a new world order system agreeable to leaders of all principal societies."[3]

Falk's assumption that no ecological catastrophe will force man to make new constitutional arrangements is, we believe, false.

We turn first to a brief inventory of the earth's biosphere and of the human systems that inhabit it and evolve within it, and to a brief evaluation of the transformations that the earth changes may well bring to these. The inventory is useful from a variety of perspectives. It underscores the earth as a limited functioning life system, capable of being acted upon and affected by intelligent collective action. It underscores the fragility of the earth and the vulnerability of the amenities of the modern society we have for centuries struggled to achieve and on whose survival our continued life depends.

2. Man's Biophysical Environment

MAN shares the fundamental biological and physical requirements of most living species: air, water, food, and various degrees of temperature and pressure. The vital difference lies in man's effect over these needs. As John McHale has pointed out, "Our distinctive human needs are complicated by the high degree of social development of the human species. Social patterns are more determinant of biophysical events than we generally concede."[1] Thus, in the sense that man relies overwhelmingly on his social organization to produce these basic needs—potable water, nutritive food, heating, and air conditioning—his ability to meet these fundamental needs in a time of catastrophe is only as great as the ability of the social system which fulfills these needs to respond and adapt to upheaval.

Water

The available evidence suggests that water resources are already in critical balance in many world regions. Population growth and urban concentration have been probably the most critical factors in the dramatic growth of the demand for water in this century. For example, the amount of water used in cities has increased seven times from 1900 to 1960 and is expected to reach twelve times the 1900 figure by 1980. In the United States alone, consumption has risen from 40 billion gallons annually in 1900 to 300 billion gallons annually in the 1960's, reflective of the growth of a highly industrialized and interdependent society. Rough estimates of the usage of water indicate that 45 percent of water is for the dilution of effluents and sewage wastes, 30 percent for the irrigation of crops, 10 percent for industrial purposes, and the remainder, 15 percent, for domestic and miscellaneous purposes.

The present world system for the supply of water is in general highly vulnerable to earthquake. Many places which are apt to serve as areas of rescue are inadequate to serve present needs, let alone the needs of an expanded population in times of disaster. Urban areas throughout the world are in many cases fed by a complex system of watersheds, reservoirs, aqueducts, and in limited cases, purification plants. Even in the more highly industrialized nations it is questionable whether these systems can adequately supply water and sewerage needs. The U.S. Department of Health, Education and Welfare concluded that "nearly half of our 20,000 community water supply systems contain defects that are serious enough to place them in a potentially unsafe status."[2] The water supply is highly critical in the less developed countries. The United Nations has estimated that 75 percent of the urban population in cities in the less industrialized countries do not have running water in their dwellings, and that only 12 percent have adequate sewerage and sanitary facilities.[3] In many cities, running water is only available during certain hours of the day.

Whatever evidence is available as to the construction of dams and reservoirs and the nature of the system which transports water to urban areas and distributes it within the cities suggests that the system may be vulnerable to seismic disturbance. Earthquakes can and have in the past destroyed or damaged critical portions of the water supply and sewerage treatment system, including dams and reservoirs, sections of aqueducts, and water mains and pipes in the urban areas. Moreover, the generally widespread nature of many watersheds, often located at large distances from cities, indicates that a city's water supply may be affected by an earthquake which does not harm the city itself but does damage to structures in the faraway watershed area. New York City is an example. Its watersheds are largely in upper New York State, an area of relatively high seismicity. It is not altogether improbable that earthquake activity there may damage or destroy important parts of the water supply system.

No significant water supply exists in areas of the world that will probably be safe spots for masses of humanity migrating to avoid the coming destruction in their own lands. Much of these land masses—central and southern Africa, large parts of Canada, the Soviet Union, and China—are largely undeveloped and have no present capacity to supply the massive water and sanitation needs that a vastly increased population would present. The suggestion is that a great deal of wisdom, rationality, and toil must go into adequately planning for man's water and sanitary needs during the coming period.

Food

The popular conception that the earth's food requirements and man's agricultural efforts are largely limited to taking care of the requirements of the 3.3 billion humans that inhabit the planet is misleading. Man's efforts in fact support a total biomass equivalent to nearly 18 billion human beings—a mass consisting of 3.3 billion humans, and livestock (cattle, hogs, sheep, buffalo, horses, poultry, mules, goats, cats, dogs) whose daily food requirements are equivalent to those of 14.5 billion additional human beings. Georg Borgstrom has quite vividly indicated the demands of the biomass on the world food supply:

> The globe is not merely inhabited by humans, but in order to maintain his present nutritional standard and retain the type of agriculture now prevailing on the earth, green plants must carry a feeding burden which is far in excess of the 3 billion humans or what amounts to approximately 17.5 billion consumers—the livestock then accounting for 14.5 billion men. In spite of all mechanization used in some parts of the world, horses still account for a protein intake that corresponds to that of 653 million people: in other words, in consumptive forces equal to that of the largest country of

the world, namely China. The Americas, with their 400 million people, as consumers represent only one-fourth of the intake of pigs, as measured on a global scale. Cattle represent an intake of primary protein which is 2.5 times that of the population-rich Asian continent.[4]

There is much to suggest that the world is not presently meeting its nutritional requirements. Asia, with approximately half the earth's population, consumes only 25 percent of its food. One report indicates that approximately two-thirds of the more than 60 million persons who die each year throughout the globe do so from malnutrition. The World Food Congress concluded in 1963 that "more than half of the world's three billion people live in perpetual hunger." There is present food shortage and famine in vast areas of Africa and India.

Borgstrom has noted that "mankind is moving into the twilight of semi-hunger and of extreme scarcity. For a few decades abundance may remain the legacy of a few fortunates with excessive resources. Frugality has already become the lot of billions." Lester R. Brown of the Overseas Development Council predicts "a chronic global food scarcity for the foreseeable future." Josué de Castro reports that only 17 percent of the earth's population receives more than 1.058 ounces of protein per day, an amount considered by nutritionists to be the minimum adequate amount. Twenty-five percent receive between .529 and 1.058 ounces per day, a substandard diet which can lead to chronic symptoms of malnutrition. Most disturbingly, a full 58 percent of the earth's population receives less than .529 ounces of protein per day, an amount which is barely enough to sustain life, let alone periods of vigorous activity.[5]

A sufficient supply of nutrition is critical to human endeavor and achievement, and the adequacy of the human response during the coming period will critically depend on its available supplies of food. In a report on chronic malnutrition in Mexico, five leading food nutritionists report:

Furthermore, the food they get is of a very low biological value. This is the reason that large groups of our people in a conspicuous way look tired, gloomy, and incapacitated. They lack sense of responsibility, they fail to take creative initiatives, nor do they have ideas of their own. In one word, they are devoid of all ambition. It is true that they do not need much to get along, but on the other hand they are not productive. They endure their nutritional misery with a stoic indifferent fatalism.[6]

Josué de Castro, a noted Brazilian nutritionist, and Borgstrom, whose theoretical work has made much of our present conceptualization of the world biomass possible, both see nutrition as a fundamental force in world history. De Castro notes, "The history of mankind could be written, without the slightest doubt, on the basis of nutrition. . . . Man's initiative, his progress, his success and his happiness have a tendency to alter along lines parallel to his available food and the type of nutrition."[7] Borgstrom takes a similar perspective:

Historians have too frequently overlooked the economic factors which both capitalists and Marxists profess and to which they give priority as driving forces. World events are to no little degree subordinate to nutritional conditions. Human endeavor and progress depends to a considerable extent upon adequate food. Conversely, lack of feeding resources continue to drastically limit and retard development, as they have been instrumental in the rise of major human migrations and large-scale hostilities.[8]

It is true that mankind has only begun to efficiently exploit the resources available to him. Colin Clark, a British nutritionist, estimates that the world is presently cultivating only one-third of its potential agricultural land. In central Africa, for example, only 3 percent of arable land is cultivated. Clark maintains that "the potential agricultural area of the world, it is seen, could provide for the consumption of . . . 35.1 billion people."[9] Aside from more extensive use of land resources, there is much improvement possible in intensive use of resources through modern agricultural methods: planned rotation, irrigation, development, and use of hybrids and other products of genetic research, pesticides, herbicides, and fertilizers. This systematic application of science to agriculture is most evident in the "green revolution" now underway in parts of Asia and recently stalled by hostile climate. "For most . . . the outstanding achievement of this generation was the landing on the moon . . . but for one billion Asians for whom rice is the staple food, the development of IR-8 (a high-yield strain) and its dissemination throughout Asia is a more meaningful achievement. It is literally helping to fill hundreds of millions of rice bowls once only half full. For those for whom hunger is a way of life, technology can offer no greater reward."[10] More recent achievements include the development of a technique to extract high protein yields from cottonseed, a crop that can be grown efficiently and quickly in most climates of the earth, and the irrigation of deserts with sea water, turning a historically void and sterile environment into productive land.

It is difficult to speculate what the impact of the coming periods of earth upheaval and meteorological change will be on world food production. The effect of weather change on food crops in the American Midwest, India, and Africa suggests that the world food system is more vulnerable to massive climatological change than is normally assumed to be the case. The seismological predictions suggest disruption in areas where the present food supply is in critical balance or in areas which are now major suppliers of food for other parts of the globe: Japan and South America in the former case; California and the Midwestern United States in the latter. The precognitive material suggests that the devastation will be far more extensive, forcing reliance at one point on world food production in Argentina, Saskatchewan, and southern Africa. There remain, moreover, the logistical considerations of storing, transporting, and distributing food to areas of devastation. There is a clear need for extensive planning and preparation to insure the earth an adequate supply of food during the coming quarter century.

Energy

Energy can be considered a basic requirement to the extent that it supplies the dense and complex population of the earth with a livable temperature range, and runs its transportation systems and its industrial and agricultural plants. In the absence of a working technological plant, it is fair to say that the earth's billions would soon perish, at the mercy of starvation or the elements. Present sources of energy include animal energy, fossil and nuclear fuels, and hydrologically generated energy. Limited amounts of energy are derived from solar sources, the wind, temperature differentials, geothermal sources, and a number of unconventional sources: thermionics and magnetohydrodynamics, for example. Much of the activity from these last-mentioned sources is still in the research and development stage.

The earth is presently facing a net energy shortage whose dimensions are apt to increase over time. Some of the energy shortage is due to short-term disruptions in world distribution systems brought about by conflicts such as those in the Middle East or by cartels of the oil-producing nations. Much is owing to increases in consumption by high-energy societies. The United States, with about one-seventeenth of the earth's population, accounted for one-third of total global industrial energy consumption. The world's consumption of industrial energy increased by approximately 19 percent during the years 1961–1964, because of increased population in this period and increased industrialization in the underdeveloped regions of the world. Still, the industrialized nations account for the lion's share of energy consumption. In 1963, they consumed 71 percent of the year's coal supply, 81 percent of its petroleum, 95 percent of all natural gas, and 80 percent of all hydroelectricity and nuclear energy. The total world consumption of fossil and other fuels for energy was 27 billion tons in 1966 and was projected to rise to 120 billion by the year 2000. The shortfall in electricity production is aptly illustrated by the consequences of attempting to bring the world to U.S. levels of energy consumption: "If the whole world were to reach our current kilowatt hour level at a time when the human population is 5 billion, it would necessitate a ninefold increase in the generation of electricity."

Much of the world's electrical energy plant is highly centralized, has a relatively vulnerable and complex transmission system, and is dependent on regular and uninterrupted shipments of fuel. One can safely argue that it is thus relatively vulnerable to the upheaval of major or even moderate earthquake. The structural vulnerability of the world electricity transmission system is most aptly illustrated by the vast blackouts that characterized the years 1962 and 1965 and were either never successfully explained or were the result of the failure of small components in the total system. In November, 1965, a blackout hit the northeastern United States, and no determining cause was ever firmly established.

The most widely accepted explanation of the failure is the malfunction of backup relay # Q-29 at the Sir Adam Beck generating station, Queenston, Ontario. Yet, Arthur J. Harris, a supervising engineer with the Ontario Hydroelectric Commission, indicated that the cause has not been fully determined. "Although the blackout has been traced to the tripping of a circuit breaker at the Sir Adam Beck No. 2 plant, it is practically impossible to pinpoint the initial cause."[11] Three years earlier, in 1962, an area in the Midwest four times as large as the New York-New England blackout area was subjected to this condition. The New York *Times* reported: "Although the 1962 wide-area failure in the Midwest was well known to power experts before the [Federal Power] Commissions survey was completed last year, the National Power Survey made no significant mention of it, while recommending an enlargement of the kind of interdependence that made Tuesday's [the 1965 North-east blackout] so extensive. The Commission has offered no explanation for the omission."[12]

Other unexplained power failures plagued much of November and December, 1965. On November 16, a series of power blackouts hit many parts of Britain. On November 26, there were unexplained power failures in St. Paul, Minnesota. On December 2, sections of two U.S. states and Mexico were without electricity as the result of a widespread power failure in the southwestern United States. On December 4, portions of East Texas lost power, affecting 40,000 households. On December 26, a power failure struck Buenos Aires and a radius of fifty miles about the city. On the same date, a power blackout attributed to the loss of a single insulator was experienced in four major cities in south and central Finland.

The best evidence suggests that these massive failures were caused by the malfunction of relatively small parts located somewhere within a transmission system which often spans areas of known high seismicity. Thus, it is not at all implausible that earthquake damage to a section of the transmission network could result in more widespread interruption of power throughout the system. Again, although it is difficult to speculate on the extent to which earthquake damage will interrupt usual transportation routes for the delivery of fuel, both the seismological and the precognitive material indicate that there will be considerable disruption of usual routes of fuel supply, thus endangering the regular and continuous supply of energy. At the very least, the evidence strongly militates for a decentralization of existing power generation and transmissions systems, and the planning and location of sufficient energy resources in what science can determine will be safe areas of the world.

3. Man's Psychosocial and Transnational Environment

JOHN McHale has coined the term "psychosocial" to refer to those aspects of the human process that define man's social organization and permit his continued existence and evolution at high levels of population. The gist of this concept is that humanity stopped evolving in a physical sense some 40,000 years ago and has since evolved in the context of a highly intricate network of social arrangements which themselves permit the species to exist in comfort and knowledge and in high numbers. In this sense, man has been effectively expanding the space available to him on the planet by developing new "conceptual spaces" based on a high degree of social interaction, trade, production, and life-supporting amenities.

> Man fully emerged as the cultural Homo Sapiens some 40 thousand years ago when he perfected his ability to elaborate conceptual space. Since then, each doubling of conceptual space has permitted an accompanying doubling of population in a very orderly manner. So effective became the ability to develop conceptual space that each successive doubling of population required only half the time as the prior doubling. Imbedded in this process of accelerating human progression lies the striving for, and realization of ever enlarging networks of communication and interdependence. From bands to clans, to tribes, to nations, to empires, to leagues, in ascending magnitude of mutual identity, support and sovereignty the web enlarges. Completion of this historic process, this first era of human evolution, will be the web of all humanity finally becoming a single accepted network before another century passes.[1]

McHale includes within the psychosocial environment all the systems which conventionally are thought to form the web of human social interaction on the earth. Social institutions, including the economy, the political system, the productive system, kinship, religious and recreational patterns. Intrapersonal patterns in societies about the earth expressed in modes of interpersonal behavior and collective interaction. Symbolic and ideological systems, including human culture's art, science, philosophy, and learning. Each of these is intimately related to the task of sustaining 3.3 billion human beings in daily life on the planet.

The history of man over the last two millennia has been of rapid and complex development in each of these spheres. The results are perhaps best measured by the activities to which present industrial man largely devotes his life. Of a life expectancy of 70 years, industrial man devotes an average of 27 years to creative and recreational activities including childhood play, 7 years to working, 4.5 years to formal education, 2.5 years to eating, 24 years to sleeping, and 5 years to miscellaneous activities. A vast improvement over the life of man at the beginning of the Christian Era, who devoted his 35-year life expectancy as follows: eight years to creative and recreational activities, 10 years to working, 1 to formal education, 1 to eating, 13 to sleeping, and 2 to miscellaneous activities.[2] While modernization has been the explicit goal, the results have in many cases fallen far short of a goal of a scientific society. McHale notes: "In general, a great many of the so-called advanced societies are faced with severe dislocation, deterioration, and obsolescence in critical areas of their socioeconomic and political structures. Many of their internal institutions are archaic, strained toward breakdown and confined by nineteenth and early twentieth century concepts and practices. . . . Though we refer glibly to the Western scientific and technological societies, no one of these has yet approached the beginnings of what might be termed a 'scientific' society, i.e. one whose motivations, goals and orientations are congruent and permeated with the scientific outlook in the larger sense."[3]

The growth of this web of systems within national boundaries has been extended in recent years to the transnational arena, where there now exists a firmly established network of international arrangements and the beginnings of a planetary society. McHale has divided this network into two spheres:

1. The noosphere, as [Teilhard] de Chardin has called the film of organized intelligence around the earth, now links myriad individuals in cooperative knowledge enterprises around the world.
2. The sociospheres, econospheres, and technospheres —all complex and interrelated networks of institutions, organizations, and interdependent technological systems —form a remarkably unified network of human service systems around the planet.[4]

One can easily detail the outlines of these systems: world communications, transportation, tourism, international organizations, international regulatory codes and standards, transnational regulatory agencies, multinational corporations, and other economic units. These again form a vital part of the "conceptual space" man has laboriously created over the centuries, and one which must be maintained if the present level of human life, activity, and culture is going to survive.

It is difficult to measure precisely the effect on this intricate and often delicate network of arrangements of a twenty-five-year period of sustained and growing earth catastrophe. Much of the catastrophe is predicted for key industrialized countries such as the United States and Japan, suggesting that the disruption to the world society at large will be substantial. In many cases, notably that of Japan, whose disappearance under the sea is foretold, the cataclysms may involve the mass migration of populations across national borders.

A disturbing tendency toward rigidity in personal relations during cataclysm can have a far-ranging effect on both cultural achievement and the efficient working of economic, political, and productive capacity of a society. The data emerging from West Virginia and South Dakota bear this out, with all the evident symptoms of deep social malaise and nonadaption; alcoholism, depression, and listlessness. A recent article on the 1973 Mississippi River floods notes that the suburbanite victims of the flooding "are angry and looking for someone to blame, not nature, but *someone*. Their suicide rate has risen sharply, as have their petitions for divorce, according to a Washington University psychiatrist, and the level of irritability and friction within the family structures has reached explosive heights."[5]

One can imagine the effect of this general pattern of maladaption writ large in a more widespread series of calamities. The effective working of economic, productive, and political subsystems is in large measure a function of services provided by individuals within the system. It is thus not altogether unreasonable to assume that the productivity of an economy and the creative activity of a society could suffer slow but steady deterioration over time merely from the loss of will of the individuals who comprise the system.

What emerges from an examination of the evidence is the deep feeling that our society's response will rest ultimately on a test of its will and resolve to survive graciously and intelligently. A failure to presently adapt social institutions to catastrophe would probably result in a significant disruption during the initial stages, and render the society more vulnerable to the succeeding stages. And so on in a vicious circle. In a word, failure breeds failure; success breeds success. In this connection one cannot overemphasize the saving effect of positive action, no matter how inconsequential it may seem in the overall scheme of things.

Two novels come to mind, each of which provides uncanny insight into man's adaptation to disaster and traces the consequences of the many tendencies he is apt to exhibit in times of major stress and profound change. In *The Four-Gated City*, Doris Lessing imagines the earth in a series of major calamities during the last quarter of the twentieth century. The book leads the reader through a world of increasing disorder, authoritarianism, anarchy in government, inflation, food shortages, failed rescue efforts, mistrust, suspicion, and violence. She notes what she calls an "inner immigration" of the spirit, an abandonment of dignity and reason. Not from one day to the next, but in a gradual and sure fashion. The early stages, in which a society attempts to recover from the trauma of catastrophe affecting other but vital parts of the earth, begin with an age of "piety and iron," a society facing a worsening economic crisis and a growing dysfunction in its system. The society turns to a government which "stood for order, self-discipline, formal religion, conformity, authority." But the government's policies are disorganized and unkempt. The new order brings only further suspicion and fear, and a crushing of creativity and initiative generally. The novel ends in a stark and ambiguous world of stagnation, jealousy, misery, and irrationality.

Another theme appears in Fred Hoyle's *The Black Cloud,* a novel of mankind's response to its threatened destruction by a large interstellar hydrogen cloud which approaches the earth from outer space and hovers around the earth for some months. The period is one of great catastrophe, resulting in deaths of "hundreds of millions" of people. Hoyle focuses mainly on the response of the world's scientific community to the event and on the reaction of various governments as they receive sometimes incomplete information about the cloud and its probable behavior from groups of scientists posted about the earth.

At one point in the drama, a group of scientists in England, under Chris Kingsley, a scientist whom Hoyle describes as the "theoretician among theoreticians," determines that the cloud is in fact a living organism with a highly evolved intelligence. In general, the scientists are able to provide the queasy world governments with information to intelligently reduce losses among the population. In a misperception based on this information, two world governments deliver thermonuclear missiles at the cloud, only to have them flung back at centers of population by a now angry antagonist. The novel ends with the cloud's departure to another solar system and the death of Kingsley under an overdose of information from the cloud. It also ends with a world now habituated to perceiving itself as a whole and as a limited system whose survival and progress is very much dependent on the intelligent application of science and reason to its structure and everyday life.

The surface similarities of plot to the course of earth events predicted for the next twenty-five years make the books interesting variations of the serious-minded social and scientific prophecy that has characterized a substantial segment of fiction since the 1930's. Importantly, the books underscore the role played by habituation in determining the nature of the system which mankind relies on to govern, feed, house, and sustain itself. In the *Four-Gated City*, a world of despair and stagnation results from an habitual view of the earth as a fragmented and ill-defined system, and of mankind as disorderly, destructive, and innately irrational. No other explanation can account for mankind's collectively undertaking steps—the increasing of authority and the destruction of individual dignity—which are themselves counterproductive to regrouping and rehabilitation after the catastrophes. Humanity was habituated to a view that a strong subjugation of the individual to the State (itself an increasingly anarchistic entity) was a proper and effective response in a time of stress.

The point is underscored in *The Black Cloud*, where it is clearly the intervention of Kingsley and his group, with their reasoned defiance of conventional scientific theory, that permits the development of information about the nature of the cloud which to some extent breaks mankind's habituation and permits collective steps to reduce losses and reconstruct the world. One can well imagine that in each of the novels humanity could have been spared suffering and the destruction of his labored civilization had individuals and societies chosen collectively to organize and respond.

* * *

The concept of conscious design in our adaptations to catastrophe is central. For Falk, the idea of conscious and explicit design is critical to new world-process, and most especially to a new process based on ecological principles rather than on the traditional division of power among nation states. He cites René Dubos, the noted ecologist, who believes that "the constraints inherent in the world of the immediate future make ideas concerned with design, rather than the accumulation of facts related to growth, the dominant need in the advancement of science and of technology." Mankind, we are told, must "concentrate upon design, not as a static image of a closed system but as an active process of learning and building; the idea of design includes the process of building over a long period of time, cathedral building in the sense of sustaining a large vision and embellishing on a basic plan of action as the occasion allows. . . ." [6]

For both Falk and Dubos the imperative for a new world-order explicitly designed as based on ecological principles grows out of a realization that "the ecological constraints on population and technical growth will inevitably lead to social and economic systems different from the ones in which we live today." However, both Dubos and Falk agree that "in order to survive, mankind will have to develop what might be called a steady state. The steady state formula is so different from the philosophy of endless quantitative growth, which has so far governed Western civilization, that it may cause widespread public alarm." Falk concludes that "human survival requires fundamental adjustments, including especially a shift from the infinity-consciousness of a growth mentality to a sense of finitiveness associated with operating within a steady state system." [7]

We dwell on René Dubos and Richard Falk's vision at length because it is both comforting and fundamentally disturbing. More than other thinkers, they have articulated the necessity of any rational and functioning human order being based on an explicit view of man as part of the life of the earth. The earth is both our parent and our spaceship, and as the rising pollution of the environment has shown, we violate this reality at our peril. Our human process in normal times—let alone in times of great earth catastrophe—must be explicitly based on man's position as a creature of the earth, responsive to its limits and seeking a balance with nature.

What is disturbing about Falk and Dubos is their conclusion that a rational human process cannot be based on material growth and that man must seek an equilibrium within nature which excludes endless quantitative growth. The lesson of history is that growth—endless growth—is a fundamental component of the human experience and that if we are subject to the operation of any iron law of nature it is.quite simply: grow or die. If the species has succeeded in reaching the modern age, it is because man throughout the last 40,000 years has consciously chosen to change the nature of the spaceship on which he travels, to enlarge and radically alter its dimensions. Though the planet today might at first glance appear to be essentially the same body it was 40,000 years ago at the dawn of our civilization, in point of fact it is a different planet, enlarged and fundamentally altered by the layers of interwoven "conceptual space" which man has added to it in his laborious path through time. The economic, productive, political, and ideational systems which now span the earth are as much a part of its fundamental life as are the rivers and trees and continents. We have in essence survived on the earth because we have in large measure created it. This is not hubris, but reality; and to ignore it is not only to do mankind a disservice, but to ignore the very nature of the planet.

This realization deeply colors our thoughts on a new world-process, one based on the imminence of catastrophic change and one designed to negotiate man through it successfully. The essence of our view is that modern man—with his amenities, knowledge, culture, and high numbers—will only survive if he can adapt his civilization to protecting himself and to growing in the midst of catastrophe. We turn to a brief discussion of conditions which we believe necessarily underlie successful adaption by humanity to the earth.

4. The Primacy of Liberty

WE choose liberty as the governing context within which human society must operate during the catastrophes and beyond for quite pragmatic reasons. The ability of mankind to survive the disruptions of catastrophe and grow beyond them is directly a function of his ability to adapt his world to conditions of extreme uncertainty, and efficiently and quickly employ his collective knowledge. Quite apart from the moral considerations involved in securing liberty for the species, it is a fact that human activity is most adaptive, creative, productive, and wise when each individual is, to the greatest extent possible, free from the coercion of other men. In choosing freedom as the primal definer of the permissible limits of human conduct, we are opting in effect for efficiency and for survival.

Our definition of liberty is like many political ideas, a goal to be approximated, but never as a practical matter to be wholly reached. It is, in the words of Friedrich A. Hayek, "that condition of men in which coercion of some by others is reduced as much as possible in society . . . it is the absence of a particular obstacle—coercion by other men." In this sense, the definition of liberty turns on the definition of coercion. We turn again to Hayek: "By 'coercion' we mean such control of the environment or circumstances of a person by another that, in order to avoid greater evil, he is forced to act not according to a coherent plan of his own but to serve the ends of another. Except in the sense of choosing the lesser evil in a situation forced on him by another, he is unable to use his own intelligence or knowledge or to follow his own aims or beliefs. Coercion is evil precisely because it thus eliminates an individual as a thinking and valuing person and makes him a bare tool in the achievement of the ends of another. Free action, in which a person pursues his own aims by the means indicated by his own knowledge, must be based on data which cannot be shaped by the will of another. It presupposes the existence of a known sphere in which the circumstances cannot be so shaped by another person as to leave one only that choice prescribed by the other."[1]

The case for liberty as a social condition which permits the maximal adaptation by man to his world, and the fullest unleashing of his creativity and efforts rests on the Socratic dictum that the recognition of our collective ignorance is the beginning of wisdom. In the context of modern society it rests on the recognition of the inevitable and profound ignorance of even the wisest of us concerning the factors on which our ends and welfare as a species depend.

Liberty, by maximizing the creative potential of the individual human spirit, is essential because it leaves room for the unforeseeable and the unpredictable. To the extent that the advance and preservation of civilization depends on a maximum of opportunity of accidents to occur, liberty permits these accidents to happen in a context of maximal knowledge, attitudes, skills, and habits of the individual men who must confront the consequences of the accident. In Hayek's words, "It is through the mutually adjusted efforts of many people that more knowledge is utilized than any one individual possesses or than it is possible to synthesize intellectually; and it is through such utilization of dispersed knowledge that achievements are made possible greater than any single mind can foresee. It is because freedom means the renunciation of direct control of individual efforts that a free society can make use of so much more knowledge than the mind of the wisest ruler can comprehend."[2]

The knowledge of the coming cataclysms is a case in point.

Both the authors are products of perhaps the freest society that has existed in mankind's history—the United States of America. We are both products of a middle-class background, anchored on hard work and competitive effort, and compassion for others. We see ourselves as neither especially talented or unusual in the conventional sense. We applied ourselves, and acquired remarkable educations through the enlightened scholarship and loan facilities of the country. We have eaten well, have traveled, and have been supported at a standard which has in history largely been the privilege of an elite. By and large, we have not been limited in expressing our opinions, however controversial these may have been to some of our elders. Although the abuses of the political system have in recent times taken on a disturbing tendency, we have enjoyed wide access to a variety of information in books, periodicals, journals, and meetings which would be tolerated in few societies on the earth. We enjoy access to libraries, scientists, research facilities, and information. No institution of society, no bureaucracy has asked us to predict the shape of the future, and yet we have stumbled in our own limited fashion on knowledge of great import. We have done so essentially as an accident, not because of the larger design of any leaders or groups within American society. We have done so because there is still enough room within this society to let us be alone to think our thoughts and pursue our individual aims and hopes.

Reliance on the individual is still the essence of societal achievement. Only under a condition of liberty can a general mobilization of mankind to meet the catastrophes be successful.

5. The Necessity of Education

IT has been suggested that "in our developing world civilization, lack of education is a form of disenfranchisement. The illiterate individual is restrained from full participation and access to his birthright as a human being—the right to man's accumulated cultural heritage and to the 'practical' augmentation of his living, which may be afforded by access to the highest scientific and technological capability."[1] Quite apart from the diminution to the individual's life that results from the lack of an education, a general deficiency in the educational level of a population can have serious repercussions on the society's attempt to develop its standard of living and level of welfare. A highly organized society—essential for sustaining us at our current level of cultural evolution—is dependent on the development of complex and specialized skills. It is also dependent on the rapid dissemination of information throughout the population. Quite simply, a society in which the proportion of illiterates is high, or in which there tends to be a deficiency in the educational system, does not work well and will tend to work even less well over time. If we are thinking of the wide mobilization of the earth's resources and the application of reason to the processes of society at unprecedented levels, we will require during the period of catastrophe a highly educated general population—both in the industrialized and nonindustrialized worlds.

The evidence indicates a serious and growing educational deficiency in both the industrialized and the less developed areas. According to a 1964 UNESCO report, a full two-fifths of the globe cannot read or write. In certain underdeveloped areas illiteracy is as high as 90 percent of the total population. In many countries, moreover, the female portion of the population is almost totally illiterate. The Center for Integrative Studies estimates that no schooling is available for about 45 percent of the 550 million children between the ages of five and fourteen. Estimates indicate the absolute number of illiterates worldwide is rising by 20 to 25 million persons each year. A comparison of the relative percentages of population in the developed and less developed regions of the world who enter the various stages of education is startling. In developed countries and 11 percent in less developed ones. primary school as opposed to 44 percent in less developed regions. Fifty-four percent will go to secondary school in developed countries and 11 percent in less developed ones. The figures for university attendance are 10 percent and 1 percent, respectively. Moreover, recent data indicates that school systems in certain areas of the developed countries may be poorly run, and producing classes of functionally incompetent graduates.

Quite apart from the question of formal education is that of the general dissemination of information throughout the society—a measure of its standard of living and its potential for development and high social organization. A report by the House of Representatives notes that "UNESCO has suggested that efficacious mass communications can be assured when for every 100 inhabitants of any country, there are at least 10 copies of a daily newspaper, 5 radio sets, 2 cinema seats, and 2 television receivers. This minimum has not been attained by 2,000 million people. One hundred states in Asia, Africa and Latin America fall below this average."[2]

One cannot underestimate the need for a literal revolution in general education, in the development of scientific and technical skills, in the training in special skills and general knowledge of natural disaster that must accompany the coming period. A wide dispersion of skills and of general educational ability is vital to an effectively functioning order. In many ways, the need for immediate mobilization in the educational field is the most imperative. The wisdom of our societal actions is in a large sense a measure of our individual wisdom. A mobilization of the magnitude of the coming quarter century cannot succeed if it is left to the hands of a few trained elite, planning contingencies for the mass. The measures must grow from, and be deeply understood by the people whom they are meant to affect. Moreover, education in this sense must be directed at more than the customary age groups and the conventional skills.

6. The Right to Survival

Mankind is one species, each member of which is entitled to at least the dignity of survival in a decent standard of welfare, and of protection against mutual calamity, irrespective of his standing in the race and irrespective of his behavior in the past. This humanitarian rule is in fact a biological imperative.

The right of individuals to the minimum provisions of the necessities of human life becomes critical in a time of rising natural catastrophe, when the primary attention is the safety and immediate needs of a stricken population, and when the normal means of distribution and supply are often disrupted. A glance at statistics on the differences in standard of living between the populations of industrialized countries and the less developed areas indicates the magnitude of the task of providing even essential needs in normal and stable times. Developed countries enjoy 110 doctors per 100,000 population, less developed countries 16. Life expectancy in less developed countries is thirty-eight years, a little more than half the life expectancy of sixty-eight in the industrialized countries. Literacy in developed countries reaches 96 percent and only 33 percent in less developed countries. Developed countries enjoy 2,800 kilowatt hours of electricity per person per year, less developed countries on 82.

As Falk has pointed out: "Any adequate world-order design needs to include as a central goal the provisions of sufficient food, housing, health and education to allow all people the conditions for a decent life." The implications of this goal are fantastic when extended to a period of catastrophe. If the precognitive material is correct, the period will probably see extensive relief and rescue of large portions of the population of Japan, South America, and the United States. Much of this work is likely to be done by nations who have traditionally been inimical or hostile. The only response can be one of general and unequivocal humanitarianism.

7. The Environmental Secretariat

ESSENTIAL to an orderly mobilization of world resources and the formulation of intelligent plans for the coming quarter century is a redirection of the chief structural elements of our embryonic world order. These have been summarized by Falk as (1) central political institutions of general authority—the United Nations and the International Court of Justice; (2) specialized agencies now devoted to specific tasks of international coordination, many of which bear directly on the effects of natural catastrophe. These include nongovernmental bodies such as the Red Cross. In Falk's words, "specialized agencies are likely to play a crucial role in the design of a new world-order system, not primarily because of the past experience and record of these agencies, but because of their greater relevance to the expected needs and conflicting value concerns of the near future." (3) Informal and tacit patterns of coordination among principal world political actors. They are important in that they possess a certain flexibility and are useful in obtaining a minimum consensus among principal nations to basic world policy. (4) Regional and subregional organizations performing tasks of a cooperative nature in economic and public welfare matters. These have been useful in beginning to move policy beyond the conception of the nation-state, and in creating a basis for a strong, one-world foundation for international order. (5) Transnational actors and movements devoted to special goals or to social or political change. The environmental movement, largely disorganized and amorphous, is an example of this.

The most appropriate forum for an initial attempt at defining world response to the coming period and at setting out levels of responsibility appears to us to be the Environmental Secretariat of the United Nations, established at the Stockholm Conference on the Human Environment in June, 1972, and presently located in Nairobi. The Environmental Secretariat itself possesses a broad mandate and a strong institutional perception of the ecological underpinning of world policy. Much of its technical skill and its ecological orientation could be easily redirected toward dealing with the natural catastrophes. Importantly, it is the only major United Nations body to be located in a less developed country and is fairly representative of the points of view of both the developing and the industrialized blocs. It has chosen to locate in an area which is highly likely to be free from upheaval. Moreover, the Stockholm Conference itself called not only for "Collaboration on a master plan for cooperation in cases of natural disasters," but formally requested the convening of a second UN conference on the human environment.

A glance at some of the policy declarations contained in the final report of the Stockholm Conference indicates their remarkably perceptive stipulation of a world order based on reason:

> A point has been reached in history when we must shape our actions throughout the world with a more prudent care for their environmental consequences. Through ignorance or indifference we can do massive and irreversible harm to the earthly environment on which our life and well-being depend. Conversely, through fuller knowledge and wiser action we can achieve for ourselves and our posterity a better life in an environment more in keeping with our human needs and hopes. There are broad vistas for the enhancement of environmental quality and the creation of a good life. What is needed is an enthusiastic but calm state of mind and intense but orderly work. For the purpose of attaining freedom in the world of nature, man must use knowledge to build, in collaboration with nature, a better environment. To defend and improve the human environment for present and for future generations has become an imperative goal for mankind—a goal to be pursued together with and in harmony with, the established and fundamental goals of peace and of world-wide social and economic development.[1]

The work of the conference was extraordinarily detailed and bore on most of the subject matters which are of primary interest in formulating a plan for the coming period. The planning stage for the conference included the preparation of a total of more than 340 detailed technical reports in a variety of subject areas, all of which bear closely on plans for adaptation to natural catastrophe: human settlements, natural resources, pollutants, educational, informational, social, and cultural aspects of an ecological world order, development and environment, and international organizational implications of an ecological world order.

The conference enjoined national governments to begin a series of far-ranging transformations of their operating structure: the institution of comprehensive planning; the revamping of legal and institutional frameworks to deal with ecological perspective; extensive water supply, sanitation, and housing policies; the development of growth poles—new cities—based on ecological considerations; the development of adequate mass media for the education of their populations; and reformation in land use policies and educational systems. International organizations were enjoined to develop new areas of specialization, increase bilateral and regional consultation among nations, encourage research in ecology, aid in information exchange and the training of populations, and, importantly, to formulate a world master-plan for natural disaster.

Moreover, the structure for effective world action on ecological policy was instituted in the form of the Environmental Secretariat. The conference established a Governing Council, composed of fifty-four nations chosen on an equitable geographical basis, to formulate world policy on the environment, and guidance to the Secretariat. The Secretariat itself was established "to serve as a focal point for environmental action and coordination" within the U.N. framework, and an environmental fund was established to finance international environmental policy.

The Environmental Secretariat in effect signals a new function for the United Nations—one of providing and defining global information, policy, and norms for the intelligent conduct of the human process.

Epilogue:
The Future World Society

In the beginning was the deed, but within it was the universal formative process. In the process of developing the community, each individual will necessarily share in some degree in the general development. The unitary emotion which inspired both religion and science will accompany and guide the further development of man. But in this process the word has a crucial role. The intellect is man's unique asset. Words are necessary for communication from man to man. The uttered word operates by calling the attention of others to the existence of a particular situation. Until a situation is jointly recognized by verbal communication no fully effective human cooperation is possible. The couple whose love remains in suspense until the first word is spoken, and the group whose emotion is impotent until the word is passed around which releases co-ordinated action, are evidence of the role of the uttered word. "Unitary" is such a word, communicating a message. Its implications are inexhaustible.

—From THE NEXT DEVELOPMENT IN MAN *by Lancelot Law Whyte (Mentor Books), pp. 52–53.*

1. Chaos

THE more we have turned over in our minds the realities of two decades of global natural catastrophe, the more our reason tells us that chaos seems the most probable result. Almost uniformly, governmental forms in key nations of the world appear incapable of acting intelligently under the coming conditions of massive stress. Despite the patina of world civilization that has characterized the mythology of the postwar globe, social attitudes in vast portions of the earth are overwhelmingly unenlightened, parochial, and highly predisposed toward dog-eat-dog solutions. The basic facts of coming natural catastrophe have been known by scientists and governments for at least several years. Yet there have been no meaningful steps taken to admit to and face this knowledge. Instead, traditional world conflicts have been permitted to dominate the focus of world attention.

There are many considerations behind this initial conclusion of likely or inevitable chaos: the physical horror and trauma of mass death, suffering, and destruction; the probability of world economic depression and of vicious competition among nations for increasingly scarce resources of food, energy, and stable land; the likelihood of increased social uncertainty and instability within stricken nations; and the threat of war as an increasingly acceptable alternative to enforce national claims and needs.

It is hard to comment on the human horrors that are the inevitable result of natural catastrophe in densely populated areas. One official estimate of the scale of coming destruction, that of the Office of Emergency Preparedness, calculates that five hundred million people are in imminent danger of death, serious injury, or substantial destruction of property due to earthquake. This figure in our opinion understates the danger. If the psychic predictions of catastrophe have even general validity, the destruction will affect vast areas of the United States, South America, Japan, and Europe. The effects of drought and constant famine will

155

affect vast areas of China, the Soviet Union, the Indian subcontinent, and Africa.

Our experience in the course of discussing the subject matter of the book with others—both laymen and professionals in the field—was the arousal of subconscious defense mechanisms of denial and avoidance. For Americans, acceptance of the reality of coming catastrophe is probably more difficult than for others. The United States has never had the devastation of a home war in modern times. The scale of destruction from the coming catastrophes is, in the absence of any preparatory measures, comparable to that of having a war bitterly fought on one's own land simultaneous with the presence of the breadlines of a deep depression.

The chaos of physical suffering is likely to be intensified by world economic depression. It takes little sophistication to elucidate the resulting breakdown in production and distribution of goods, stable sources of energy and raw materials, and reliable and adequate world food supplies. Moreover, the breakdown would in all probability take on the aspects of a self-reinforcing cycle. Given the high degree of interdependence among the subsystems of our world economy, a serious bottleneck in one of the systems would serve increasingly to amplify disturbances and dislocations in the remainder.

A significant predictable component of the breakdown would be a return to vicious competition and protectionist economic measures by regions or nations seeking to enforce their claims on successively scarce resources. This was certainly one hallmark of the depression of the thirties, and there is no obvious reason to believe that such misfortune would not reoccur. The measures would have wide detrimental impact on the global exchange of raw materials, goods, and services. Restrictive measures on labor and population migration, on control over natural resources, on free trade, and on monetary policy, would in all probability occur.

There is some evidence that even in the United States, a country which in this century has gone to considerable lengths to promote free trade, popular opinion is swinging toward irrational protectionism. A recent poll of 1,600 readers of the *National Enquirer* indicated that over 91 percent were opposed to the exportation of food from the United States, whether by sale or by grant. One may conclude that this represents a shift from attitudes held in 1966, a year in which the United States exported 20 percent of its wheat crop to then starving India.

A deeply unsettling aspect of the possible chaos is the blanket of increased social uncertainty and instability that would settle on the world during the decades of catastrophe. The probable ineffectiveness of governmental authority to operate sensibly in an atmosphere of continual crisis is bound to lead to a profound loss of confidence both in the governmental apparatus and in other institutions of society. The result could be anarchical, with interest groups within a society appropriating to themselves whatever goods, services, and security they could. More likely, the result would be totalitarian, with threatening chaos temporarily avoided by increasingly harsh and repressive governmental measures over the allocations of goods and the permissible movement of persons.

The harm would not be limited to short-term dislocations and inconveniences to the civilian population. One can point to the long-term detrimental effects that social chaos would have on basic systems—such as education—which require a high degree of stability and certainty.

In an atmosphere of social chaos we are bound to see an increased general awareness among the population of the individual's growing ineffectiveness in relation to his surroundings. Here is the "alienation" of modern society writ large. Deep mental depression and pathological inertia appear inevitable.

Furthermore, it is highly likely that under conditions of chaos, military and economic warfare will become an increasingly acceptable alternative employed in enforcing national claims on scarce economic resources. Although habits of cooperation among nations have at least on the surface been consolidating, these habits do not appear sufficiently well structured to resist the stress of extreme scarcity.

Let us take, for example, the problem of food allocation during a period of worldwide drought. If the free market were the only operative force in supplying and distributing food, the rich nations would eat and the poor would starve. The rich would be able to afford the expensive commodity of food and the poor would not. Weak, poor areas such as India, the Philippines, and Africa would have no effective recourse. Their populations would be decimated. A militarily strong nation with little foreign exchange, such as the Soviet Union, might well be inclined to use its military capacity to enforce its claim over food-producing areas and to divert food supplies toward itself.

This is not an unlikely scenario, and one can perceive the seeds of future military conflict over food and other resources in present trends. For reasons that escape most Western military observers, the Soviet Union has in recent years begun an alarming increase of its force under arms and in its military presence in key areas of the globe. At a time of alleged détente, the Soviet government is moving to increase its compulsory military service from two years to three, thus substantially increasing its number of trained men under arms. It has begun to deploy substantial naval forces near regions of the world which are likely to be areas of common food production for the species during the period of catastrophe.

Edgar Cayce indicates three areas of the world will be key to the common provision of food during the period of high catastrophe: central Canada, southern South America, and southern Africa. Assuming that there is some general validity to his predictions, the character and levels of production of food in these areas should be dictated by global needs. This in turn implies a high degree of access to the product of these areas by any needy nation, with no single nation having predominant control.

We have confidence that the agricultural product of central Canada will be available to world markets. Our confidence rests on North America's deep tradition of nondiscriminatory trade. There is, however, some cause for concern that the distribution of foods produced in southern Africa and southern South America may be subject to military pressure from the Soviet Union.

The nondiscriminatory distribution of food produced in southern South America and southern Africa depends on unimpeded access by ships of all nations to the waters of the Indian Ocean and of the South Atlantic. Southern Africa is nestled between the Indian Ocean and the South Atlantic. Southern South America rests between the South Atlantic and the impenetrable barrier of the Andes. These two bodies of water have traditionally been free from the predominating naval presence of any single nation.

For reasons yet to be fully elucidated, the Soviet Union has increased its naval presence in the Indian Ocean to the point where it can effectively impede the free passage of ships. Its naval presence there now exceeds that of the West by a factor of almost 5 to 1. It has, moreover, begun to establish a military presence in the South Atlantic, a zone traditionally free of warships and increasingly important to world shipping traffic. At last report, the Soviet Union has established a military base on the west coast of Africa, in Guinea, a country of high potential strategic value due to its location on the pinch-waist separating the North and South Atlantic. The base is to serve as a center of operations for continual air reconnaissance of the South Atlantic, which is puzzling since the area is of little present strategic importance. According to some observers, the base could eventually become a home port for a substantial Soviet naval force in the South Atlantic.

Our alarm at these provocative trends does not itself stem from anti-Soviet feeling but rather from the foreboding implications of the trends for a globe facing imminent and catastrophic upheaval. One implication, entirely within conventional geopolitical analysis, is that the trend signals a further escalation in world military expenditures at a time when national budgets should be heavily weighted in favor of preparation for natural catastrophe. The second implication, with even darker meaning, is that the increased military presence in these areas could set the stage for armed conflict over food. It would be difficult to conceive that the Soviet Union would allow its population to starve when it can employ an overwhelming military might to forcefully secure supplies of food.

This parade of social and economic horrors has not sprung whole-cloth from our imaginations. Each of these outcomes follows logically from a systematic consideration of the effects of extensive natural catastrophe on an ill-prepared society.

* * *

2. Millennium

THERE is some objective data for belief that chaos will not occur, despite its apparent high probability. These data consist of the predictions of high psychics, all of whom uniformly converge on the millennium, a peaceful and creative society growing out of an era of great natural catastrophe. These psychics—the Hebrew prophets, Edgar Cayce, and others—have had a high record of accuracy in the past. Unlike most scientists and observers, we conclude from the data that their millennial prophecies may on the whole if not in detail be fulfilled.

There are numerous references in the prophetic literature to a promised land, a land of peace, prosperity, happiness, and freedom. Uniformly, this society is postcataclysmic, and occurs hard on the heels of a period of sustained natural catastrophe. If we assume that these predictions contain a generally accurate representation of the near future, the conditions for such a society would perforce be laid immediately prior to and during the period of cataclysm. Otherwise, cataclysm would most likely produce a dark age for man.

It is surprising that so few students of the future have

examined the psychic predictions of millennium in their attempts to outline the direction of human culture. Perhaps this oversight stems from the highly religious rhetoric which characterizes most millennial prophecies. It is not at all difficult, however, to conceive of concrete qualities which would characterize a society that matches the millennial predictions.

It runs against common sense to imagine the achievement of a millennium through an abrupt and miraculous rupture with the historical course of societal and cultural evolution. It seems most reasonable to imagine the coming of the millennium as the *de facto* achievement of a successful human society. The values which characterize a millennial society are thus the values which characterize a successful society.

There is no clear general consensus as to what constitutes a successful society. As a matter of principle, it is safe to say that whatever the characteristics of a successful society may be, the society itself must be conducive to material and moral prosperity, to happiness, and to the development of personal creativity and individual fulfillment among the general population. These are in the widest sense the goals of human life, and any society which fosters these values deserves for itself the title "promised land."

One disturbing tendency among a small but influential sector of the Western intellectual community has been to characterize postindustrial society as fundamentally inimical to the achievement of human happiness. A notable example is the Club of Rome, a group which counsels retreat from the recent gains of societal evolution. The core defect in their argument for an abrupt break with economic progress is their deep lack of trust in human ingenuity.

Major problem solving in society is typically done by people with upward social aspirations. There is no greater mobilizer of personal energies to useful ends than the desire to "make it" in established society. Large numbers of such people can only be fostered in a society that is economically progressing. To argue for a policy of economic retreat is to automatically cut off a wide number of potential routes for social creativity and needed problem solving. Ingenuity demands a concrete social and economic route for its expression. Individual career advancement in a generally prosperous society provides that needed route.

A successful society is thus a productive one, and one which consciously fosters the conditions for individual advancement. Fortunately, the social sciences are sufficiently advanced to provide us with a list of conditions which objectively promote the maximal degree of individual opportunity within a society. The list is not a surprising one, and includes most of the social prerogatives which we now accept as commonplace. A successful society exhibits a high degree of education, economic prosperity, accelerated scientific advance, domestic tranquillity, individual liberty, high personal mobility, high technology, representative government, rational military policies, free trade and liberal immigration policies, and a high standard of living for the population.

From this perspective it is startling to realize that for a limited segment of the human race the millennium has essentially been achieved. Man has already realized millennial goals. Although no single nation to date has achieved a completely successful society, there is strong evidence that at least some of the more advanced industralized nations are premillennial.

The non-Socialist, poor nations of the world, by and large characterized by feudalistic or mixed economies and a generally low level of education, fulfill very few of the necessary prerequisites of a promised land. Indeed, they are generally deficient in almost all the listed criteria. The Socialist or Communist countries are on the whole better educated than the non-Socialist poor nations. Yet they, too, fulfill rather few of the criteria. It is the advanced capitalist nations of North America, Western Europe, and Japan which have most nearly achieved a condition of promised land. Within this group, Holland and Denmark come to mind as examples of nations which today most approximate promised-land status.

Our conclusion that millennial prophecies may on the whole be fulfilled is thus based on an analysis of present societal trends using readily available data and employing the fundamental tools of the social sciences.

The list of millennial goals is useful in that it provides the single most meaningful framework within which to evaluate both national and global policy measures taken in response to natural catastrophe. These policies must be calculated to maintain to the greatest extent possible the equilibrium of those nations which now enjoy premillennial status. They must be calculated to bring those nations which now find themselves varyingly distanced from success into a premillennial condition. These are necessary steps to achieving a global promised land in the aftermath of catastrophe, an outcome which we believe is not beyond the realm of possibility.

From this viewpoint, the most objective and reliable criterion for judging the wisdom of a particular policy measure is whether the measure tends on the whole to foster or impede the achievement of millennial goals. A prudent and conscientious application of this principle of fostering millennial goals will make the public servant of the future beware of a short-term panacea that may in the long run be counterproductive. The importance of the cautionary function of this principle cannot be overemphasized in a condition of high environmental stress.

The catastrophes will present many novel and at first apparently insoluble dilemmas. Whether and how to ration food? When and if to evacuate cities? Where and how to build new nations? These are questions whose resolution involves many decisions requiring a high level of creativity and a balanced perspective. They require decision making of a sophisticated order, consciously employing our most advanced organizational techniques. In the language of the systems analyst, the list of millennial goals provides an objective matrix of values for complex problem solving.

* * *

3. The Federalist Party

THREE dimensions appear critical to a society's successfully negotiating the age of cataclysm. One of these is a balanced and imaginative use of expertise in the development of social policy and in the management of institutions. A second is the maintenance of a fluid political system, capable of governing firmly and of grappling with a rapidly .shifting balance of interests and values within its jurisdiction. The last is the rise of new talent in a nation's political and social leadership.

It is the political leadership of a country which is responsible for formulating wise and acceptable social policies and for firmly guiding the nation to the attainment of its declared goals. Without intelligent and responsible heads of society, the probabilities of government formulating good policy and of the nation enjoying secure guidance become vanishingly small.

If the system for choosing political leadership is faulty, and tends toward the production of mediocre public servants, then the nation will suffer no matter how talented and noble its wider population might be. If the system is adroit in selecting its leadership, a nation initially unprepared for stress and crises can rise above itself.

The history of American postwar economic predominance in the world has been the history of the achievements of the American managerial system. It is beyond any doubt that the United States possesses the highest degree of managerial sophistication and ability. The computer revolution was fostered in America and it is America's computer technology which largely runs the world. Its schools of organizational administration have pioneered systems analysis, computer model-building, simulation and complex programming, and the science of decision making. More than any other single nation, the United States is strongest in the first critical dimension for success: expertise. It is not unlikely that the world will draw on American managerial expertise and know-how as a communal resource in the coming period of stress.

Moreover, America is well capable of carrying out the plans of its experts. It is a country well endowed with natural wealth and it possesses a resourceful population capable of healthy reaction in times of great national crises. The country's conduct during World War II and its development and execution of the Marshall Plan is striking evidence in this regard.

It is in the second two critical dimensions for success that America must improve itself. Its political system, once considered a genius of flexibility and farsightedness, is showing increasing strain and inability to successfully cope with the unforeseen. The competency of America's present generation of political leadership is subject to grave public doubt, and no practical and quick solution to the problem of inadequate leadership appears at hand. The country is blossoming with new talent which is not being put to proper work.

Political systems should be open to new talent. Government is not fundamentally different from any other social organization, and the heart of a successful and well-run organization is its ability to attract well-qualified people and place them in positions of major responsibility.

With some significant exceptions, the present system of selecting candidates for public office in the United States ensures the success of individuals with limited vision. This flows from the generally archaic and antidemocratic character of our two dominant political parties and from the effective monopoly which they possess in the political marketplace.

In a fluid and well-run political marketplace, the electoral system is expected to provide the following products: competent and talented contenders for political office, a campaign which involves and educates the electorate on the important policy issues of the day, and the election of officials who are well qualified for their offices.

There is evidence that the rate of occupant turnover in elected positions is far less than one would expect of a system that is functioning fluidly and well. Thus for example, out of 435 seats in the House of Representatives, only 50 were seriously contested in the 1972 general election, and only 10 of these challenges against incumbents were actually successful. Moreover, the average cost of defeating an incumbent was $126,000.[1]

There are a total of approximately 522,000 elected political offices in the United States, at the local, state, and federal level. These correspond to: President and Vice President, 100 Senators, and 435 Congressmen at the federal level; 50 Governors, approximately 7,400 state legislators, and approximately 5,700 other officials at the state level; and elected officials of counties, municipalities, townships, school districts, and special districts totaling approximately 74,000, 144,000, 130,000, 108,000 and 57,000 respectively.[2] In competitive terms, this is a listing of the potential job market for seekers of elected political office.

The occupants of these offices are chosen by the electorate in a general election in which the names of official contenders appear on a ballot. There are three major methods by which a person seeking public office may secure his or her name on the ballot in a general election.

1. *Nomination by Primary Election.* This is the predominant method for the selection of nominees to appear on the ballot in a general election and is mandatory by state law for the candidates of established political parties in most states. Under this method, any member of an established political party may petition to have his name placed on the primary ballot. The party's contender in the general election is the candidate receiving the largest number of votes in the primary. The electorate in the primary is generally limited to registered party members. Under most state laws, an established political party is defined as a party which has polled a specified minimal percentage of the votes cast at the last general election. Thus a new political party would not be

permitted by state law to have its candidates selected in a primary. Only after it has established a track record is a new party permitted to conduct a primary.

2. *Nomination by Party Convention.* This method, used in a handful of states, leaves the selection of an established party's candidate for local, state, or federal (other than Presidential and Vice Presidential) office to a convention of selected delegates who are presumed to act in the party's and the public's ultimate interest. The composition of state convention delegates may vary widely between parties and from state to state within a party. The nominee selected by the convention appears on the ballot in the general election. Again, the privilege of holding a nominating convention is generally limited to established political parties.

Party nominees for President and Vice President of the United States are of course chosen by a national convention of state delegates.

3. *Nomination by Petition.* Most independent candidates or candidates of new parties appear on the ballot in the general election by this method. A candidate seeking to appear on the general ballot is generally required to show that he is not the candidate of an established party, and to present a predetermined minimal number of signatures of legal voters. This method is available for all or almost all elected offices in the United States. The individual requirements for each office vary widely from office to office and from state to state. Thus for example a new party or independent candidate for U.S. Senator is required to obtain the signatures of 500 qualified voters in Rhode Island, while the same candidate would have to obtain the signatures of 25 percent of the voters according to the state vote for Governor cast in the last gubernatorial election in North Carolina.

It is now the case that candidates who have qualified themselves by petition do not enjoy wide public appeal. They are predominantly sectarian and even when their appeal is truly directed to the broad public interest they rarely gain sufficient public limelight.

Petition candidates are typically supported by some third party organization. It is important to emphasize that there is nothing inherent in state law which specifies how a new party should select its nominees. The law only requires that a nominee present a requisite number of signatures. Unless specifically prohibited by law, a new political party could well decide to choose its nominee—in advance of the petition stage—by lot, by a battery of psychological tests, by professional accomplishments, or by scientific polling of the preferences of the general electorate.

On its face, the primary system appears to be a democratic procedure, and one which does not present unnecessary barriers to the entry of new talent into the political marketplace. A person who considers himself a viable candidate for public office could enroll in an established party, collect the required number of signatures, and compete against others in a primary election. In theory, he or she would have an equal chance or opportunity of convincing the party electorate of his or her qualifications. In some cases, this theory may be realized in practice. The various contenders for political office may agree to debate with each other on the crucial issues of the day, the debates may receive adequate media attention, and the campaign may generate wide public interest. In these cases, well-qualified candidates are probably drawn into the political competition in the first place, and we may assume it is one of the best of these who wins.

This democratic ideal is not the usual state of affairs. There is a weak tradition of open and public debates among contenders in modern primary campaigns. Where debates occur, they are rarely taken as integral and significant to the campaign. This is unfortunate since it is difficult to publicly measure the relative leadership qualities of contenders without open confrontation. Thorough and hard-hitting debates provide the best means available for defining the major issues of the day and permitting free competition among differing visions. They are the best insurers of a well-informed and educated choice by the voting population.

A significant consequence of the lack of frequent debate among primary contenders is the increased significance of the relative financial resources of the contenders. Those who possess greater financial resources have a greater ability to manipulate public attitudes through one-way advertising techniques. Much of the current outcry over excessive campaign spending is misdirected. The core problem is not how much money is spent but how it is spent. An excessive proportion of campaign funds is presently devoted to manipulatory advertising techniques, rather than to sponsoring open debate.

In addition, true competition among candidates in a primary is often distorted by the support given to one of the candidates by the "party machine." By the party machine we mean dependable party workers at the precinct, ward, district, county, state, or federal levels; party members who hold elective or appointive political office; persons who owe their jobs to the patronage of the party; and financial interests—both legal and illegal—who have benefited from party policy. There is generally a cohesive party machine in every electoral district. The influence of the machine varies widely from one area to another. In some areas, the political machine of a single party is for all practical purposes the only functioning political entity. In other areas both major parties have machines and some influence is further divided among a variety of insurgent or reform groups.

It is frequently the case that there is a conflict between the interests of the party machine and that of the public. The party machine is often beholden to private financial interests and when in power tends to support policies that further these interests. Moreover, much of the power of the machine resides in its ability to dispense jobs within the governmental system. These vary from relatively high-paid executive positions in the governmental hierarchy to the more mundane jobs at the bottom of the governmental ladder: clerk, laborer, sewerage and sanitation worker, and the like. The relative importance of this power of patronage in any single community is a function of the relative size of the public payroll. With government assuming an increasingly important role as an employer in most communities, the power of the machine that controls appointments increases correspondingly.

The machine thus has much at stake in the outcome of a general election. For example, the loss of a mayoral campaign can mean the loss of control over thousands of jobs, and of a wide influence in the economic life of the community. Any political machine acting in its own self-interest will thus be very careful in determining who its favored candidate for nomination will be, and will assiduously use its powerful resources to insure the nomination of that candidate over his competitors in the primary election.

These constraints on the selection of the candidate to be backed by the party machine severely limit the available pool of talent upon which the party draws. In the statistician's language, the candidates of a political machine are selected from a highly skewed population. They are drawn from a pool of men and women who are party members, have a high degree of interest in the affairs of the party, and are sufficiently active within the party as to have impressed the leadership of the party machine. Most importantly, they must be judged by this leadership as "dependable" persons who if elected to office could be counted on to act in the party's interest. The issue of capacity for public service is only one among many competing demands the potential candidate must meet, and often comes in a poor second. The primary consideration is most frequently past service to the party.

At no point in the decision to back a particular candidate are the opinions of the general electorate taken into account in a formal way. For more important offices, an informal polling of the public as to a particular candidate's desirability may be one of the factors taken into account in the political machine's private deliberations. In the more severe cases of political monopoly—unhappily a far too common condition—the leadership of the machine will make the classical judgment of "what the traffic will bear" in selecting its candidates.

Once the machine has selected its preferred candidate, it is in a position to bring to bear formidable resources on behalf of his nomination in the primary. The main effect of this is to distort true competition among contenders, and it is typically the case that only contenders with large private wealth or significant financial contacts are able to realistically compete with the machine candidate.

The power of the political machine to "get out the vote" typically results from the advantages it possesses in financial resources, from its control of oft-played-with administrative details of voting, and from a vast number of party or patronage workers and families and friends whose jobs are on the line. These workers are highly motivated from personal rather than public interest to do the many menial but important tasks required to induce the largest vote for the machine candidate. Furthermore, if the machine currently enjoys political power, the workers may be in a position to use the privileges of their public offices for partisan political advantage.

For no apparent good reason, the nation has remained tied to an antiquated and inefficient voting technology—the ballot box and the voting machine. These present considerable inconvenience to the average voter who has many competing demands on his time. They also provide an inherent advantage to the political power structure which controls the administrative details of ballot-box voting and is capable of "getting out the vote." American business has shown remarkable ingenuity in the development of computerized technology to service a wide variety of customer functions. There is no inherent reason why such technological innovation could not be quickly applied to the business of voting.

An especially harmful aspect of a political-machine-run campaign is its tendency to hamper the true competition of ideas that must occur if the electorate is to make an informed choice. The most typical strategies of incumbent machines are to avoid debate among candidates, to suppress any objective evaluation of its prior performance in office, and to carefully orchestrate the information which becomes public during the campaign. The political atmosphere in this regard has been so corrupted over the past several decades that active suppression and cover-up are taken as commonplace political tactics. The demand for genuine debate in open forums appears in the present atmosphere as a naïve request.

A further distortion of fair and full competition is the requirement that only members of established political parties can compete in a primary. The predominant trend among the American electorate appears to be an increasing disaffection with the parties and a disinclination to join them. An otherwise well-qualified person who is neither a Republican nor a Democrat would in all probability find no viable outlet for his or her talents. This is a highly irrational waste of our most needed national resource, competent and farsighted leaders.

These criticisms of severe limitation of entry into the political marketplace and of distortion of competition among contenders by machine interests apply even more strongly in the case of candidates nominated by conventions. Delegates to political conventions primarily have the party's interests at heart, and rather than far-ranging vision and leadership qualities, partisan interest is typically the prime consideration in selecting a candidate.

Nomination by petition has been the traditional way by which new parties have attempted entry into the political marketplace. New parties have generally been of two basic types. Groups such as the Socialist, Constitution, Tax Cut, Prohibition, Peace and Freedom, and National States' Rights parties have been primarily concerned with espousing a particular point of view rather than winning broad popular support. Another class of new political parties have evolved as spin-offs from one of the major parties and have attempted to win broad popular support. Examples in this category include the Populist Party, the various Progressive movements (Theodore Roosevelt, Robert La Follette, Henry Wallace), and the American Party (George Wallace). To date none of these parties have achieved significantly broad-based national power at the local, state, and federal level.

It is fair to say that these third parties encountered the strong opposition of deeply entrenched political forces. Moreover, these parties focused on differentiating themselves policy-wise from the dominant political parties by emphasizing party unity behind a specific platform. None of them emphasized the singular aim of attracting new competent talent to political leadership.

Our claim is that the most fruitful analysis of an ideal system for choosing political leaders is best done using the principles of competitive economic theory. According to classical economic theory, the best insurer of the quality and value of a product is ease of entry of competitors into the marketplace and a well-informed consumer population. These conditions encourage the development of new ideas and ensure that only the best of these new ideas will survive. The sum result is, within sometimes gross limitations emphasized by welfare economists, the optimal use of scarce resources in a society.

These principles of competitive theory can be transferred wholesale to the political marketplace. The quality of elected political leaders is thus best ensured by ease of entry of potential competitors into the market, and by a well-informed electorate. This analysis underlies the observation that the inherent genius of democracy is its assumption that the truly popular choice is by and large the best choice for society. Under a democratic system, if there are unnecessary barriers to the entry of new contenders for office, or if the electorate is poorly informed or not interested, the quality of the final product—elected political leaders—will necessarily suffer. This is Adam Smith's "Invisible Hand" transferred to the political marketplace. If we are to reap full advantage of the principles of healthy competition, the American electorate must be presented with the country's best talent, and the voters must be fully informed and educated with respect to the relevant issues of the day. The system for selecting candidates must involve intelligent consumer evaluation at as many stages as possible.

Our judgment is that these goals cannot be achieved as a practical matter within the structure of the two dominant political parties. The parties lack an effective mechanism for attracting new talent and permitting it to compete fairly and effectively against the opposition. There are deep habits of favoritism and self-interest within these parties, and these are positively reinforced by an array of both legal and illicit political and financial interests. Those in a position of authority to amend party procedures are precisely those who most profit by the present arrangements. The likelihood of effective change within the Republican or Democratic parties in the foreseeable future is dim.

We are hesitant to propose a new party as a solution to our present state of political stagnation. The history of third parties in America has not been a successful one. Moreover, there is a maze of often arcane and tortuous legal obstacles to the formation of third parties created by the state election laws. To have any practical hope of significant success in the election game, a new party would of necessity have to galvanize public opinion to a degree unprecedented in American political history.

What makes the present times different from others are the threatening crises of an age of cataclysm—some of them already beginning to be felt in the shortages of energy, food, and raw materials—and the generally acknowledged failure of the American political system to supply leaders equal to the times. Our trust is that the vision of a new political party dedicated solely to the rise of competent leadership through fair and hard competition will galvanize America's imagination and mobilize the personal energies required for success.

We know of nothing under state election laws which prevents the establishment of a system for choosing candidates that draws on the largest pool of possible talent and puts the contenders to hard tests before a wide audience. To this end we are proposing a new political party, the Federalist Party. We have two reasons for selecting this name. The name best describes in a single word what history has found after long struggle to be the optimal governmental form for man. The name also associates to the concerns of the men who founded our country and is intended to remind the electorate of our deep Constitutional roots.

We conceive of the party as self-organized and highly decentralized, with the formulation of party policy left in the hands of the contenders. Its candidate selection procedures are designed to facilitate the candidacy of any qualified person, thus drawing on the total pool of national talent. The procedures are designed to rigorously expose each candidate to the widest possible segment of the voting population so that it may make an informed choice. There is no uniform party platform, no simple party ideology, no party discipline, no party doctrine. Only fair and impartial rules for the selection of candidates.

Because the rules are designed to value individual merit rather than conformity to party image, it is likely that there will be a large diversity of opinion among party candidates as to proper social policy. We do not see this diversity of opinion as a barrier to effective governmental action. We believe that the open competition of ideas from all realms of the political spectrum that will be generated by Federalist Party procedures is the best method to ensure the weeding out of infirm or unsound policy directions.

The Federalist Party must of necessity employ nomination by petition as its method of appearing on the ballot in local, state, and federal elections. In diagrammatic terms, the course of ultimately presenting a Federalist Party candidate for contention in a general election would run as follows:

1. Internal Federalist Party nominee
   selection procedure

2. Selection of Federalist Party
   nominee

3. Gathering and presentation of legally
   required petitions on behalf of each
   Federalist Party nominee to
   appropriate governmental authority

4. Placement of Federalist Party nominee
   on ballot for general election

5. General election

The heart of this process is the first stage: internal Federalist Party nominee selection procedure. These procedures must of necessity be designed to foster open competition among contenders who consider themselves qualified for public office, and they must involve the evaluations of the widest possible segment of informed public opinion. The essential ingredients of the procedure are a high degree of initial self-selection by potential candidates, public debate and intimate conversations on the media among contenders, and the judicious use of scientific audience opinion polling techniques.

In brief, the procedure for selecting a Federalist Party nominee for any political office consists of rounds of debates and intimate conversations among potential contenders, aired on local advertised television or radio time purchased on the open market. Immediately after each of the rounds, a scientific opinion poll of a representative sample of the listening audience will be taken. The contender scoring the highest in the poll is the winner of that round. The ultimate nominee of the Federalist Party for a particular office is that contender who successfully avoids elimination in the successive rounds. Potential contenders self-select themselves into the procedure in the first place by petition, the number of signatures required varying with the particular office sought. For the more important offices contenders will be required to appear in the debates and conversations with a principal adviser. This requirement permits the audience to observe the quality of at least one of those who would surround the contender in office.

In order to ensure that each of the Federalist Party contenders is fully informed of the positions of his opponents prior to the debates, contenders will be required to circulate detailed position papers among their opponents some time prior to the scheduled round. These papers would also be available to the press. This will decrease the likelihood that the debates would be won by a person who excels in public appearance but who has no substantial content behind his position.

The procedure accomplishes a number of goals. First, it ensures ease of entry into the political marketplace by permitting any person who has collected a nominal number of signatures of persons of voting age to present himself as a candidate. In a successful democracy it should be relatively simple for the interested and qualified citizen to present himself or herself as a candidate for public office. This is what we mean by self-selection. At its ideal, the only significant barrier which a potential candidate should face is that of convincing enough of his fellow citizens that he or she is viable and might be a good leader. In competitive terms, ease of entry into the political marketplace is thus ensured. The high emphasis on initial self-selection is the best method for intelligently drawing talent from a largely unknown population. Long experience in democratic processes has shown that petition—formal subscriptions of support by the qualified electorate—is a viable procedure for initial self-selection.

Secondly, the procedure ensures deep scrutiny of the contenders by a broad segment of voter opinion. The process is designed to emphasize an informed choice concerning the relative leadership abilities of the contenders. Public debates are a good measure of a candidate's vision and his or her ability to think quickly and coherently under conditions of limited time. These are characteristics which any good political leader must possess. Public debate does not, however, test all the necessary qualifications of a good political leader. He must be successful in dealing with many often conflicting groups of people and resolving disputes or getting his or her way in a creative and politic manner. Publicly aired intimate conversations among contenders provide this latter measure. They permit the electorate to view the leader in his chambers, as it were, and to take good stock of his ability, sophistication, and leadership qualities. Contenders for Federalist Party nomination will face each other in successive rounds of debate and conversation, giving the public a chance for deep insight into their worth.

Lastly, the process is designed to ensure that the ultimate Federalist Party nominee will be acceptable to a wide segment of the voting population. This is a precondition to success which many of the third parties in America's history have ignored. The successive rounds of aired debates and conversations that form the heart of the Federalist selection process are in a sense commercial programs, competing with other commercial programs for listener attention. To the extent that Federalist Party contenders succeed in drawing the interest of a wide listening audience, they will necessarily be raising issues of deep interest to the American public. By significantly educating the public on the issues of the day, Federalist Party candidates will be seen as viable contenders against Republican or Democratic opponents in the general election. The fact that the nominee is deemed the most popular candidate by a wide listening audience almost guarantees his or her desirability by the electorate as a whole.

There are many details which remain to be resolved. Let us take first the question of money. Under an ideal electoral system television or radio time for public debate or intimate conversation among contenders for public office would be financed from public funds. We stress that this is different from "free time," where the actual cost of air time is borne by the individual broadcaster. Under the ideal, the market cost of air time for public debate would be borne by the taxpayer.

Until the passage of legislation enabling this subsidy, the Federalist Party procedure would have to be self-financed, with party funds purchasing the required advertising and air time for rounds, and conducting the necessary polls of the listening audience at its own expense. There are a number of possible sources of funds. The most preferable of these is the funding of party selection procedures, official petition gathering, and the general election campaign through private donations, both large and small. A second possible source of money lies in the traditional fund-raising techniques, including direct mail, benefits, dues, and the like. If these procedures fail to raise sufficient funds, the reliance of the party for funds will rest perforce on the candidates themselves. There are some cost-saving techniques which the national committee of the party could employ, such as providing a low-cost polling organization to service the entire party and providing institutional advertising of the party at the national level, which would have significant beneficial effects at the local level.

A second issue is the role that direct campaigning would play in the nominating process. "Pressing the flesh" or personal campaigning is a long and noble tradition of democratic elections, and there is no reason to deny the candidates this valuable outlet during any stage of the electoral process. What the particular value of personal campaigning during the nominating process might be is of question. Our present judgment is that the debates and intimate conversations will play a dominating role in the selection of candidates for nomination. Individual candidates would naturally be free to do whatever personal campaigning their imagination, energy, and resources deem fit. During the general election, the full resources of the party will be behind each candidate, with the division of available funds following as much as possible predetermined rules.

A third problem is simply that of numbers. One can easily envision a situation where far vaster numbers of potential candidates will have qualified themselves for the Federalist selection procedure by petition than can be accommodated on air time. Our solution, as fair and equitable as we can think, is that those who go on to the nominating rounds be chosen by lot from qualifying contenders. Given the law of averages, it is likely that on the whole well-qualified candidates would be represented in the process.

The final issue is that of practicality. For the Federalist Party to be successful, a series of intricate logistical and procedural problems, requiring for solution much professional expertise and popular energy, would have to be resolved. These include the formation of a national party structure, the adaptation of Federalist Party procedures to individual state election laws, the holding of initial state organizing conventions, the adoption of a charter and bylaws for each state, the designation of a state governing committee for each state, the encouragement of candidates and the organization and conducting of a Federalist nomination process in each state and community, the gathering of qualifying petitions for placement on the ballot for general election, and the conducting of competent political campaigns for offices across the nation.

The realities of modern politics require the systematic use of the most advanced organizational and information-processing techniques at each stage of this process. It would involve the collective efforts of many experts in law, systems analysis, information processing, social sciences, media, and other fields as well as the outpouring of unprecedented popular energy. The many crises of our times demand nothing less.

In our more optimistic moments, we have contemplated the possibility of a substantial Federalist Party victory in the general elections of 1976. This would indeed be a political miracle. At the expense of possibly appearing excessively unrealistic and tendentious, we offer the following timetable for its accomplishment. The timetable needless to say is applicable for the general elections of 1978, 1980, and so on into the age of cataclysm.

We see no practical possibility of holding a national organizing convention prior to the holding of state organizing conventions. Public interest at this early stage would be too weak to sustain a meaningful national convention; considerations of travel distances and costs appear significant as well. These same considerations do not apply in the case of the state organizing conventions. Travel distances and costs are considerably less. Moreover, the overwhelming majority of electoral offices fall under the jurisdiction of the state party apparatus, thus providing motivation for individuals to participate in the state process. In the absence of feasible alternatives, the authors intend to take upon themselves the responsibility of forming a national governing committee.

One cannot provide generally applicable deadlines for completion of each stage in the creation and development of the Federalist Party. Filing requirements and procedures vary drastically among states, and each state Federalist organization would have to tailor its own internal timetable to the requirements of applicable state law. However, we may estimate approximate durations of each of the stages.

A previously formed national committee would have to determine the rules for accreditation of delegates to the state organizing conventions. Our present inclination is to have accreditation to the state convention by self-selection; that is, any person of voting age who presents a nominal number of signatures and a modest admission fee to defray costs to the national committee by a specified date would automatically be accredited as a delegate to his state convention. The national committee of the party would thus act as initial referee in drawing up a list of state convention delegates and in seeking out those delegates who would take on responsibility for organizing the convention.

The principal tasks of the state organizing convention appear to be the adoption of a charter and bylaws for the state party and the designation of a state governing committee whose responsibility would be to administer the Federalist Party procedures for local, state, and federal offices. The concerns of the convention would thus be entirely procedural—there would be no need to adopt a convention platform—and it is likely that much of the acrimony and extended debate which characterizes most political conventions would be avoided. The adoption of a model charter and bylaws with minor variations for each state would go a long way to ease the task of the convention. The selection of members of the state governing committee would be by vote of the convention.

Our present estimate is that the work of the state organizing convention could be completed on four successive three-day weekends, thus minimizing inconvenience for members of the working population who wish to attend. In terms of the 1976 general elections, the work of state organizing conventions must be completed by between November, 1975, and February, 1976, depending on the requirements of relevant state election laws.

The next stage in the Federalist program is the nominee selection procedure. This includes initial advertising of the procedure by the state governing committee, applications by potential contenders, the holding of successive rounds of aired debates and conversations, and the final designation of Federalist nominees for a wide variety of offices. We have estimated that the advertising, the self-selection of candidates, and the program of debates and conversations would each take approximately one month, adding to a total of three months for this phase of the program. The timetable for 1976 has thus moved to some variable date falling between February and May, 1976, again depending on the peculiar requirements of relevant state law.

The next stage in the process is the gathering of qualifying signatures and their presentation to the relevant state election officials. The costs and difficulties of this procedure will vary enormously between the states. Some states require a nominal handful of signatures; other states require a formidable percentage of the voting population. Thus the time required for this procedure could be as little as a few days and as long as three months.

Again, the time interval between completion of this stage and the holding of the general election varies with state law. The intent of state law is generally to provide a decent interval between the deadline for qualifying petitions and the general election. Federalist nominees would at the very least have this interval to devote to their campaigns in the general election.

A final though not unimportant topic is the selection of the Federalist Party nominee for President and Vice President of the United States. Under state election laws candidates of a new party for President and Vice President must qualify by petition in each of the individual states. One possible and absurd outcome of this requirement is that a contender for Federalist Party nomination for President or Vice President would be required to compete in fifty separate selection procedures. It seems best to have a single Federalist selection procedure for President and Vice President, broadcast on national television or radio. This process would be administered by the national committee of the party and the winner would have the privilege of seeking qualification by petition as Federalist Party nominee in each of the fifty states.

The authors can think of a number of individuals who

would make able contenders for Federalist Party nomination as candidates for the Presidency, and who would not be likely to attain nomination otherwise. Kingman Brewster, President of Yale, and a man who brought the university successfully through the tensions of the late sixties and early seventies, is an example.

The authors have opened a post office box in order to facilitate communication with interested persons and groups. It is PO Box 704, Canal Street Station, New York, N.Y. 10013.

4. A New Constitution

A reasonable and not altogether speculative scenario is that the decade of the 1980's will be one of a steady stream of destructive cataclysm. The high psychics tend to place the most cataclysmic earthquakes in the middle and late 1980's, and seismological opinion does not make this at all unlikely.

If this is the case, then the 1970's will be the years of preparation. Questions of enormous consequence must be debated. Needs and goals must be systematically analyzed and resolved. Logistical undertakings on an unprecedented scale must begin.

The needed mobilization of human energies is global. It is difficult because it comes at a time when man is only beginning to establish himself in the prosperity and certainty of the postwar world. To ask man to drastically rearrange the first widespread condition of comfort he has achieved in his history seems an impossible undertaking. The inertia appears overwhelming.

The only appeal against this inertia is reason. We have built a house of cards which we know will fall. Surprising. One would have thought that with the advances of seismology the scientific community would have informed those who plan our cities that they were proceeding unwisely.

Perhaps this scientific community has not sufficiently in-
gested the lessons of game theory. Whatever the reason, it is
we who are left with the result.

We are left with a practical problem: how to gather our
wits and painfully begin again. Let us assume, in the absence
of more specific predictions, that we have from five to fifteen
years for the slow business of gearing to the coming shaking
of the earth. We have always assumed the human race will
muddle through. What differentiates our present position is
the foreknowledge that it might not.

We are dealing with conditions of limited time. Man must
respect time and use it wisely. There are many directions
toward which our energies could flee. Conversation, worry,
citizen groups, public outcry, fits and starts. The style of the
past ten years has been toward self-assertion, and the
beginnings of cataclysm would see this trend run wild.
Feverishness might fill our time; it would perforce solve
little.

The logic of redemption seems inescapable. It is a long,
slow process. The world is not changed overnight. The first
step seems clear: the selection of new talent and competent
leaders. That is not infeasible and is well within our grasp. It
is in the air; in the necessities of the times. Even without the
cataclysms, these changes would come naturally.

But, one can ask, of what consequence will this new talent
be once it is elected? This is a fair question. In our recent
past, men of noble intentions and personal ability have been
elected to office with the promise of reform and of action.
On the whole they have not succeeded; otherwise our world
would be far from what it is today. It is a familiar story that
men of talent enter government only to find themselves
rendered ineffective by institutions that permit no significant
change.

Let us take the situation of the United States, a country
which in all probability will face cataclysm in its most densely
populated areas in the 1980's and 1990's. Suppose one were
to succeed in electing to Congress and to the Presidency men

who by and large are competent and who have assimilated the implications of the coming catastrophes. The divergence of opinions and recommendations emanating from Congressional halls would be near chaotic. It would be inexpert. Most damaging, it would be delaying; it would not respect the exigencies of limited time.

There are two monopolies in the present American constitutional system. One is inherent; the other *de facto*. The Executive Office is filled by a single man. That is inherited with the Constitution. Its effects are to place the choice of experts, the direction of government, and the formulation of policy under the will of one man. Effective decision making is derived from the competition of ideas. No single man is capable of selecting the right combination of experts who will reconcile substantial but widely divergent societal interests.

How to make the most of the fundamentally limited knowledge man has—that is the problem of society, and of the constitution society designs to govern itself. A constitution should be designed to make the most of the extremely decentralized and individualistic form man's knowledge takes. It should prevent men of magnanimous but limited vision from setting up barriers to the entry of novel and possibly superior thought.

The *de facto* monopoly of the American Constitutional system is the assumption by the Executive of Congress' function to formulate law and social policy. Congress has lost its role. The formulation of good law in postindustrial society depends intimately upon access to information and upon expertise. Only the Executive Branch can command that information and expertise. Congress has not abdicated its function by an act of conscious will. Because of its nonexpert and crowded composition it is structurally incapable of sustaining the organization and analysis required to formulate law.

Congress was originally designed to ensure the infusion of opinion from representatives of all member states of the nation in the making of law. This design was the natural result of a concern among the fledgling states about the viability and the potentially threatening character of a strong centralized government. There was, furthermore, a strongly felt need to balance the power between large and small states. This design reflected the high degree of decentralization and duplication of the postcolonial economy. The economic integration of the United States through free trade had not yet fully occurred.

It is no longer the case that the separate states have fundamentally conflicting political and economic interests. This is especially so since the single and most compelling political, economic, and social constraint of the next several decades will be natural catastrophe. The development of intelligent social policy for this period will be a function primarily of expertise and of an understanding of the integrated nature of the national and world economy.

It is misleading to state that governmental power has been excessively concentrated in the Executive Branch during recent years. One can more accurately say that the Executive is improperly designed to efficiently discharge its present duties. It would be wishful thinking to believe that the concentration of power in the Executive is apt to diminish in the near or distant future.

A constitution is a set of social rules which forms government and broadly characterizes its domain. The rules of government that optimize the conditions for human happiness are far from fully known. They are in a state of evolution.

The first Constitution of the United States of America is by all admission a document of extraordinary moral force. It incorporated the best of the ideals of the European Enlightenment and has since served as a basic model for balancing power in progressive government. It was a remarkable document for the eighteenth century and has served our country well for nearly two centuries.

A true balance of power in our government has been lost. Divergent social interests require divergent representation.

Many deep social interests are not being represented in government. Effective power lies in the hands of the Executive, a result not intended by the framers of our first Constitution. This balance must be restored in a manner not inimical to the efficient running of government and to the preservation of the essentials of constitutional democracy.

We are led to speculation on the wisdom of Constitutional reform. It is a difficult subject, and we are far from experts in the matter. The times lead us to venture where angels fear to tread. We are offering radical suggestions for revision of the first Constitution. Their content is by no means definitive. Their intent is to initiate wide public debate.

Our suggested reform involves two significant changes in the present Constitution:

1. The abolition of Congress, and,

2. The transformation of a single Executive into an executive led by a group.

The reform has little direct influence on the role of the Judiciary, which despite its many defects has proved itself to be the most successful of the three branches instituted by our first Constitution.

There is no apparent reason for prolonging the life of Congress. The principles of euthanasia seem to apply. If Congress does not formulate law, it has no purpose. Most Congressmen now perform an ombudsman function for their constituency and for the interests they represent. There is a granted need for ombudsmen. If government is to have this function, it should be by design rather than happenstance.

In postindustrial society there is no escaping the fact that the Executive must formulate as well as execute the law. The formulation and execution of social policy must be done in full public view and with the meaningful representation of diverse societal interests. It must also be done in a manner which permits expeditious and firm leadership. With all considered, a group of three, each elected by different constituencies, appears sufficiently numerous to represent the main bodies of public opinion and interest and yet small enough to lead the nation firmly.

Under the new Constitution legislation would, as now, be developed by the staff of the Executive Branch. Upon thorough public debate and, in major cases, unanimous approval by the group leadership, it would be administered by the full Executive.

How to ensure separate constituencies for the three? The group of three would be elected by the voting population at large. The final voting for candidates seeking membership in the group would be done on a one-voter, one-vote basis, out of a final field of six. That is, a single voter could vote for only one candidate of the six.

The three would thus represent and be responsive to differing political constituencies. If each voter had three votes, then it would be quite possible for a bare majority of the population to elect the full three members of their choice, who could in turn act against substantial minority interests. By limiting each voter to a single vote, it is virtually ensured that a healthy diversity of views and interests would characterize the three members of the group.

To minimize abuse of their considerable powers, all major decisions of the group would be made unanimously. Our proposed electoral reform, already discussed, permits the election of candidates only after a deeply probing series of debates and intimate conversations on major issues. It is thus unlikely that individuals unqualified for the office or unable to work effectively with each other would be elected.

Let us examine two major blessings of this proposed system. The first is a restoration of healthy competition to the formulation of law. The second is popular education.

Proposed legislation would be debated in an open and public forum by three persons each beholden to a sizable and separate segment of the public will. Unlike individual Congressmen, they would each have equal access to the full information and analytical expertise of the Executive Branch of government. Due to their somewhat differing values, each would start off with a differing notion of proper social policy.

Take for example the issue of military policy, an issue on which widely divergent opinions are held among the American populace. It is fair to assume that the three members of the group would each represent differing opinions on this issue. In order to come to unanimous agreement, each would try to convert the others to his view. As a practical matter, this conversion to a common view can only be done by a broad appeal to a well-informed popular consensus. A member of the group who is attempting to accrue the broadest possible spectrum of national opinion to his position would not hesitate to make use of important data which is now held in secrecy by the Executive. The internal dynamic of the group and a hard analysis of where each member's best political interests lie argue against the degeneration of the process into a series of back-room deals.

We can see some obvious difficulties with the proposal in its present form. In issues requiring unanimous decision, there could be effective veto power exercised by one member of the group. This could immobilize potentially important policy issues such as budgetary approval. Whether the motivation to compromise within the group will be dominant is unclear. Moreover, it is difficult to Constitutionally draw sharp lines between those issues which should require only two-thirds majority and those which should require a unanimous group decision.

Although the manner in which the final three group members are elected makes more probable the representation of significant minority interests than does the present system, the proposal does not ensure such an outcome. Thus in a close election, the three who are most popular might agree on a position with which the losing three disagree. The interests of the constituencies of the losing three would thus be unrepresented.

These are difficulties which may be ironed out after appropriate study and discussion by Constitutional experts and observers. We are by no means offering a final version of a new Constitution. We are arguing that a reexamination and redesign of our present Constitution is in order, and have offered some preliminary suggestions in this regard.

The internal structure of the Executive and the manner in which its organizational functions are divided among Cabinet posts, commissions, agencies, boards, administrations, and offices is not strictly a Constitutional one. In an era of burgeoning duplication, bureaucracy, red tape, and ineffective government, it is of particular importance to rationalize Executive functions into a few coherent, tightly run and efficient units. Although we have by no means undertaken an extensive management analysis of the present structure of the Executive Branch, we offer the following preliminary suggestions for reorganization. We believe that coherent and economical governmental administration could be provided by a minimum of four administrative units which would collectively undertake to discharge public functions.

The four units would correspond in area of responsibility to the four main functions of government: budgeting; liberty and property; health, education, and welfare; and foreign and military affairs.

More precisely, this plan would consolidate the Executive into the following units:

1. a central budgeting, planning, and coordinating unit, charged with determining the total number and functions of the other units, coordinating their efforts, and determining the share of the budget allocated to each of them and to itself;

2. a liberty and property unit, charged with developing and administering the laws that directly determine people's civil and property rights and obligations, and with the administration of justice. It is anticipated that the majority of present Executive agencies would be consolidated into this unit;

3. a health, education, and welfare unit charged with

fostering the social welfare of the public at large; and,
4. a foreign and military affairs unit charged with conducting the international responsibilities of the nation.

Deep habit and lack of sufficient imagination often account for monopoly. One small, though important, example
is the failure of the Congress to extend antitrust legislation to
labor monopolies. This has resulted in monopolies in areas
as diverse as construction and medicine. The effect of such
failure has been an unnecessary constriction in the number
of qualified and skilled craftsmen and professionals, and
severe shortages in the number of specialized personnel
available for the national economy. These deficiencies will
gleam large during an era of natural catastrophe.

The solution of least effort to the problem of provision of public services is to grant a governmental monopoly. This solution is almost never the wisest one. Governmental employees have little incentive to cut costs and
improve efficiency. Indeed, bureaucratic status is most
often determined by the size of a bureaucracy's budget.
There is thus a built-in incentive to increase the total cost of
providing needed public services. Most importantly, the
individual citizen is left with no effective alternative of
consumer choice.

The traditional argument for placing the provision of
public services under the government is that public services
are natural monopolies, and that the needs of the public can
only be protected by a sovereign and official entity. These
are false notions. The management of a large bureaucracy
differs in no significant respect from the management of any
large business corporation. The professionals who now
administer our public services realize this, and the more
successful ones behave no differently than if they were
managing a large-scale private enterprise.

There is no good reason why government should not
purchase from competitive firms those services which it now
itself provides. In many cases this shift of burden to the
private sphere would significantly lower costs and greatly

improve the quality of services offered. A prime example is that of the prison system. The prisons are a monopoly and are offering society an extremely perverted product. Instead of rehabilitating criminals, the prisons create them.

Prisons are educational institutions and should be dealt with as such. Their control should be in the hands of the educational industry. This result can best be served by having prison functions provided by competing educational firms.

An important component to the ongoing health of the reorganized Executive is its deep self-investment in the acquisition of new knowledge. There exists an intimate relationship between the degree of sophisticated knowledge possessed by a government and its capacity to perform its duties. Only a government which acknowledges its deep ignorance about the workings of society can hope to develop sufficient understanding of social functioning to act responsibly.

5. Global Society

THE millennial society is a global society, emphasizing the free movement of people, goods, and services anyplace throughout the world. It is also a society which has achieved as broadly as possible the full range of millennial goals, especially peace, prosperity, and individual liberty. It thus presumes a high degree of integration among its component economic systems and political structures.

Natural catastrophe is a double-edged sword. Although it could very well produce a disintegration of society, from the millennial viewpoint it may well bring the world together. Man's historical failure to intelligently and successfully unite could be explained by the lack of any compelling reason to do so. One important effect of the stress of natural catastrophe is to render the conventional rules of international behavior obsolete. The looming proliferation of nuclear weapons leads to a similar conclusion.

Two significant barriers toward the achievement of a globally integrated response to an age of cataclysm are the insufficiency of habits of cooperative problem solving among nations and the absence of legal frameworks that would mobilize world energies.

The long-range goal of mankind is the establishment of a world federalism in which the energies of the world are directed within a single cohesive legal and social framework. From any practical viewpoint, the attainment of this condition is, as the prophetic literature seems to indicate, post-cataclysmic. The structure and dynamic of national policies adopted in the interim, however, must be consciously supportive of this goal.

Foremost among the required collective policy changes is a systematic reduction of world tensions. A primary effect of massive natural catastrophe is to render the games of war and of excessive national defense counterproductive. The resources, effort, time, money, and temptations now characteristic of the war and defense establishments add little useful product to the world economy. They divert considerable manpower and resources into highly specialized areas which have no direct and practical application to preparation for natural catastrophe, and add to rather than detract from the probability of destruction.

This reduction of military tensions and budgets is a necessary component of the global coordination of disaster preparedness plans. Other components include the mutual relaxation of national immigration barriers, a high degree of integration in economic, trade, and monetary policy, and the coordination of emergency relief.

The goal of world federalism depends intimately upon the ability of people to live and work wherever they wish. It is probable that general catastrophes will occur in areas of the world that are now densely populated. Many areas that are now underpopulated and underdeveloped, such as Africa, will be relatively stable during the coming period and may form the heavily populated areas of the future.

The collective effect of national immigration standards should be to facilitate a resettlement of the earth in as speedy and nondiscriminatory a fashion as possible. The major single policy reason underlying the restrictive immigration barriers which now characterize much of the world has been individual nations' reluctance to accept large numbers of poor and unskilled laborers who have little to offer the national economy. The relaxation of immigration barriers can only occur with the extensive development of useful skills among the poor. The educated nations of the world must perforce invest themselves deeply in this undertaking. Governments must support and subsidize modern educational technologies for the development of knowledge and skills among the poor of the world.

A singularly important function of government during an age of cataclysm is its heavy involvement in the development of productive skills among many sectors of the population. It will be especially important in the case of persons whose existing career skills will be made obsolete by the demands of the economy. Since an individual's sense of personal well-being and security in a period of rapid, confusing, and stressful changes is intimately linked to his job opportunities, governments must make sophisticated models of the future economy and subsidize training of its populace in the job skills most apt to be in short supply.

This training, moreover, must be nondiscriminatory. In purely functional terms, a pattern of class, racial, ethnic, or sexual discrimination in skill development serves to deprive a national economy of the full range of talent it might otherwise profitably employ. Although a nation may well absorb the loss of this talent in normal times, the stress of natural catastrophe requires that the full range of human potentialities be exploited.

Although we are by no means experts in comparative

government, the electoral and perhaps Constitutional changes which we have outlined for the United States appear applicable to most other nations. The selection of competent and truly popular political leaders by an educated electorate, and of expert decision making at the highest governmental levels, are values which must be emphasized in a period of world catastrophe. These values apply whether the country is rich or poor, capitalist or Socialist, parliamentary or nonparliamentary. We can think of no single nation whose government could not be improved by reforms which incorporate the substance of our suggested electoral and constitutional revisions.

The proper economic form of a successful society has been long debated. The objective data of history indicate strongly that the most successful societies to date in achieving millennial goals have combined a fluid capitalist economic system with a high degree of social welfare. By capitalism we mean the free movement of people, goods, and services within an economy and the preservation of a healthy and competitive marketplace by an appropriate legal structure. By social welfare, we mean the provision from public funds of minimal needs for the well-being and development of the populace, where the marketplace has shown itself inadequate.

It seems to us that if Socialist economies are to achieve millennial goals, they will have to move toward a capitalist form. Such a transformation of Socialist economies cannot occur without close cooperation with the advanced capitalist nations and must occur gradually through intelligently programmed stages.

It is highly likely that under conditions of natural catastrophe a growing proportion of the total product of the economy would be distributed by the government rather than by the free market. This is because the minimal demand for necessities such as food, housing, energy, and vital raw materials during a period of catastrophe will be either relatively constant or will increase, while the supply will be drastically reduced. If the free market were the only principle operative in distributing goods throughout the world during a period of global catastrophe, the resultant inequities would be incalculable and deeply offensive.

Appendix I

A READER'S GUIDE

In addition to the references provided in the footnotes and in Appendix II, the following books are included to indicate to the interested reader our general orientation.

1. An excellent introduction to general science is George Gamow's *One, Two, Three . . . Infinity* (New York: Bantam, 1971).

2. Emanuel Swedenborg's *True Christian Religion*, obtainable from the Swedenborg Foundation, 139 E. 23 St., New York, N.Y., is a major useful work of one of man's most important scientists.

3. The educational potential of children is treated with considerable sensitivity and hope in Madeleine Goutard's *Mathematics and Children*, obtainable from Schools for the Future, 821 Broadway, New York, N.Y.

4. A guide to the relationship between psychic capacity and creativity is Harmon Bro's *Edgar Cayce on Religion and Psychic Experience* (New York: 65-216 Paperback Library).

5. Friedrich A. von Hayek's *Constitution of Liberty* (Chicago: Henry Regnery) is, as we mention in the text, our major constitutional guide.

6. Milton Friedmann's *Capitalism and Freedom* (Chicago: University of Chicago Press, 1962), provides a valuable analysis of the social implications of competition.

7. *The Pulse of the Planet*, a State of the Earth Report from the Smithsonian Institution Center for Short-lived Phenomena (New York: Harmony Books, Crown Publishers Inc., 1972), is a useful summary of major natural catastrophes occurring about the earth during the years 1968 through 1971. This center also provides a weekly information summary on global natural catastrophes, available for fifteen dollars per year from the Center at 60 Garden St., Cambridge, Mass. 02138.

8. John McHale, *World Facts and Trends* (New York: Macmillan, 1972), contains valuable perspectives on our resource needs and survival systems.

9. *Disaster Preparedness,* a Report to the Congress, Office of Emergency Preparedness, January, 1972, U.S. Government Printing Office, is a good summary of the present state of disaster preparedness. It contains a thorough bibliography of research and reports. Available from the Superintendent of Documents, U.S. Government Printing Office, Washington, D.C. 20402. Stock Number 4102-0006. $2.75.

Appendix II

Robert W. Kates *et al.*, "Human Impact of the Managuan Earthquake," *Science*, Vol. 182, December 7, 1973, pp. 981–989.*

This article is one of the more concise summaries of the effect of a moderate earthquake on the life of a city. It contains a range of information important to any person seriously concerned about the effect of earthquake on human populations. Since the periodical in which it appears is of specialized circulation, it is included here in its entirety to make it more available to the general public.

HUMAN IMPACT OF
THE MANAGUA EARTHQUAKE

Transitional societies are peculiarly vulnerable to natural disasters.

Robert W. Kates, J. Eugene Haas, Daniel J. Amaral,
Robert A. Olson, Reyes Ramos, and Richard Olson†

... [T] *he framers of the existing constitution of the State, in view of the rivalry and jealousy which exist between the cities of Granada and León, and in order to relieve the Legislative Assembly from the overawing political influence of the latter, designated the city of Managua as the place of its meeting. The choice was in many respects a good one; Managua is not only central as regards position, but its inhabitants are distinguished for their attachment to "law and order," and their deference to constituted government.*

When the men of Granada and the men of León made a compromise decision in 1855 to locate the capital of Nicaragua on the shores of Lake Xolotlán (*1*), they made a political accommodation and a geophysical blunder. No other city of similar size has had

* Copyright 1973 by the American Association for the Advancement of Science.
† Dr. Kates is professor of geography and Mr. Amaral is a Ph.D. candidate, Graduate School of Geography, Clark University, Worcester, Massachusetts 01610. Dr. Haas is professor of sociology and head, Program on Technology, Environment and Man, Institute of Behavioral Science, University of Colorado, Boulder 80302. Robert Olson is assistant director, Metropolitan Transportation Commission, Berkeley, California 94705. Dr. Ramos is assistant professor, Department of Sociology, University of California (San Diego), La Jolla 92110. Richard Olson is a Ph.D. candidate, Department of Political Science, University of Oregon, Eugene 97403.

a more recurrent record of destruction than Managua. It has experienced severe shaking in 1885, destruction in 1931, severe but localized damage in 1968, and enormous destruction in 1972. Thus it is not surprising that, in the days and weeks following the 23 December 1972 disaster, at least 39 groups of geologists, seismologists, and engineers from seven different countries converged on Managua to examine in detail this latest experience, for each such major geologic event provides field data for earthquake science and engineering.

Less common was the mission that we, as geographers, sociologists, and political scientists specializing in natural hazard and disaster preparation, prevention, and research, undertook. Of some 40 major earthquakes in the last 25 years for which detailed scientific and engineering reports are available, only four have been seriously studied and reported upon by social scientists. Reasons for this discrepancy lie partly in the organization of science: earthquake study is a well-organized component of the disciplinary structure of the physical sciences and of engineering, but comparable organization is only beginning to emerge in the social sciences. Underlying such organization is the view that the measurement and observation of earthquakes and their physical impacts is the proper activity of the physical sciences and engineering; the measurement and observation of human impact and response is in the purview of journalists, relief organizations, and governments.

But the extraordinary quality of the 23 December earthquake in Managua cannot lie in its magnitude, physical mechanisms, impact on the crustal structure, or assemblage of seismic observations. An estimated 1000 shocks of equal or greater magnitude occur each year, the fault traces and mechanisms are unexceptional, and the seismic record is sparse. What brought at least 114 geophysicists, seismologists, and engineers to Managua in the month following the earthquake was the extraordinary destruction wrought by this earthquake, the potential for recurrence, and the hope of gaining from the Managuan experience insights that would reduce earthquake loss elsewhere in the world. We share this hope and consider this article complementary to the extensive geophysical, scientific, and engineering documentation that will surely appear. But we also place our brief and hurried observation of human response (2) in the context of the major questions of natural hazard and disaster research: How do men survive and even prosper in environmental settings of high risk and recurrent loss? What is the nature of human response to catastrophe?

Human Adjustment to Natural Hazards

Society, groups, and individuals risk natural hazards in the search for that which is useful in the natural world. Resources and hazards are linked, however—the rain that waters the fields poses, in its maximum and minimum, the threats of flood and drought. Particularly attractive for human settlement have been boundary areas, those between land and water, mountain and plain, hill slope and valley. Such areas pose opportunities for exploiting or integrating two different resources and climates and are especially advantageous for settlement and travel. The circum-Pacific seismic risk area is one such attractive zone—a band of intense settlement where mountains meet the sea. If men are to reap the climatic, locational, and topographic benefits of a Japan, California, or Nicaragua, they must risk seismic hazard.

In all societies, men survive and even prosper in such areas by accepting the occasional, even catastrophic, loss; by making adjustments to modify the impact of natural events or to reduce human vulnerability; and, more rarely, by making fundamental adaptive changes in their livelihood, habitation, or location. Empirical findings from studies of 15 natural hazards in varied settings within 20 countries now enable us to specify more carefully this process and to identify trends (3). In every case, adjustments are determined both by the characteristics of the natural events and the material and organizational resources of the society.

Severe earthquakes, compared to other natural events, rarely recur in a small area, release a great deal of energy, and occur extremely suddenly. Such a hazard does not favor extensive human adjustment, and what adjustment does take place is strongly oriented toward building earthquake-resistant structures, controlling the secondary effects, and minimizing pain and loss of life.

Developing countries are peculiarly vulnerable to natural disasters. Their societies normally contain substantial elements of an industrial society, which are concentrated in a capital or primary city, as well as elements of a folk society, which are found in outlying areas. Adjustments in the folk society, while often mystical and arational, are aimed more at modifying human behavior than at controlling nature, are flexible and easily abandoned, are low in capital requirements, and require action only by individuals or small groups.

In contrast, adjustments in modern industrial societies involve a limited range of technological actions that emphasize the control of nature; are uniform, inflexible, and difficult to change; have high capital requirements; and require interlocking and interdependent social organization, but tend to be individually more effective than those in a folk society. In developing societies that combine aspects of both folk and industrial society, much of the folk wisdom may disappear or atrophy. The expectation of support and relief may shift from the family and clan to government or other organizations before their actual capacity to provide such aid has been realized. And the applications of technology, limited by scarce resources, may actually increase the potential for catastrophe. Thus a series of national comparisons (4) for drought, flood, and tropical cyclone show the costs of hazard for the three developing countries studied (Tanzania, Sri Lanka, and Bangladesh) to be 10 to 20 times greater in average relative income and up to 1500 times greater in annual loss of life than the industrialized countries (Australia and the United States). The urban history, seismic record, and social organization of Managua created a similar setting of heightened vulnerability.

Urban History of Managua

Managua, on the south shore of Lake Xolotlán, is no stranger to massive human tragedy. In the past 400 years, this site has witnessed repeated bloody wars, uneasy truces, and natural catastrophes of great magnitude. At the time of the Spanish Conquest, it was the location of an extensive settlement of Dirianes, whose condition then and whose fate thereafter are concisely summarized by Spaniard Gonzalo Fernández de Oviedo y Valdés (5):

> It [Managua] was inhabited by Chorotegans, and, to tell the truth, it was a beautiful and populous village ... composed of isolated houses, at considerable distance from each other ... at the time of

its prosperity, it was the finest place of the province, and contained 40,000 inhabitants, of which 10,000 were archers, or slingers. But when I visited it, six years after the Conquest, it was the most completely abandoned and desolate place of the government. It now contains 10,000 souls. . . .

In the 1840's, when E. G. Squier traveled extensively in Nicaragua (*1*), the population of Managua had barely increased. Except for the fact that the town had become the de facto capital (it did not become the official capital until 1855) of a nation torn by internecine conflict between the Liberales of León and the Conservadores of Granada, Squier's description leads one to believe that it had also changed little in ethnic makeup and daily custom (*1*, pp. 402–415).

The total number of inhabitants of Managua probably did not exceed 20,000 until the early years of the 20th century; it did not again reach its pre-Columbian estimate of 40,000 until the late 1920's, a period of growth in the commodities export economy and of civil war, replete with U.S. intervention (*6, 7*). Recovery (in terms of population) from the Conquest took 400 years; recovery from the 1931 earthquake took considerably less than a decade. By 1940, the city's population had passed 50,000; by 1963, it had passed the quarter-million mark, and the best estimates on the eve of the December 1972 earthquake put it at somewhat greater than 400,000 (Fig. 1).

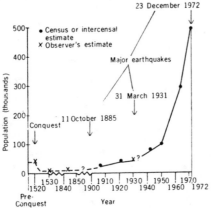

Fig. 1. Population of Managua over the last 400 years (*6*).

From a town of predominantly Indian tradition and culture, Managua, under the impetus of commodities export and a growing commercial industrial sector, had become a city typical of its kind in the developing world. The city's streets were filled with cars, trucks, and buses during the working day and were nearly empty after 6 p.m. and on weekends. North American and European foodstuffs might be purchased in a modern, shiny supermarket, and iguana and pitahaya might be bought from wicker baskets in the Mercado Central. Wood shanties sheltered thousands in the shadow of high-rise bank buildings. The now-dead heart of Managua was archetypical of the contrast in the developing world.

Seismic History

The plains of Managua lie in the Nicaraguan Graben, a long laguna-dotted depression lying 30 to 40 kilometers inland from the Pacific Ocean and cut by innumerable fault lines, generally running parallel to the coast (Fig. 2). Made up of recent alluvial and volcanic sediment, the plains are bounded on the north by Lake Managua, on the west and south by the Sierra de Managua, a chain of volcanic material and collapsed craters, and on the east and south by a major chain of volcanoes having a northwest, southeast orientation (8).

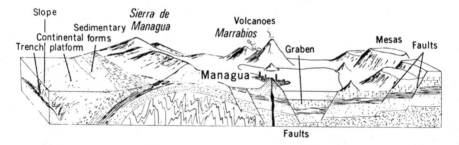

Fig. 2. A block diagram [adapted from J. Incer (7)] showing the setting of Managua, city and lake, in the graben that is parallel to the coast and offshore trench.

In the century prior to the 1972 earthquake, Managua was damaged in 1885, 1931, and 1968. Comparative data are presented in Table 1 and brief descriptions follow.

1885. As might be expected, very little information exists other than the fact that a very damaging earthquake struck Managua on 11 October. There were no estimates of casualties or damage except as implied by statements that the earthquake produced enormous material damage.

1931. This devastating earthquake has been well documented (*9*). It occurred at 10:10 a.m. on 31 March. In addition to the 1000 to 2000 deaths, there were several thousand injuries. About 35,000 were made homeless. Property losses were estimated at $15 million to $30 million (1931 values). Serious damage covered an area of about 10 square kilometers, and minor damage was noted over about 23 square kilometers. Reinforced concrete buildings were reported to have fared well, even those poorly constructed, but the dominant wood frame with mud and rubble-filled walls survived poorly, and fire contributed to the overall damages.

1968. Unlike the 1931 and 1885 earthquakes, this one strongly affected a highly localized area on the southeast outskirts of Managua. It occurred at 4:04 a.m. on 4 January. Except for two housing developments, the area was lightly populated. These two developments and nearby schools, a dormitory, and orphans' home were damaged. There were no reports of deaths or serious injuries, and we could not locate any figures for property damage.

Social Organization

A large city provides essentially a complete life-support system for its inhabitants and its visitors. For this to occur, however, there must be extensive interchange with the city's external environment. Managua, as is the case with many cities in developing countries, was very dependent on both the rural countryside and foreign sources and markets. Within the city itself, however, the range of basic activities relating to the community was fairly typical. The list includes activities centering around (i) preservation of life and health; (ii) provision of food, clothing, and shelter; (iii) economic functions (production, distribution, sales, and so forth); (iv) provision of basic community services (utilities, transportation, communications systems, and so forth); (v) maintenance of public order; (vi) leisure and recreation; and (vii) socialization (education, provision of information).

There were few unusual features in the conduct of these basic activities immediately prior to the earthquake. Schools were out for the Christmas holiday season, and the stores had the usual upsurge in buying. But there were some patterns of activity that would not be considered typical in a U.S. city of comparable size and that are particularly related to evaluating the earthquake experience.

Nicaragua, like other Latin American countries, has a pervasive, extended family system (*10*). Any given individual may reasonably anticipate assistance and social and psychological support when needed, not only from members of the immediate household, but also, to a significant extent, from uncles, aunts, cousins, and members of their households. While this pattern shows up in a variety of ways, it is perhaps most noticeable in the provision of food, clothing, and shelter. The nuclear family in Managua is not a little island unto itself as is often the case in U.S. cities, although most families did have their own dwelling unit, however small. The pattern of residence also differed. The central city contained many small commercial establishments within which the owner-operator family also lived. Thus there was more residential occupance in the commercial district than is typical for the United States.

Nicaragua was undergoing a year-long drought when the earthquake struck. During the preceding months, some voluntary relief organizations such as Caritas had operated a food distribution program for the most needy. However, Managua had no welfare clientele in any way comparable to that in most U.S. cities. The poor, no matter how desperate their plight, knew that no agency, whether government or private, would care for them on a continuing basis.

Citizens of Managua could move around the city with relative ease because of the large number of bus lines and the frequent schedules. Only the moderately well-to-do could afford automobiles, so the buses were heavily used and, except in the center city, traffic jams were quite rare. Many of the poor were accustomed to walking. Managua was not a city dominated by private automobiles and thus differs significantly from the prevailing patterns in the high-risk seismic areas of North America.

Managua did not have a city police force to maintain public order—no Nicaraguan city does. The National Guard was the only organization involved in law enforcement. It was reported that in recent years a small movement had been made toward dividing the city into something like police precincts, with a designated military officer responsible for law enforcement in each area. Reportedly there were only 5000 persons in the entire National Guard in all parts of the country before the earthquake. It is not known what proportion of the National Guard were in and around Managua on 23 December 1972. There was certainly no competing law enforcement agencies, as is sometimes the case in the United States. A related pattern was the watching and guarding of property. Yards of upper-class dwellings are almost always surrounded by a fence with sharp pickets or a wall with glass shards imbedded in the top. A private home is seldom left unattended. Either a family member remains home or a hired watchman is present. The underlying assumption seems to be that anything of value that is left unguarded is fair prey.

Thus the special quality of the situation in Managua prior to the earthquake was the unusually high occurrence of damaging earthquakes in a relatively new and rapidly growing city that contained 20 percent of the population, as well as the major industrial, commercial, and governmental capacity, of a small nation. Yet despite its seismic history and special, centralized vulnerability, pre-earthquake disaster prevention or preparedness measures were almost nonexistent (Table 1).

Table 1. Selected characteristics of damaging earthquakes, Managua, Nicaragua.

Date	Population	Magnitude (Richter scale)*	Estimated duration of strong shaking (seconds)	Lives lost	Property damage
11 October 1885	20,000 (1906)	Unknown	30	Unknown	Enormous material damage
31 March 1931	40,000†	5.3 to 5.9†	6	1000 to 2000	$15 to $30 million
4 January 1968	317,600 (1963)	4.6	5	0	Unknown
23 December 1972	420,000†	5.6	5 to 10	4000 to 6000	$400 to $600 million

* For the earlier earthquakes (1885 and 1931) there were either no or poor quality instrumental records.   †Estimated.

At least six major structures had been designed and constructed in accordance with U.S. design standards applied in seismically active areas. A law requiring seismic-resistance of major structures had been recently passed but not implemented. Insurance was in force on upper-income housing [with a coverage, perhaps 50 percent, exceeding that for comparable housing in California, about 4 percent (*11*)], by virtue of being required by the local mortgage lenders. A radio frequency had been set aside for emergency broadcasts as part of a Central American network. To the best of our knowledge, this was the extent of significant pre-earthquake disaster prevention, planning, and preparedness.

The Earthquake of 23 December 1972

Three shocks produced most of the damage to Managua. They occurred at 12:30, 1:18, and 1:20 a.m. local time on 23 December 1972. A magnitude of 5.6 on the Richter scale has been computed for the first and largest of the three shocks. Foreshocks were reported locally, beginning about 10:00 p.m. on 22 December. As a result of these foreshocks, some persons slept outdoors that night. Aftershocks continued for many weeks.

Surface faulting was located in four zones (Fig. 3). The area has been mapped extensively by the U.S. Geological Survey (*12*). The greatest zone of damage was in the older downtown area (Fig. 3). Moderate to extensive damage, including collapses, extended virtually everywhere in the vicinity of Managua. Damage was caused by shaking, faulting, and fire in the downtown area. It is probable that these earthquakes had a shallow focus (epicenter close to the surface), which often intensifies damage. The epicenter of the main shock has been tentatively located northeast of the city under Lake Managua.

When the sun rose over the city of Managua on Sunday, 23 December, out of an estimated population of 420,000 at least 1 percent were dead, 4 percent injured, 50 percent (of the employed) jobless, 60 percent fleeing the city, and 70 percent temporarily homeless. In this nation of 2 million people, at least 10 percent of the industrial capacity, 50 percent of the commercial property, and 70 percent of the governmental facilities were inoperative. To restore the city would require an expenditure equal to the entire annual value of Nicaraguan goods and services. In a country where the per capita gross national product is about $350 per year, the 75 percent of Managua's population affected by the earthquake had, on the average, a loss of property and income equivalent to three times that amount.

There is a unique epistemology of disaster reporting. No one will

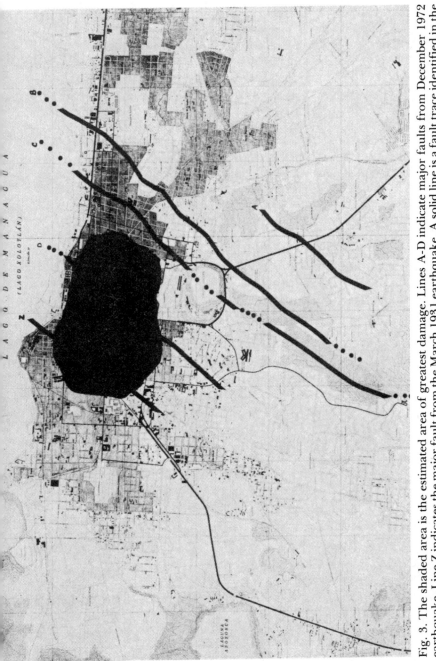

Fig. 3. The shaded area is the estimated area of greatest damage. Lines A-D indicate major faults from December 1972 earthquake. Line Z indicates the major fault from the March 1931 earthquake. A solid line is a fault trace identified in the field, a dotted line is inferred only. [Based on preliminary data from U.S. Geological Survey]

ever really know the precise magnitude of the human disaster. Estimates of death ranged from 2000 to 20,000; estimates of damage are almost certainly overstated. The methodology of loss estimation itself is not clear. Damages differ depending on whether they are considered as replacement value, restoration value, or the depreciated value of assets or property. In the aftermath of disaster, the actual costs and expenditures may become seriously inflated. Conversely, much opportunity for repair and salvage is underestimated initially. Losses differ by accounting stance as well. Much money will change hands among Nicaraguans. There are winners as well as losers in times of great tragedy.

Two weeks after the earthquake, a National Committee for Economic Reconstruction, with specialists from government, industry, and the Central American Institute of Business Administration, prepared the damage estimates given in Table 2. The estimates are based on simple and crude measures of damaged area, of employment, and of the distribution of rental and owned property, as well as assumptions about the average amount of space required per worker for commercial, industrial, and governmental purposes. These are not really damage losses; rather, they reflect, in the main, replacement costs. They include many transfer payments; for example, emergency expenditures for locally grown food stocks may only reflect a shift in the cost of food from private individuals to the government. Nevertheless, the estimates and the documents accompanying them are impressive when compared with early estimates made in other disasters [for example, in the

Table 2. Estimate of damages (millions of dollars) caused by the earthquake of 23 December 1972 (21).

Sector	Buildings	Equipment and furniture	Inventories	Emergency costs unrecoupable*	Accounting losses and others	Total
Government	22.5	9.0	1.0	38.6	30.3	101.1
Industry	3.0	15.0	2.9	2.6	17.1	40.6
Commerce	60.6	12.0	31.5	3.0	21.3	127.8
Housing	312.3	50.0	2.1			364.4
Services	28.5	11.4	4.5	4.4		48.8
Infra-structure	101.4	30.8	5.8	20.8	3.3	162.1
Total	527.7	128.2	47.8	69.4	71.7	844.8

*This column includes costs of feeding, medicine, temporary facilities, wages, and so forth, that have been incurred as a result of the earthquake, as well as government income that will be lost.

1964 Alaska earthquake (13)]. Based on our review of these estimates, we would calculate the losses of material wealth as between $400 million and $600 million.

Where the burden of this enormous loss falls can only at this stage (and perhaps forever) be guessed at. A review of estimates of rents and the value of housing lost suggests that 40 percent of the homeless were among the poor, 50 percent were salaried or self-employed middle-class, and the balance well-to-do (14). The psychic distress, widely reported but inordinately difficult to assess, cut across the entire society (15).

A comparison of the 1972 Managua earthquake with the San Fernando Valley earthquake of 9 Febuary 1971 illustrates the special vulnerability of the transitional society. For a seismic event an interval of magnitude lower, Managua's deaths were 100 times greater and injuries 10 times greater. Property losses were roughly comparable, but the relative impact in terms of income was 15 times greater (Table 3).

Table 3. Comparative data for human impact of 23 December 1972 Managua, Nicaragua, earthquake and 9 February 1971 San Fernando, California, earthquake; n.a., not available.

Disaster characteristics and human impacts	Managua (22)	San Fernando (23)
Magnitude (Richter scale)	5.6	6.6
Duration of strong shaking	5 to 10 seconds	10 seconds
Area of Mercali intensity		
VIII–XI	66.5 km²	500 km²
VII–VIII	100.0 km²	1,500 km²
Estimates		
Population of affected area	420,000	7,000,000
Dead	4000 to 6000	60
Injured	20,000	2,540
Evacuees	220,000 to 250,000	80,000
Housing units		
Destroyed (unsafe)	50,000	915*
Damaged	n.a.	29,560†
Commercial-industrial		
Destroyed	n.a.	575
Damaged	n.a.	1,125
Hospitals	4	20
Schools	740 classrooms	180‡
Unemployment	51,200	?
Damage (restoration value)	$400 to $600 million	$504,950,000§
Per capita loss	$1050	$70

* Includes 65 apartments.   † Includes 1707 mobile homes and 58 apartments.   ‡ Of which 35 received major damage and 18 were located as unsafe.   § Of which $250 to $257 million was public property.

Response to Disaster

When massive physical and human damage is caused by natural forces, without significant prior warning, a reasonably well-known series of activities ensues. The following account of typical, immediate responses to disaster is based on what reportedly has occurred in modern times in North American, European, and Japanese communities struck by a large earthquake or similar natural disaster (13, 16). The sequence in which the activities are discussed is thought to be a rough approximation of the typical sequence following disaster, but the various activities overlap in time (17).

1) Initial assessment of physical and human effects: through direct observation and contacting others, seeking to discover what has happened, who is hurt and who safe.

2) Efforts to secure self, family, and organization: a quick, initial attempt to shore up and save those persons and property immediately around the individual.

3) Spontaneous search and rescue activity: cries for help and the sight of rubble are quickly followed by spontaneous, mostly individual, efforts to search for the injured, trapped, and dead.

4) Attempts to ensure or reestablish public order: responsible officials and other persons believing that public order has broken or is about to break down take hurried action to keep the curious and most of the altruistic out of the damaged area, to direct vehicular traffic, and to take steps to minimize the likelihood of looting.

5) Spontaneous, sporadic attempts to limit secondary effects: for example, a blockade is quickly thrown up next to a fallen bridge, valves are shut off to stem the flow from obvious ruptures in the water system, attempts are made to stamp out small fires and to take quick corrective action against a few obvious fire hazards, and so forth.

6) Attempts made to mobilize previously existing organizations relevant to the emergency: calling in off-duty personnel, preparing directives for action, getting equipment and supplies assembled, all combined with a continuing effort to ascertain needs and priorities.

7) Beginning actions of emergent groups and organizations: where certain needs are obvious and are not being met (for

example, search and rescue, traffic control, examination of buildings for safety), new groups form and carry out activities.

8) Systematic attempts to limit secondary effects, including systematic evacuation: preexisting local organizations, in some instances with assistance from nonlocal organizations, take immediate steps to reduce any further threat to life and property.

9) Systematic efforts to provide needed emergency services: careful search and rescue with records being kept, assured care for the injured found, identification of the dead, programs of inoculation, organized distribution of food and water, organizing shelter for the homeless, provision of critical services to emergency organizations.

10) Organized debris removal and the beginning of emergency repairs: efforts to normalize the physical setting so that the full range of activities can be carried out with relative efficiency.

11) Efforts by public officials to boost the morale of local citizens: through news releases and public appearances, citizens are told that the worst is over, that help is forthcoming, that the community will be rebuilt, that "we shall overcome."

Word of a disaster spreads quickly. The result is that the affected area acts as a magnet for persons, food, medicines, clothing, and all manner of material. In the early hours and days, much of the influx is not in response to specific requests or expressed need. This convergence appears to spring largely from a naive, altruistic impulse to help those who have suffered unexpected loss for which they are not responsible.

In addition to the convergence of persons and material, there is a communications convergence. Every mode of communication is soon jammed with inquiries concerning the location and health of residents and of offers of help. Representatives of the news media quickly arrive at the disaster scene and attempt to question already harried public officials. The convergence is a mixed blessing. It creates all manner of logistical and other problems, but often in the cornucopia are some of the critically needed specialists, equipment, and supplies.

The Managua Response

Community-relevant activities in and around Managua differed from the typical response of industrialized societies previously studied in the following ways.

The early, spontaneous actions involving the assessment of effects and search and rescue were almost totally oriented to family, friends, and neighbors in dire need. With large dispersed families for whom responsibility was felt, immediate assessment and survival efforts were lengthier and more laborious. Public and private organizations and institutions, some of crucial importance in the emergency period, were given little or no attention.

Very early attempts to ensure or reestablish public order simply did not develop. Indeed, some evidence suggests that those persons who might be expected, in the countries previously studied, to initiate such early actions either reported in later or abandoned their posts of public responsibility. Looting began almost immediately and was apparently widespread. Commandeering of private property (for example, automobiles and trucks) took place to an unknown extent without any effort at record-keeping or promise of compensation. The flow of traffic, although slow, did not become a major problem.

Early, usually sporadic, efforts to limit secondary effects seem to have been absent, with only a few exceptions.

Generally speaking, serious attempts to mobilize previously existing emergency organizations started late and proceeded slowly. It appears that for approximately 48 hours the city's population had no significant support or direction from public or private organizations in the country.

Emergent groups from the local populace consisted principally of neighbors assisting each other in rescue and, less frequently, in retrieving property from damaged homes. One emergent group conducted a survey of the families still in the Managua area.

Systematic attempts to limit secondary effects did not begin until the third and fourth day, later than is typical for North American and European cities.

Systematic provision of needed emergency services was mixed. Organized search and rescue with careful record-keeping never did take place. It was assumed that families would bring their dead and injured to a few centralized locations. Organized care for the injured started later than usual and was built around field hospitals sent in by other countries. Some injured were flown to other countries. Identification of the dead would have been a monumental task, even in a well-prepared city. In Managua, most of the dead were buried without any written record. Mass inoculation efforts were considered but, on the advice of foreign medical experts, were not initiated. No epidemics developed.

The distribution of potable water, although later than in the industrialized countries, was better organized, in the beginning, than the distribution of food. The latter was a source of friction among different parts of the government and between the government and the voluntary agencies helping distribute food. The government declared itself the sole distributor of food, and all others had to cease doing it or else come under government supervision. As a result, it took much longer than usual for organization in the food distribution process to develop.

Much of the usual need for planned emergency shelter for the homeless was obviated by the extended family system. An estimated 75 percent of the refugees went to live in or around the homes of relatives. An enormous, spontaneous, self-reliant evacuation and relocation to cities up to 80 kilometers away took place in the immediate aftermath, only later to be organized and enforced by governmental services.

The provision of work space and utilities for emergency organizations was a very difficult task because most buildings were no longer usable. Tents and the homes of agency heads became temporary offices since these persons had some of the basic utilities available by the end of the first week. Only the electric power company came close to the usual timing for industrialized countries in getting its service to emergency organizations, possibly because its headquarters and maintenance equipment survived well and a power surplus was available elsewhere in the grid.

Efforts by officials to boost the morale of citizens were usually late and meager. Even the provision of simple information about what was taking place was very late and sporadic in presentation.

Interpreting the Social Response

The ways in which any city performs in disaster are determined by a variety of factors. Principal among these is the community normative structure. It includes widely held values, which are rather general and abstract notions about what is right and important, and social norms, which encompass fairly specific ideas about required, preferred, and forbidden behavior. Some social norms appear in the form of legal statutes, but the majority are simply understood by most adults without ever existing in written form. The significant point is that, during normal periods in the ongoing life of any city, there is a comprehensive normative structure, widely known, which can act as a blueprint for almost any set of circumstances that may arise.

In this context, there are three principal observations that help in understanding the social response in Managua. The first is that there was a highly centralized government, thin on human and material resources and operating in a delicate political matrix. Second, the tradition of the extended family was still very strong in this urban setting. Finally, there was wide disparity in socioeconomic status among the population, combined with high visibility of these differences.

It is not at all unusual to have highly centralized governments, military or nonmilitary, in developing and near-industrial societies. Their pervasiveness, however, should not blind us to the significance of such centralization in times of disaster. These governments rarely have an established civil service force of adequate size and discipline to continue administrative and operational functions when the physical or political environments are undergoing upheaval. Nicaragua was no exception. And the more centralized the power structure of such governments, the less dependable and effective will be the civil service units that do exist. When communications break down and directives from the sole source of power are not being received as usual, the actions of usually subservient organizations become less predictable. They are not likely to conduct business as usual. And when, in addition, there is ignorance as to whether the government may be in power at all, organizational functioning becomes even more problematic.

It appears to us that the early, near total absence of concerted action, effective or otherwise, by governmental agencies must be viewed in this context. It is true that these organizations had not considered and planned for such an emergency and that lack of preparedness did take its toll on the organizational response. In disasters elsewhere, however, other organizations have been caught without any semblance of preparation, and yet, with some innovation and inputs of heroic energy, they have managed to get going again within 12 to 24 hours. In addition to the usual disbelief and shock, agency heads in Managua hesitated to take early actions because their attention was first turned to their families. In the midst of the confusion, there was also an unwillingness to act without new directives from top authorities.

In addition, at the time of the earthquake, the nation was governed by a three-man junta—an uneasy alliance of the two major parties—with former president Anastasio Somoza Debayle at the helm of the National Guard. The disaster left the nation in political conditions of extraordinary ambiguity. Effectively, the government began operating only when the Somoza family took charge of emergency operations and located them on their own estate. Fernando Agüero Rocha, the leader of the opposition party, resigned from the junta.

Immediately after a disaster strikes, the family, especially the extended family, is both a boon and a hindrance for societal functioning. Within the family unit, all sorts of help including social and psychological support, are available because the well-being of the family is usually given exceedingly high priority. Individuals survive and recover in large measure because of this strong tendency to seek out, help, and protect members of one's own family first.

In Nicaragua, this family priority provided an amazing resource. An estimated 75 percent of the homeless of Managua found shelter in and around the homes of relatives on the fringes of the city or in more distant towns. The food stored in these host homes constituted a huge, dispersed warehouse, which supported an estimated 200,000 persons for several days.

But for persons who hold positions in organizations responsible for emergency operations to give priority to their families at the expense of their organizations means that those activities in which the community as a whole functions will suffer unnecessarily. Only specialized organizations are good at fighting large fires, restoring electric, gas, water, phone, and sewer facilities, and treating the badly injured. Emergency organizations can function effectively, if at all, only when most of their trained and disciplined regular members are available for operations. For 3 to 5 days, most of the emergency organizations in Managua were denuded of personnel, principally because of this family-organization role conflict. Much of the looting and perhaps many of the fires are attributable to the absence of law enforcement personnel. One can only guess how many of the injured need not have died and how many of the dead could have been identified before burial. But the normative structure of communities in Nicaragua specifies that the family must come first, and organizational responsibility is, at best, a distant second.

Socioeconomic differences are also related to the response to the earthquake in Managua. The differences in life-style between the small, very wealthy upper class and the large lower class that exists in poverty is obvious even to the casual observer. One gets the impression that they are almost two separate cultures. In Managua, as in other cities, the material products from industry are clearly visible in the small shops of the emergent middle class and in the large stores. Everywhere the poor can see what they might have but can't afford.

When, then, in the middle of the night the walls came tumbling down and windows shattered and the affluent, in the form of hired guards or the National Guard, were not there to protect these much-desired possessions, the result was almost inevitable. The overwhelming evidence suggests that people took what they could get from homes, shops, supermarkets, department stores, and even warehouses. Persistent rumor has it that many of the fires were intentionally started as a means of diverting attention from organized looting or qualifying for fire insurance benefits if earthquake coverage were not in effect. The community normative structure provided a justification, if not positive support, for the taking of unguarded property. In the absence of special norms for disaster situations, it would be assumed that the usual community norms regarding property would apply after the earthquake. They did.

The Unplanned Experiment

For those interested in reducing losses resulting from earthquakes, a major earthquake becomes an unplanned experiment testing building materials and construction techniques, on the one hand, and social organizations and human endurance, on the other, against the accumulated experience of past disasters in the same location and similar disasters in other parts of the world. What seem to be the significant lessons that can be learned at this early writing?

Each decade, a cumulative toll of lives and property equivalent to a city of half a million disappears beneath mud or ash, is reduced to rubble and splinters, or shrivels in the parched ground. Managua underscores the global inequity of such loss. In comparison with the San Fernando earthquake, losses in lives were 100 times greater, per capita losses of material 10 times greater.

But if developing countries suffer more from natural disasters, they also do less to prepare for and prevent them. Many features of the 1931 earthquake were faithfully reproduced in 1972, yet no significant emergency planning, seismic-resistant construction, or redundancy and decentralization of emergency services was developed during the 40 years between earthquakes. The low national priority given to reduction of seismic losses, however, is not peculiarly Managuan. Natural disaster may be costly to developing countries, but so is disease, unemployment, and public disorder. Planning horizons are short—attention is centered on increasing economic wealth. The international community is relied on to provide for the exceptional need; the small national surplus is needed daily.

In the emergency phase, the international community seems to have responded well. While organized assistance in Managua was fragile, sporadic, and unreliable during the period immediately after the earthquake (48 hours), when our observations began on 7 January relief and emergency restoration were well advanced (in comparison, for example, with the Sicily earthquake of 1968). In part this was due to the fact that the earthquake occurred in a capital city; the location amplified the damages, but also enabled the government to draw on the largest pool of skilled manpower in the nation. In good part, however, the relative speed with which relief was provided was due to the growing sophistication of the international community in providing relief. Central American countries functioned as neighboring states or provinces; U.S. disaster stockpiles in the Canal Zone were providential; organized units of engineers from the U.S. military, the Mexican highway department, and the Southern Bell Telephone Company played strategic roles in restoring services. Symbolic of the increased skill in both providing and receiving aid, and coupled with the best humanitarian responses, were the offer and the acceptance of a Cuban relief team, despite a decade of enmity. While we were impressed by the speed with which aid was marshaled and the improved skill with which it was used, there is reason for both some hope and serious concern for the future.

A central weakness in reducing the high cost of natural disasters for humankind lies in our understanding and handling of the critical post-emergency policy decisions for reconstruction (*18*)—and the need for this understanding is not limited to developing countries. With the haste to restore facilities, encourage economic activity, and reassert the security of familiar surroundings in the face of disaster, great pressure is generated to put back things exactly as before.

In Managua, the public arguments for maintaining the existing location of the city noted such factors as the survival of 90 percent of the heavy industry, 20,000 housing units, and the enormous investment in waterlines, sewers, connecting highways, and the like. Also cited was the deep attachment of Managuans to their city, the lack of alternative, risk-free land nearby, and the potential to rebuild with structures that could withstand future earthquakes. Privately, it was widely believed that the city would remain where it was because of the value of land held therein by wealthy, influential families.

Six months after the earthquake, relocation is not a serious consideration, but alternative patterns of reconstruction are still possible. Such patterns include: (i) regional decentralization, the provision of housing and employment, and the diversion of future growth to the major refugee centers as alternatives to the return of the refugees to their pre-disaster locations; (ii) reduced urban density—a decrease in intensity of land use by relocation to the periphery, controlled reconstruction in the center city, and increased open space; and (iii) increased seismic resistance by improving construction techniques and discouraging repair of greatly weakened structures.

Some progress in all three of these directions can be observed. External aid agencies have moved rapidly, compared to their normal pace, to provide alternative housing and employment opportunities. Large sections of the center city have been leveled and await further planning and risk delineation studies. Guidelines for seismic reconstruction techniques have been published, and a new building code patterned on Acapulco, Mexico, is being reviewed. New building permits have been restricted mainly to single-family dwellings.

Countering these trends is the return to Managua of a sizable portion of the refugee population, the low utilization rate of the refugee settlements on the periphery, the many pressures for laissez-faire speculation and reconstruction, the enormous difficulties in code enforcement and inspection, the absence of critical information as to microzonation and long-term environmental risk, and a general atmosphere of indecision and confusion in a period in which major decisions are still to be made and the dissemination of public information is limited.

If the past is any guide to the future, Managua will experience further earthquake damage within the lifetime of most of the current earthquake victims. The seriousness of that damage is still very much in the balance.

Finally, Managua reminds us in North America of our own vulnerability. While we can be encouraged somewhat by the comparative experience of the San Fernando earthquake, there is much in the Managua experience that is sobering. The Managua earthquake was a low-energy, short-duration earthquake, and another, perhaps 1000 times greater, can be expected to occur on the West Coast of the United States within the lifetime of most readers of this article. One set of scenarios for the San Francisco Bay area envisages between 10,360 and 100,000 deaths and property damage of up to $1.4 billion (19). The realism of such scenarios is underscored by three relevant aspects of the Managuan experience.

First, while the experience in Managua is reassuring as to the ability of construction built to current standards of seismic resistance to avoid structural failure, it is not reassuring with respect to functional failure. A building may be safe—that is, no one is killed or even injured by its collapse—but it may also be useless, unable to effectively house the functional activity contained therein. Managua provides a grim lesson as to what occurs when all the major hospitals that do not collapse become nonfunctional. Recent legislation in California now calls for hospital buildings to be not only safe but functional. Literal enforcement of such an act should require drastic changes in design practice (20).

Second, a center city disaster of the type envisaged in the scenarios, with a major fire, will necessitate massive evacuation of the surviving population. Three elements made the transport logistics in Managua possible: a simplified, one-level road transport system, a large pool of public transport equipment and a minimum of private automobiles, and the fortuitous survival of the oil refinery and its initiative in distributing gasoline to suburban stations. None of these elements would necessarily be present in

California— inded, the contrary could be expected. The freeway system can be fail-safe structurally but be rendered inoperative by unavoidable minor breaks and offsets. The everyday operation of private automobiles under normal circumstances can result in massive traffic jams, and gasoline, while ample in the area, might be unattainable where and when needed.

Third, if a breakdown of public order takes place during such a major disaster and if extended aid, while forthcoming, is unable to penetrate effectively into the stricken area, a large West Coast urban center might suffer much of the social dislocation and none of the compensatory supports found in Managua. Already a norm similar to that of Managua prevails in many of our central cities—what is not watched is likely to be stolen. But the compensating norm of broad familial responsibility is missing. Thus, while 200,000 Managuans moved in with their kin and lived there for months, will 4 million Californians be able to double up with kin and strangers for an extended period?

These questions are perhaps the most one can derive from transferring the results of an unplanned experiment. In any event, the experiment of major earthquake disaster will be repeated somewhere else, possibly in similar fashion. If there is any conclusion to be reached, it is that the Managua-type experiment need not recur, but it probably will.

References and Notes

1. The quotation is from E. G. Squier, *Nicaragua: Its People, Scenery, and Monuments and Proposed Interoceanic Canal* (Appleton, New York, 1851), vol. 1, p. 396.

2. We were in Managua from 7 to 15 January 1973 with support provided through NSF grants No. GA-03184 and No. GI-32942. Our data were collected from published materials and maps; semistructured interviews, many of which were tape-recorded; reports and other written records; and observation and note-taking at governmental and private sector meetings. More than 100 interviews were conducted: 30 with top officials of the national ministries, relief agencies, U.S. government representatives and visiting scientists, local leaders in banking, commerce, housing, education, engineering, and related professions; 30 casual interviews with relief workers, enlisted military personnel, volunteer workers of all types, both Nicaraguan and foreign; and 40 with refugees and host families crudely stratified by social class and shelter type. Time constraints required the use of purposive sampling.

3. G. F. White, Ed., *Natural Hazards: Local, National, Global* (Oxford Univ. Press, New York, in press).

4. I. Burton, R. W. Kates, G. F. White, *The Environment as Hazard* (Oxford Univ. Press, New York, in press).

5. G. F. Oviedo, in E. G. Squier (*1*, p. 416).

6. The Conquest in Nicaragua (Francisco Hernández de Córdova's expedition) occurred in 1524; we have employed Oviedo's estimate for the eve of the Conquest and for the date of his own visit [about 1530 (*5*)]. Squier estimates the population of Managua at about 12,000 in the 1840's (*1*, p. 32). Jaime Incer (*7*, pp. 382–384) gives census dates of 1778, 1867, 1906, 1920, 1940, 1950, 1963, but no data for Managua proper before 1920. The figure for 1906 has been interpolated from departmental (Departmento de Managua) data found in Incer (*7*, p. 383) for that year. The *Christian Science Monitor* (4 April 1931, p. 14) estimates Managua's population at 40,000; this figure accords with Incer's population graph (*7*, p. 384). The intercensal estimate for 1971 found in Convenio Ministerio de Economía, Industria y Comercio-Banco Central de Nicaragua (No. 19-AE 3, 1970–1971, p. 46) has also been employed. The question marks refer to unverified drops and recoveries in the population of the city after the earthquake disasters of 1885 and 1931; the drop in population after the recent earthquake was verified in our interviews with public officials and relief organizers during the second week of January 1973.

7. J. Incer, *Nueva Geografía de Nicaragua* (Editorial Recalde, Managua, 1970).

8. The site description is adapted from J. Incer (*7*, p. 209).

9. J. R. Freeman, *Earthquake Damage and Earthquake Insurance* (McGraw-Hill, New York, ed. 1, 1932), pp. 589–595.

10. R. A. Clifford, *The Rio Grande Flood: A Comparative Study of Border Communities in Disaster* (Disaster study No. 7, National Academy of Sciences–National Research Council, Washington, D.C., 1956); J. Gillin, in *Integración Social in Guatemala*, J. L. Arriola, Ed. (Seminario de Integracion Social, Guatemala City, 1956); N. Hayner, *J. Marriage Fam. Living* 16, 369 (1954); W. Sayres, *Am. Sociol. Rev.* 21, 348 (1956).

11. K. V. Steinbrugge, F. E. McClure, A. J. Snow, *Studies in Seismicity and Earthquake Damage Statistics 1969, Appendix A* (U.S. Coast and Geodetic Survey, Rockville, Md., 1969), p. 90.

12. R. O. Brown, Jr., P. L. Ward, G. Plafker, *Geological and Seismological Aspects of the Managua, Nicaragua, Earthquakes of December 23, 1972* (U.S. Geological Survey professional paper No. 838, Government Printing Office, Washington, D.C., 1973).

13. Committee on the Alaska Earthquake, Eds., *The Great Alaska Earthquake of 1964: Human Ecology* (National Academy of Sciences, Washington, D.C., 1970).

14. Such figures, based on census reports and housing count, would tend to undercount the poor.

15. *New York Times* (4 May 1973), p. 12.

16. G. W. Baker and D. W. Chapman, Eds., *Man and Society in Disaster* (Basic Books, New York, 1962); W. Form and S. Rosow, *Community in Disaster* (Harper & Row, New York, 1958); R. R. Dynes, J. E. Haas, E. L. Quarantelli, "Some preliminary observations on organizational responses in the emergency period after the Niigata, Japan, earthquake of June 16,

1964," Research report No. 11, Disaster Research Center, Ohio State University, December 1964; J. E. Haas and R. S. Ayre, *The Western Sicily Earthquake Disaster of 1968* (National Academy of Engineering, Washington, D.C., 1969); A. H. Barton, *Communities in Disaster* (Doubleday, New York, 1969); R. R. Dynes, *Organized Behavior in Disasters* (Heath, Lexington, Mass., 1970).

17. D. Yutzy and J. F. Haas, in *The Great Alaska Earthquake of 1964: Human Ecology*, Committee on the Alaska Earthquake, Eds. (National Academy of Sciences, Washington, D.C., 1970), pp. 90-95.

18. These and related issues are now being investigated with financial support provided by grant GI-39246 from the National Science Foundation.

19. National Oceanic and Atmospheric Administration, *A Study of Earthquake Losses in the San Francisco Bay Area: Data and Analysis* (report prepared for the Office of Emergency Preparedness, Washington, D.C., 1972). The damage estimates refer only to residential structures. Other estimates place the *total* loss at $11 to $25 billion.

20. State of California, Senate Bill No. 519, 21 November 1972.

21. Source of data: "Evaluación preliminar de daños a consequencia del terremoto de Managua—23 Deciembre 1972," emergency report prepared by a task force of persons in private enterprise and authorized by the Comité Nacional de Reconstrucción Económica.

22. Sources: author's evaluations of data in (*21*); Mercali intensity summarized from S. T. Algermissen, J. W. Dewey, C. Langer, W. Dillinger, "Managua, Nicaragua, earthquake of December 23, 1972: Location, focal mechanism, and intensity distribution," paper presented at the annual meeting of the Seismological Society of America, Golden, Colorado, 16 May 1973.

23. Sources: "San Fernando earthquake. February 9, 1971," report of the Los Angeles County Earthquake Committee, 1971; "The San Fernando earthquake of Feburary 9, 1971, and public policy," report of the Special Subcommittee of the Joint Committee on Seismic Safety, California Legislature, 1972.

24. The following persons provided significant assistance to our research activity: Ing. Carl Ahlers, Lic. William Baéz, Fundación Nicaragüense de Desarrollo; George Baker, National Science Foundation; Ernest Barbour, U.S. Agency for International Development; Gary Bergholdt, Instituto Centroamerica de Administración de Empresas; Carlos H. Canales, Ministry of Health and Hospitals; Edgar Chamarro C.; Arq. Eduardo Chamarro C.; Ing. Filadelfo Chamarro C.; William Dalton, U.S. Agency for International Development; Orlando Espinosa B., Ministry of Labor; Ing. Alfonso Guerrero, Empresa Nacional de Luz y Feurza; Pdr. Ramiro Guerrero, University of Central America; Janice Hutton, University of Colorado; Verona Norton; Cap. Ortegaray, La Guardia Nacional; Doña María Elena de Porras, Emergency Relief Committee; Carlos Ramón Romero, Ministry of Health and Hospitals; Ing. Cristóbal Rugama Nuñez, Ministry of Public Works; Renée Spinosa, Caritas; Harry Strachen, Instituto Centroamerica de Administración de Empresas. The authors alone are responsible for any omissions or errors in fact and interpretation.

Appendix III

The Disaster Preparedness and Assistance Act
of 1973 (S.1840) and related materials

*Included in Appendix III are the Disaster Preparedness and
Assistance Act of 1973 (S. 1840), and three statements delivered in
hearings before the Subcommittee on Disaster Relief, U.S. Senate
Committee on Public Works, on September 12 and 13, 1973.*

*The statements of Senator James Abourezk (Democrat-South
Dakota) and of the Honorable Harold A. Swenson (Mayor of
Harrisburg, Pennsylvania) are important in that they reflect the
views of public officials whose communities have recently suffered
major disaster and who have had firsthand experience with the
adequacy of present disaster preparedness plans. They project the
effect that S. 1840 would have on the nation's capacity to respond to
catastrophe. Both critics of the Administration's bill emphasize the
lack of a comprehensive long-range federal disaster relief program,
and the failure of S. 1840 to facilitate the development of such a
program. In fact, S. 1840 represents a regressive step in the
development of a rational and cooperative federal role in disaster
preparedness.*

*The statement of Dr. Joel A. Snow, of the National Science
Foundation, presents the present state of scientific research in the
United States on major aspects of disaster preparedness and social
policy. It demonstrates that although competent research is now
underway, expert answers to major policy issues do not yet exist.*

A. Disaster Preparedness and Assistance Act of 1973 (S. 1840).

TITLE I—FINDINGS, DECLARATIONS, AND DEFINITIONS

FINDINGS AND DECLARATIONS

SEC. 101. (a) The Congress hereby finds and declares that—

(1) because disasters often cause loss of life, human suffering, loss of income, and property loss and damage; and

(2) because disasters often disrupt the normal functioning of governments and communities, and adversely affect individuals and families with great severity; and

(3) because there is need for special measures to assist the efforts of the States and local governments in preparing for and effectuating expeditious rendering of emergency services and of assistance for the reconstruction and rehabilitation of devastated areas; therefore

(b) It is the intent of the Congress, by this Act, to provide an orderly and continuing means of supplementary assistance from the Federal Government to State and local governments and individuals, in fulfilling their basic responsibilities for alleviating damage and suffering resulting from disasters.

(c) In order to accomplish these objectives, this Act is designed to—

(1) achieve greater coordination among disaster preparedness and assistance programs;

(2) provide for supplementary Federal funding to State and local governments in their disaster recovery efforts;

(3) revise the scope of existing disaster programs and make them more compatible with and responsive to local needs;

228

(4) encourage the development of comprehensive disaster assistance capabilities, including plans, programs, and organizations, by the States and by local governments;

(5) encourage individuals, States, and local governments to protect themselves by obtaining insurance coverage to supplement or replace governmental assistance; and

(6) encourage hazard mitigation measures to reduce losses from disasters, including development of land use and construction regulations.

DEFINITIONS

Sec. 102. As used in this Act—

(a) "Disaster" means any hurricane, tornado, storm, flood, high water, wind-driven water, tidal wave, earthquake, drought, fire, or other catastrophe in any part of the United States.

(b) "Major disaster" means any disaster which, in the determination of the President, is of sufficient severity and magnitude to warrant disaster assistance under this Act above and beyond emergency services by the Federal Government to supplement the efforts and available resources of States, local governments, and disaster assistance organizations in alleviating the damage, loss, hardship, or suffering caused thereby.

(c) "United States" means the fifty States, the District of Columbia, Puerto Rico, the Virgin Islands, Guam, American Samoa, and the Trust Territory of the Pacific Islands.

(d) "State" means any State of the United States, the District of Columbia, Puerto Rico, the Virgin Islands, Guam, American Samoa, or the Trust Territory of the Pacific Islands.

(e) "Governor" means the chief executive of any State.

(f) "Local government" means any county, city, village, town, district, or other political subdivision of any State, and includes any rural community or unincorporated town or village or any other public or quasi-public entity for which an application for assistance is made by a State or political subdivision thereof.

(g) "Federal agency" means any department, independent establishment, Government corporation, or other agency of the executive branch of the Federal Government, except the American National Red Cross.

TITLE II—DISASTER ASSISTANCE ADMINISTRATION

PROCEDURES

SEC. 201. All requests for disaster assistance from the Federal Government under this Act shall be made by the Governor of the affected State. Such Governor's request shall be based upon a finding that the disaster is of such magnitude and severity that effective response is beyond the capabilities of the State and the affected local governments and that Federal assistance is necessary. Based upon such Governor's request, the President may declare that a major disaster exists, or take whatever other action he deems appropriate in accordance with the provisions of this Act.

FEDERAL ASSISTANCE

SEC. 202. (a) In the interest of providing maximum mobilization of Federal assistance under this Act, the President is authorized to coordinate, in such manner as he may determine, the activities of all Federal agencies providing disaster assistance. The President may direct any Federal agency, with or without reimbursement, to utilize its available personnel, equipment, supplies, facilities, and other resources including managerial and technical services in support of State and local disaster assistance efforts. The President may prescribe such rules and regulations as may be necessary and proper to carry out any of the provisions of this Act, and he may exercise any power or authority conferred on him by any section of this Act either directly or through such Federal agency or agencies as he may designate.

(b) Any Federal agency charged with the administration of a Federal assistance program is authorized, if so requested by the applicant State or local authorities, to modify or waive, for the duration of a major disaster, such administrative procedural conditions for assistance as would otherwise prevent the giving of assistance under such programs if the inability to meet such conditions is a result of the disaster.

(c) All assistance rendered under this Act shall be provided pursuant to a Federal-State disaster assistance agreement unless specifically waived by the President.

COORDINATING OFFICERS

SEC. 203. (a) When the President determines assistance under this Act is necessary, he shall request that the Governor of the affected State designate a State coordinating officer for the purpose of coordinating State and local disaster assistance efforts.

(b) The President shall, after determining that disaster assistance is necessary, appoint a Federal coordinating officer for the affected area.

(c) In order to effectuate the purposes of this Act, the Federal coordinating officer, pursuant to the authority delegated to him, shall—

(1) make an initial appraisal of the extent and nature of the assistance most urgently needed;

(2) establish such field offices as he deems necessary;

(3) coordinate the administration of disaster assistance from all Federal sources, in cooperation with the State coordinating officer;

(4) take such other action, consistent with the authority delegated to him, and consistent with provisions of this Act, as he may deem necessary.

REIMBURSEMENT

SEC. 204. Federal agencies may be reimbursed for expenditures under this Act from funds appropriated for the purposes of this Act. Any funds received by Federal agencies as reimbursement for services or supplies furnished under the authority of this Act shall be deposited to the credit of the appropriation or appropriations currently available for such services or supplies.

NONLIABILITY

SEC. 205. The Federal Government shall not be liable for any claim based upon the exercise or performance of or the failure to exercise or perform a discretionary function or duty on the part of a Federal agency or an employee of the Federal Government in carrying out the provisions of this Act.

PERFORMANCE OF SERVICES

SEC. 206. (a) In carrying out the purposes of this Act,

any Federal agency is authorized to accept and utilize the services or facilities of any State or local government, or of any agency, office, or employee thereof, with the consent of such government.

(b) In performing any services under this Act, any Federal agency is authorized—

(1) to appoint and fix the compensation of such temporary personnel as may be necessary, without regard to the provisions of title 5, United States Code, governing appointments in competitive service;

(2) to employ experts and consultants in accordance with the provisions of section 3109 of such title, without regard to the provisions of chapter 51 and subchapter III of such title relating to classification and General Schedule pay rates; and

(3) to incur obligations on behalf of the United States by contract or otherwise for the acquisition, rental, or hire of equipment, services, materials, and supplies for shipping, drayage, travel, and communications, and for the supervision and administration of such activities. Such obligations, including obligations arising out of the temporary employment of additional personnel, may be incurred by an agency when directed by the President without regard to the availability of funds.

USE OF LOCAL FIRMS AND INDIVIDUALS

SEC. 207. The selection of private organizations, firms, or individuals to enter into contracts with the Federal Government for the performance of work authorized by this Act shall be made with preference given, to the extent feasible and practicable, to those private organizations, firms, and individuals which reside or do business primarily in the disaster area.

LEGAL SERVICES

SEC. 208. Whenever the President determines that needy individuals are unable to obtain legal services adequate to meet their needs as a consequence of a major disaster, the President shall, in coordination with the State, assure that such legal services are provided with the advice and assistance of the State and local bar associations.

NONDISCRIMINATION IN DISASTER ASSISTANCE

SEC. 209. (a) The President shall assure that all disaster assistance shall be rendered in an equitable and impartial manner, without discrimination on the grounds of race, color, religion, nationality, sex, age, or economic status prior to the disaster.

(b) As a condition of participation in disaster assistance under this Act, all governmental bodies and other organizations shall be required to comply with all regulations promulgated by the President pursuant to section 209 (a).

DUPLICATION OF BENEFITS

SEC. 210. (a) The President shall issue regulations to assure that no government, person, business concern, or other entity will receive any disaster assistance under this Act with respect to any part of a loss as to which a recipient has previously received or will receive assistance under any other Federal or State program or any insurance policy, or for which it is eligible for compensation under an insurance policy.

(b) Partial compensation for a loss or a part of a loss resulting from a disaster shall not preclude additional Federal assistance for any part of such a loss otherwise eligible for compensation.

INSURANCE

SEC. 211. (a) An applicant for assistance under section 401, 402, 501, or 602 of this Act shall comply with regulations prescribed by the President to assure that, with respect to any property to be replaced, restored, repaired, or constructed with the assistance, such types and extent of insurance will be obtained and maintained as may be reasonably available, adequate, and necessary to protect against future loss to the property.

(b) No applicant for assistance under section 401, 402, 501, or 602 of this Act shall receive such assistance for any property or part thereof for which he has previously received assistance under any of these sections, unless all insurance required pursuant to this section has been obtained and maintained with respect to such property.

REVIEWS AND REPORTS

SEC. 212. The President shall conduct annual reviews of

the activities of Federal agencies and State and local governments providing disaster preparedness and assistance, in order to assure maximum coordination and effectiveness of such programs, and shall from time to time report thereon to the Congress.

CRIMINAL AND CIVIL PENALTIES

SEC. 213. (a) Any individual willfully violating any order or regulation under this Act shall be fined not more than $10,000 or imprisoned for not more than one year or both for each violation.

(b) Any individual who violates any order or regulation under this Act shall be subject to a civil penalty of not more than $5,000 for each violation.

(c) Whoever wrongfully misapplies the proceeds of a loan or other cash benefit obtained under any section of this Act shall be civilly liable to the Federal Government in an amount equal to one and one-half times the original principal amount of the loan or cash benefit.

TITLE III—EMERGENCY ASSISTANCE

PRESIDENTIAL AUTHORITY

SEC. 301. If the President determines, upon request of the Governor of an affected State, that a major disaster is imminent, or that emergency services are necessary to save lives and protect the public health and safety, he is authorized to use Federal departments, agencies, and instrumentalities and all other resources of the Federal Government to provide such emergency services under this title as he deems necessary to avert or lessen the effects of such disaster or danger.

EMERGENCY ASSISTANCE

SEC. 302. (a) Under this title, the President is authorized to direct Federal agencies to provide assistance by—

(1) utilizing or lending, with or without compensation therefor, to States and local governments, equipment, supplies, facilities, personnel, and other resources, other than the extension of credit under the authority of any Act;

(2) distributing or rendering, through disaster assistance organizations or otherwise, emergency assistance, including medicine, food, and other consumable supplies;

(3) donating or lending surplus Federal equipment and supplies to State and local governments for their use or distribution by them for the purposes of this Act; and

(4) performing on public or private lands or waters any emergency work or services not within the capability of State and local governments and essential for the protection and preservation of public health and safety where endangered by a disaster, including but not limited to: search and rescue, emergency medical care, emergency mass care, and provision of food, water, medicine, and other essential needs, including movement of supplies or persons; clearance of roads and construction of temporary bridges necessary to the performance of emergency tasks and essential community services; demolition of unsafe structures that endanger the public; warning of further risks and hazards; public information and assistance on health and safety measures; technical advice to State and local governments on disaster management and control; and reduction of immediate threats to public health and safety.

(b) Emergency work or services for purposes of this section shall not extend beyond thirty days following the President's initial determination that emergency services are required, except that this limitation may be waived by the President where he deems extraordinary circumstances warrant such waiver.

(c) Emergency work or services performed under this title shall not preclude Federal assistance under any other title of this Act.

USE AND COORDINATION OF RELIEF OR DISASTER
ASSISTANCE ORGANIZATIONS

SEC. 303. (a) In providing emergency assistance the President may utilize, with their consent, the services and personnel of any relief or disaster assistance organization to the extent necessary in the rendering of emergency assistance.

(b) The President is authorized to enter into agreements with any relief or disaster assistance organization whereby the disaster assistance activities of such organizations shall be coordinated with other Federal activities pursuant to this Act and in accordance with the regulations promulgated thereunder.

TITLE IV—DISASTER LOANS

DISASTER LOANS TO INDIVIDUALS, BUSINESS CONCERNS, AND OTHER LEGAL ENTITIES

SEC. 401. (a) The President is authorized to make or guarantee disaster loans to individuals, business concerns, and other legal entities in a major disaster area to replace, restore, or repair private property damaged or lost in the disaster, to the extent it is not covered by insurance. No proceeds of any disaster loan made or guaranteed pursuant to this section shall be disbursed unless the applicants have complied with the insurance requirements of section 211 of this Act.

(b) The President is authorized to make or guarantee loans to small business concerns for working capital and operating expenses, to the extent that a major disaster has created a need for such loans.

LOANS TO MAJOR SOURCES OF EMPLOYMENT

SEC. 402. (a) The President is authorized to make or guarantee disaster loans to any industrial, commercial, agricultural, governmental, or other enterprise that has constituted a major source of employment in an area suffering a major disaster and is no longer in substantial operation as a result of such disaster. Such disaster loans shall be for the purpose of enabling the enterprise to resume operations in order to assist in restoring the economic viability of the disaster area. No such disaster loans shall be made or guaranteed unless the applicant has complied with the insurance requirements of section 211 of this Act.

(b) Assistance under this section shall be in addition to any other Federal disaster assistance, except that such other assistance may be adjusted or modified to the extent deemed appropriate by the President under the authority of section 210 of this Act.

COMMUNITY DISASTER LOANS

SEC. 403. (a) The President is authorized to make disaster loans to any local government that demonstrates a need, as a result of a major disaster, of financial assistance in order to perform its governmental functions. The amount of any such disaster loan shall be based on need, and shall not exceed 10 per centum of the annual operating budget of that local government.

(b) Any disaster loans made or guaranteed under this section shall not reduce or otherwise affect any grants or other assistance under this Act.

TERMS AND CONDITIONS

SEC. 404. (a) Notwithstanding the provisions of any other law, loans made or guaranteed under this Act shall be on such terms and conditions as the President may prescribe, except that—

(1) No loan or guarantee shall be extended unless the President finds that credit is not otherwise available on reasonable terms and conditions, and that there is reasonable assurance of repayment.

(2) Loans made or guaranteed shall provide for complete amortization within a period not to exceed thirty years, or 90 per centum of the useful life of any physical asset to be financed by the loan, whichever is less as determined by the President.

(3) No loan shall be guaranteed unless the President determines that the lender is responsible and that adequate provision is made for servicing the loan on reasonable terms and protecting the financial interests of the United States.

(4) No loan shall be guaranteed if the income from such loan is exempt from Federal taxation.

(5) Loans made by the President under title IV of this Act shall bear interest at a rate comparable to the current rates prevailing with respect to similar loans guaranteed under this Act.

(6) Guaranteed loans shall bear interest (exclusive of guarantee fees and service charges) at rates not to exceed such per centum per annum on the principal obligation outstanding as the President determines to be reasonable, taking into account the range of interest rates prevailing in the private market for similar loans and the risks assumed by the United States.

(7) (A) The President is authorized to make, and to contract to make, periodic debt service payments on loans made or guaranteed under this Act in amounts sufficient to

reduce the periodic payments of interest payable under section 404 (a) 5 and 6 of this title to not less than the interest payments resulting from (i) a rate determined by the Secretary of the Treasury taking into consideration the current average market yield on outstanding marketable obligations of the United States with remaining periods to maturity comparable to the average maturities of such loans, adjusted to the nearest one-eighth of 1 per centum, plus (ii) an allowance adequate in the judgment of the President to cover administrative costs and probable losses under the program.

(B) The total amount of debt service payments contracted to be made under this Act shall not exceed $100,000,000. There are authorized to be appropriated to the President, without fiscal year limitation, such sums as may be necessary to make debt service payments under this section.

(8) The approval of the President shall be required of the interest rate, timing, and other terms and conditions of the financing of guaranteed obligations, except that the President may waive this requirement with respect to the financing of any guaranteed obligation when he determines that such financing does not have a significant impact on the market for Government and Government-guaranteed securities.

(9) The President shall charge and collect fees in amounts sufficient in his judgment to cover administrative costs and probable losses on guaranteed loans.

(10) Any guarantee made by the President shall be conclusive evidence of the eligibility of the loan for such guarantee, and the validity of any guarantee so made shall be incontestable in the hands of the holder of the guaranteed loan, except in the case of fraud or material misrepresentation on the part of the holder. The full faith and credit of the United States is pledged to the payment of all guarantees.

(b) The President is authorized to adjust and readjust the schedule for payments of principal and interest and to extend the maturity date of any existing Federal loan to a date not beyond five years from the original maturity date when he determines such action is necessary as a result of a major disaster. He is further authorized to refinance any note or obligation when he deems such refinancing is necessary as a result of a major disaster.

PAYMENT OF LOSSES

SEC. 405. (a) If, as a result of a default by a borrower under a guaranteed loan, after the holder thereof has made such further collection efforts and instituted such enforcement proceedings as the President may require, the President determines that the holder has suffered a loss, the President shall pay to such holder 90 per centum of such loss, as specified in the guarantee contract. Upon making any such payment, the President shall be subrogated to all the rights of the recipient thereof. The President shall be entitled to recover from the borrower the amount of any payments made pursuant to any guarantee entered into under this Act.

(b) The Attorney General shall take such action as may be appropriate to enforce any right accruing to the United States as a result of the issuance of any guarantee under this Act. Any sums recovered pursuant to this section shall be paid into the fund created by section 406 of this Act.

(c) Nothing in this section shall be construed to preclude any forbearance for the benefit of the borrower which may be agreed upon by the parties to the guaranteed loan and approved by the President.

(d) Notwithstanding any other provision of law relating to the acquisition, handling, or disposal of property by the United States, the President shall have the right in his discretion to complete, recondition, reconstruct, renovate, repair, maintain, operate, or sell any property acquired by him pursuant to the provisions of this Act.

REVOLVING FUND

SEC. 406. (a) There is hereby created within the Treasury a separate fund (hereinafter in this section called the fund) which shall be available to the President without fiscal year limitation as a revolving fund for the purpose of this title. The total of any loans made or guaranteed from the fund in any fiscal year shall not exceed limitations specified in appropriation Acts. A business-type budget for the fund shall be prepared, transmitted to the Congress, considered, and enacted in the manner prescribed by law (sections 102,

103, and 104 of the Government Corporation Control Act ((31 U.S.C. 847-848) for wholly owned Government corporations.

(b) (1) There are authorized to be appropriated to the fund from time to time such amounts as may be necessary to provide capital for the fund. All amounts received by the President as interest payments or repayments of principal on loans, fees, and any other moneys, property, or assets derived by him from his operations in connection with this title shall be deposited in the fund.

(2) All loans, expenses, and payments pursuant to operations of the President under this title shall be paid from the fund. From time to time, and at least at the close of each fiscal year, the President shall pay from the fund into the Treasury as miscellaneous receipts interest on the cumulative amount of appropriations available as capital to the fund, less the average undisbursed cash balance in the fund during the year. The rate of such interest shall be determined by the Secretary of the Treasury, taking into consideration the average market yield during the month preceding each fiscal year on outstanding marketable obligations of the United States with remaining periods to maturity comparable to the average maturity of loans made or guaranteed from the fund. Interest payments may be deferred with the approval of the Secretary of the Treasury but any interest payments so deferred shall themselves bear interest. If at any time the President determines that moneys in the fund exceed the present and any reasonably prospective future requirements of the fund, such excess may be transferred to the general fund of the Treasury.

(c) If at any time the moneys available in the fund are insufficient to enable the President to discharge his responsibilities under guarantees under this title, he shall issue to the Secretary of the Treasury notes or other obligations in such forms and denominations, bearing such maturities, and subject to such terms and conditions, as may be prescribed by the Secretary of the Treasury. Redemption of such notes or obligations shall be made by the President from appropriations or other moneys available under subsection (b) of this section. Such notes or other obligations shall bear interest at a rate determined by the Secretary of the Treasury, taking into consideration the average market yield on outstanding marketable obligations of the United States of comparable maturities during the month preceding the issuance of the notes or other obligations. The Secretary of the Treasury shall purchase any notes or other obligations issued hereunder, and for that purpose he is authorized to use as a public debt transaction the proceeds from the sale of any securities issued under the Second Liberty Bond Act, and the purposes for which securities may be issued under that Act are extended to include any purchase of such notes or obligations. The Secretary of the Treasury may at any time sell any of the notes or other obligations acquired by him under this subsection. All redemptions, purchases, and sales by the Secretary of the Treasury of such notes or other obligations shall be treated as public debt transactions of the United States.

TITLE V—DISASTER GRANTS FOR NEEDY FAMILIES

SEC. 501. (a) The President is authorized to make a grant to any State in a major disaster area for the purpose of assisting the State in indemnifying the uninsured property losses of needy families, and thereafter, to aid such families in meeting such other extraordinary disaster-related expenses as the State may recognize. The amount of such grant shall be determined by the President on the basis of evidence supplied by the Governor of the affected State as to the number of low-income families affected by the disaster; but the grant to the State shall not exceed an amount equal to $3,000 per low-income family. The evidence supplied by the States as to the number of low-income families affected by the disaster shall be based upon a definition of low income to be determined by the President. An initial advance to States may be provided which shall not exceed 25 per centum of the estimated funds required to implement the purposes of this title.

(b) The actual disbursement of the funds made available to the State under this title shall be made by the Governor or his designated representative according to eligibility requirements to be determined by the Governor or his designated representative. The Governor or his designated representative shall have complete discretion in determining such eligibility requirements and the amount of the individual grants except that the administration of the grants under this title shall be subject to the following provisions:

(1) No funds from any grant made pursuant to this title shall be disbursed by the State unless individual applicants have complied with the insurance requirements of section 211 of this Act.

(2) No grants under this title shall be disbursed to individuals or other entities for business purposes.

(3) No payments by a State for replacement, restoration, repair, or construction of real or personal property shall be made to any family in excess of its actual uninsured loss.

(4) No family shall receive payments under this title in excess of $4,000.

TITLE VI—GRANTS TO STATES
PURPOSES

SEC. 601. (a) The President is authorized to make grants to States for the benefit of persons or parties adversely affected by a major disaster, for the following purposes—

(1) provision of essential human needs and services, including but not limited to food, communications, water, clothing, utility services, and public transportation;

(2) replacement, restoration, repair, or construction of—

(A) State and local public facilities;

(B) private nonprofit educational, utility, emergency, medical, and custodial care facilities, including those for the aged and disabled; and

(C) facilities of Indian reservations, as that term is defined by the President.

(3) debris and timber removal from public or private lands and waters, when in the public interest.

(b) The amount of funds to be granted under this section shall be based upon 75 per centum of the estimated cost of relief for losses sustained as a result of the major disaster in the categories of assistance specified in subsection (a) of this section. The amount of funds granted for losses of the types included in section 601 (a) (2) above shall be based upon the estimated cost of performing work in conformity with applicable codes, specifications, and standards in effect at the time of the disaster: *Provided,* That the estimated cost for such purposes shall be based on the design capacity of such facilities as they existed immediately prior to the major disaster. For those facilities which were in the process of construction when damaged or destroyed by a major disaster, the grant shall be based on the net costs of restoring such facilities substantially to their predisaster condition and of completing construction not performed prior to the major disaster to the extent the increase of such costs over the original construction cost is attributable to changed physical conditions resulting from a major disaster.

(c) The President is further authorized to make grants to the States to provide to any individual unemployed as a result of a major disaster such assistance as he deems appropriate while such individual is unemployed. Such assistance as the President may provide shall not exceed the maximum amount and the maximum duration of payment under the unemployment compensation program of the State in which the disaster occurred, and the amount of assistance under this section to any such individual shall be reduced by any amount of unemployment compensation available to such individual for such period of unemployment.

(d) The President is further authorized, for the purposes of this section, to provide reemployment assistance services under other laws to individuals who are employed as a result of a major disaster.

(e) The President is further authorized to make grants to the States for temporary housing or other emergency shelter for individuals and families displaced as a result of a major disaster. The amount of such grants shall be determined by the President on the basis of the number of families requiring such housing, but shall not exceed a fixed amount per eligible individual or family, and shall be in accordance with criteria to be established in regulations to be promulgated by the President. Such housing may include payment to occupants for relocation costs.

ADMINISTRATION

SEC. 602. (a) The Governor or his designated

representative shall be responsible for administering the grant program authorized by this title. An initial advance may be provided which shall not exceed 25 per centum of the estimated funds required to implement the purposes of this title. No grant shall be disbursed unless the Governor or his designated representative has assured compliance with the insurance requirements of section 211 of this Act. Such administration shall be subject to Federal audit for purposes of determining whether the criteria, standards, and procedures herein have been complied with.

(b) The use of funds granted under subsection 601 (a) shall be left to the discretion of the States, except that funds granted on the basis of replacement, restoration, repair, or construction of private nonprofit educational, utility, emergency, medical, and custodial care facilities or of facilities of Indian reservations specified in subsection 601 (a) (2) (B) and (C) shall be utilized specifically for those facilities.

(c) The President shall promulgate regulations that shall include criteria, standards, and procedures for the administration of grants made under this title.

(d) Not more than 3 per centum of the total grant provided to an affected State shall be utilized for administrative purposes.

TITLE VII—DISASTER PREPAREDNESS ASSISTANCE

FEDERAL AND STATE DISASTER PREPAREDNESS PROGRAMS

SEC. 701. (a) The President is authorized to establish a program of disaster preparedness that utilizes services of all appropriate agencies and includes—

(1) preparation of disaster preparedness plans for mitigation, warning, emergency operations, rehabilitation, and recovery;

(2) training and exercises;

(3) postdisaster critiques and evaluations;

(4) annual review of programs;

(5) coordination of Federal, State, and local preparedness programs;

(6) application of science and technology;

(7) research;

(8) assistance in updating disaster legislation.

(b) The President is authorized to provide technical assistance to the States in developing comprehensive plans and practicable programs for preparation against disasters, including hazard reduction, avoidance, and mitigation; for assistance to individuals, businesses, and State and local governments following such disasters; and for recovery of damaged or destroyed public and private facilities.

(c) Upon application by the States, the President is authorized to make grants, not to exceed $250,000, for the development of plans, programs, and capabilities for disaster preparedness. Such grants shall be available for a period of one year from the date of enactment. Any State desiring financial assistance under this section shall designate or create an agency to plan and administer such a disaster preparedness program, and shall, through such agency, submit a State plan to the President, which shall—

(1) set forth a comprehensive and detailed State program for preparation against, and assistance following, a major disaster, including provisions for emergency and permanent assistance to individuals, businesses, and local governments; and

(2) include provisions for appointment and training of appropriate staffs, formulation of necessary regulations and procedures, and conduct of required exercises.

DISASTER WARNING

SEC. 702. (a) The President is authorized to insure that all appropriate agencies are prepared to issue warning of disasters to State and local officials.

(b) The President may authorize the Federal agencies to provide technical assistance to State and local governments to insure that timely and effective disaster warning is provided.

(c) The President is further authorized to utilize or to make available to Federal, State, and local agencies the facilities of the civil defense communications system established and maintained pursuant to section 201 (c) of the Federal Civil Defense Act of 1950, as amended (50 U.S.C. app. 2281 (c)), or any other Federal communications system for the purpose of providing warning to governmental authorities and the civilian population in areas endangered by imminent disasters.

(d) The President is further authorized to enter into agreements with the officers or agents of any private or commercial communications systems who volunteer the use of their systems on a reimbursable or nonreimbursable basis for the purpose of providing warning to governmental authorities and the civilian population endangered by imminent disasters.

TITLE VIII—MISCELLANEOUS PROVISIONS
MINIMUM STANDARDS FOR PUBLIC AND
PRIVATE STRUCTURES

SEC. 801. As a condition of any disaster loan or grant made under the provisions of this Act, the recipient shall agree that any repair or construction to be financed therewith shall be in accordance with applicable standards of safety, decency, and sanitation and in conformity with applicable codes, specifications, and standards, and shall furnish such evidence of compliance with this section as may be required by regulation. As a further condition of any loan or grant made under the provision of this Act, the State or local government shall agree that the natural hazards in the areas in which the proceeds of the grants or loans are to be used shall be evaluated and appropriate action shall be taken to mitigate such hazards, including safe land-use and construction practices, in accordance with standards prescribed by the President, and the State shall furnish such evidence of compliance with this section as may be required by regulation.

FEDERAL FACILITIES

SEC. 802. (a) The President may authorize any Federal agency to repair, reconstruct, restore, or replace any facility owned by the United States, and under the jurisdiction of such agency, which is damaged or destroyed by a major disaster, if he determines that such replacement, restoration, or repair is of such importance and urgency that it cannot reasonably be deferred pending the enactment of specific authorizing legislation or the making of an appropriation for such purposes, or the obtaining of congressional committee approval.

(b) In order to carry out the provisions of this section, such replacement, restoration, or repair may be begun notwithstanding a lack or an insufficiency of funds appropriated for such purpose, where such lack or insufficiency can be remedied by the transfer, in accordance with law, of funds appropriated to that agency for another purpose.

(c) In implementing this section, Federal agencies shall evaluate the natural hazards to which these facilities are exposed and shall take appropriate action to mitigate such hazards, including safe land-use and construction practices, in accordance with standards prescribed by the President.

TIMBER SALE CONTRACTS

SEC. 803. (a) Where an existing timber sale contract between the Secretary of Agriculture or the Secretary of the Interior and a timber purchaser does not provide relief from major physical change not due to negligence of the purchaser prior to approval of construction of any section of specified road or of any other specified development facility and, as a result of a major disaster, a major physical change results in additional construction work in connection with such road or facility by such purchaser with an estimated cost, as determined by the appropriate Secretary, (1) of more than $1,000 for sales under one million board feet, (2) of more than $1 per thousand board feet for sales of one to three million board feet, or (3) of more than $3,000 for sales over three million board feet, such increased construction cost shall be borne by the United States.

(b) If the Secretary determines that damage is so great that restoration, reconstruction, or construction is not practical under the cost-sharing arrangement authorized by subsection (a) of this section, the Secretary may allow cancellation of the contract notwithstanding contrary provisions therein.

(c) The Secretary of Agriculture is authorized to reduce to seven days the minimum period of advance public notice required by the first section of th Act of June 4, 1897 (16 U.S.C. 476), in connection with the sale of timber from national forests, whenever the Secretary determines that (1) the sale of such timber will assist in the construction of any area of a State damaged by a major disaster, (2) the sale of such timber will assist in sustaining the economy of such area, or (3) the sale of such timber is necessary to salvage the value of timber damaged in such major disaster or to protect undamaged timber.

RELOCATION ASSISTANCE

SEC. 804. Notwithstanding any other provision of law, no person otherwise eligible for any kind of replacement housing payment under the "Uniform Relocation Assistance and Real Property Acquisition Policies Act of 1970" (Public Law 91-646) shall be denied such eligibility as a result of his being unable, because of a major disaster as determined by the President, to meet the occupancy requirements set by such Act.

REPEAL OF EXISTING LAW AND TECHNICAL AMENDMENTS

SEC. 805. (a) The following Acts are hereby repealed:

(1) The Disaster Relief Act of 1970, as amended (Public Law 91-606).

(2) The Act of August 16, 1972 (Public Law 92-385), except section 2 thereof.

(3) Notwithstanding the repeal herein of Public Law 91-606 and Public Law 92-385, section 7 of the Small Business Act (15 U.S.C. 636) is amended—

(a) by deleting paragraphs (1) and (2) from subsection (b) thereof;

(b) by amending all after paragraph 7 of subsection (b) thereof to read as follows:

"No loan under this subsection, including renewals and extensions thereof authorized by any provision of this Act, may be made for a period or periods exceeding thirty years. Notwithstanding the provisions of any other law, the interest rate on the Administration's share of any loan made under this subsection shall not be more than the average annual interest rate on all interest-bearing obligations of the United States then forming a part of the public debt as computed at the end of the fiscal year next preceding the date of the loan and adjusted to the nearest one-eighth of 1 per centum plus one-quarter of 1 per centum per annum. In agreements to participate in loans on a deferred basis under this subsection, such participation by the Administration shall not be in excess of 90 per centum of the balance of the loan outstanding at the time of disbursement."; and

(c) by deleting subsection (f) thereof.

(b) The following provisions of law are hereby repealed:

(1) Section 7 of the Act of September 30, 1950 (20 U.S.C. 241-1).

(2) Section 16 of the Act of September 30, 1950 (20 U.S.C. 646).

(3) Section 408 of the Higher Education Facilities Act of 1963 (20 U.S.C. 758).

(4) Sections 7 (b) (1) and (2) of the Small Business Act (15 U.S.C. 636 (b) (1) and (2)).

(5) Section 7 (f) of the Small Business Act (15 U.S.C. 636 (f)).

(6) Sections 761 through 766 of Public Law 92-318 (title VII, D), Higher Education Act, as amended.

(7) Subtitle (C), sections 321 through 327 of the Consolidated Farm and Rural Development Act of 1961 (7 U.S.C. 1961–1967).

(c) The following provisions of law are hereby amended:

(1) Section 2 (2) of the United States Housing Act of 1937 (42 U.S.C. 1402 (2)) is amended by striking out "in areas determined by the Small Business Administration, subsequent to April 1, 1965, to have been affected by a natural disaster," and inserting in lieu thereof "in an area affected by a major disaster declared by the President pursuant to the Disaster Preparedness and Assistance Act of 1973,".

(2) Section 101 (c) (2) (E) of the Housing and Urban Development Act of 1965 (12 U.S.C. 1701s (c) (2) (E)) is amended by striking out "determined by the Small Business Administration, subsequent to April 1, 1965, to have been affected by a disaster," and inserting in lieu thereof "affected by a major disaster declared by the President pursuant to the Disaster Preparedness and Assistance Act of 1973,".

(3) Section 221 (f) of the National Housing Act (12 U.S.C. 17151 (f)) is amended by striking out of the last paragraph "the Disaster Relief Act of 1970." and inserting in lieu thereof "the Disaster Preparedness and Assistance Act of 1973.".

(4) Section 165 (h) (2) of the Internal Revenue Code of

1954 relating to disaster losses (26 U.S.C. 165 (h) (2)) is amended by striking out "Disaster Relief Act of 1970." and inserting in lieu thereof "Disaster Preparedness and Assistance Act of 1973.".

(5) Section 5064 (a) of the Internal Revenue Code of 1954 (26 U.S.C. 5064 (a)) relating to losses caused by disaster is amended by striking out "Disaster Relief Act of 1970." and inserting in lieu thereof "Disaster Preparedness and Assistance Act of 1973.".

(6) Section 5708 (a) of the Internal Revenue Code of 1954 (26 U.S.C. 5708 (a)) relating to losses caused by disaster is hereby amended by striking out "Disaster Relief Act of 1970." and inserting in lieu thereof "Disaster Preparedness and Assistance Act of 1973.".

(7) Section 701 (a) (3) (B) (ii) of the Housing Act of 1954 (40 U.S.C. 461 (a) (3) (B) (ii) is amended by striking out "Disaster Relief Act of 1970." and inserting in lieu thereof "Disaster Preparedness and Assistance Act of 1973.".

(8) Title V, section 521 of the Housing Act of 1949 (42 U.S.C. 1490a) is amended by striking out the last proviso.

(9) Section 3 of the Act of June 30, 1954 (48 U.S.C. 1681) is amended by striking out the following: "There are hereby authorized to be appropriated such sums as the Secretary of the Interior may find necessary, but not to exceed $10,000,000 for any one year, to alleviate suffering and damage resulting from major disasters that occur in the Trust Territory of the Pacific Islands. Such sums shall be in addition to those authorized in section 2 of this Act (set out as a note under this section) and shall not be subject to the limitations imposed by section 2 of this Act. The Secretary of the Interior shall determine whether or not a major disaster has occurred in accordance with the principles and policies of section 102 (1) of the Disaster Relief Act of 1970."

PRIOR ALLOCATION OF FUNDS

SEC. 806. Funds heretofore appropriated and available under Public Laws 91-606, as amended, and 92-385 shall continue to be available for the purpose of completing commitments made under those Acts as well as for the purposes of this Act. Commitments for disaster assistance and relief made prior to the enactment of this Act shall be fulfilled.

EFFECTIVE DATE

SEC. 807. This Act shall take effect one hundred and twenty days from the date of enactment, except as otherwise indicated.

AUTHORIZATION

SEC. 808. Funds are hereby authorized to be appropriated for the purpose of this Act.

B. SENATOR JAMES ABOUREZK (DEMOCRAT-SOUTH DAKOTA) STATEMENT, SEPTEMBER 13, 1973.

STATEMENT BY SENATOR JAMES ABOUREZK
Subcommittee on Disaster Relief
Senate Committee on Public Works

Thursday, September 13, 1973

MR. CHAIRMAN, Once again I thank you for the opportunity to present a perspective on Federal disaster relief programs. Your close attention to this vital area is gratefully appreciated.

It has been nearly 16 months since the tragic flood in Rapid City, South Dakota and the surrounding area.

In my statement today, I would like to offer my general thoughts about what Federal disaster relief programs ought to be, the direction they should go, and take a few minutes to discuss some specific problems we are having in the recovery effort out there.

The most important thing I have learned since June 9 of last year is that disaster assistance programs ought to be as generous, flexible, comprehensive and long-range as we can make them.

The Disaster Relief Act of 1970 reflects a giant step in the right direction. We should be expanding that basic approach, not retreating from it. Major disaster relief is a logical and legitimate Federal function.

We have learned that a cadre of people with very special skills and knowledge is necessary in the wake of disaster. It would be impractical, inefficient, expensive and unworkable to insist that each of the fifty states provide such a cadre on their own.

But the major point is the ability to provide comprehensive, far-reaching assistance which can be provided in a flexible manner suitable to special local situations.

The direction taken by S. 1840 is exactly the opposite of the direction we should be travelling. Instead of minimizing the Federal role, we should expand it.

Federal disaster relief programs ought to include long-range community reconstruction.

Such long-range community reconstruction programs should include a workable program to guarantee the replacement of permanent housing, especially for those at the lower and moderate ends of the income scale. They should include what would be the equivalent of urban renewal or neighborhood development programs. They should provide for expanded mental health care. A legal service/advocacy/ombudsman component should be provided. A special entity to help the elderly, the disabled, the disadvantaged and the poor to cope with the bureaucratic wake of a disaster is needed in addition to the legal services component.

Presently, communities must look outside of Disaster Relief programs to provide those needed components. The results are uneven, to say the least. There is no guarantee that funds will be available, and there are all kinds of problems involved in trying to fit non-disaster Federal grant-in-aid programs to disaster situations. I will get to each of these areas separately in a moment.

First, I want to acknowledge that what I propose is not cheap. There is no cheap way out of a major disaster. It is a question of priorities. It is a point not everyone may be able to appreciate until they have been in a meeting where their local community leaders discussed, in bitter tones, seceding from the nation in order to apply for foreign aid.

On the question of housing, these points argue for making a program of permanent housing assistance a component of Federal disaster relief:

—Federal housing programs are fragmented. Some rely on the existence of a local public housing authority. Half the counties in the country are not covered by such authorities. Other programs rely on the presence of non-profit or limited divided sponsors, and

other institutions which also appear erratically across the countryside. Moreover, they are layered—one program takes care of
one income group, and there is another approach for still another
group. They all have too much red tape. Assuring smooth delivery
of the right kind of programs to the right people in the right place
under the existing programs is highly difficult. There are no
guarantees that you will get what you need where you need it. It's
catch-as-catch-can.

—There is no assurance that a community will be able to get the
kind of housing funds it needs on the scale it needs them. In Rapid
City, we were comparatively lucky. We were allocated 460 units of
low-rent public housing and a variety of Sec. 235, 236 and rent
supplement units. We got these units because the regional office
bent over backwards to find them—and also because the flood hit
in June, only a few weeks before the new fiscal year's allocations
became available. Somewhere in our region, some community
surely did not receive housing it had been promised. There is
another side to the coin, too: it seems unlikely that after such a
dramatic one-shot infusion of housing funds, that Rapid City is
going to be very high in the pecking order for further program
reservations in the foreseeable future.

—On the catch-as-catch-can basis, a number of problems arise:
flood victims have been given priority on the subsidized units.
What happens to the families who were not flood victims but who
do need better housing? Secondly, there is no central coordination
of the programs—no one place to apply for permanent housing. As
a result, there is much confusion on the part of victims and
non-victims alike. Some families will miss benefits they might have
had on account of this. Thirdly, you end up with a lot of mobile
homes in your permanent housing inventory. About 120 Rapid
City flood victims have already or will soon buy their HUD
temporary trailers. To me, this reflects at least two things: uncertainty about the availability of assisted permanent housing, and the
fact that the programs we got just didn't seem to fit everyone who
needs permanent housing. The mobile homes are a bad housing
investment. They depreciate rapidly and they are built to
minimum standards. In the best of all possible worlds, those
monthly payments should be invested in appreciating assets. This is
especially important where people have been put heavily in debt by
a disaster.

—Finally, a coordinated, flexible housing approach would provide a hedge against inflation in land, building and material costs which follows disaster. It would not be too far afield to suggest that the price of a house on a sewered site is increasing $1000 per month in Rapid City right now. Mr. Burns, in his wisdom over at the Federal Reserve, is not helping any—but regardless of however the Fed is currently mismanaging the money market, the plain truth in a localized situation is that when you suddenly dump 1500 families with varying abilities to pay into a previously-tight housing market you are going to have inflation. Mass purchasing of materials and a coordinated effort to develop sites would tend to abate those pressures somewhat.

I see no reason, once the post-disaster units are in place, why they could not be spun off to HUD or Farmers Home for mortgage servicing. But to start it, you should have some entity capable of accurately measuring long-range housing needs, efficiently matching individual families to financing and developing that housing with a centralized approach. Perhaps there ought to be a pool of appropriations set aside at the national level for permanent housing development in the wake of a disaster. Once the mortgages are written, whatever mix they may be, then those funds could be spun off to the regular agencies for management.

Now to the subject of long-range community development programs. In the Rapid City case, this is the classic example of the problems which arise when you try to twist a non-disaster grant-in-aid program into something it was not intended to be.

Rapid City has received a $48,000,000 urban renewal grant. The City is obligated to contribute $16,000,000—for a total project cost of $64,000,000. We asked for $87,000,000. That would have done the job much better.

The urban renewal project—which is by the way blessed with superb people at the local level and excellent cooperation from the Denver regional office—was intended to do two things: first, redevelop a flood zone which consumes approximately a third of the city's land area, mostly into parks, and secondly, trigger the Uniform Relocation Assistance Act as sort of a backdoor way to increase loan forgiveness.

Here's how that latter program might work in a typical situation: Mr. and Mrs. Flood Victim had a $25,000 mortgage on a house worth $30,000 when the flood hit. They receive a $65,000 load from SBA, with $5000 forgiven. They replace $5000 worth of personal property and purchase a $30,000 house. At this point they have a $60,000 mortgage at one per cent on a $30,000 home. Urban renewal acquires their flood-devastated property for $13,000. In addition, they receive a relocation housing assistance payment of $15,000 —leaving them with a $32,000 mortgage on a $30,000 home. That was the goal, and by and large it is being achieved.

There are, however, a number of serious inequities which result from this attempt to twist one program into something else. First, not everyone is covered by urban renewal. People outside of Rapid City are not covered, and several who are living inside the flood plain in Rapid City are outside of the urban renewal area. Thus, there is some inequity. While on the one hand you have a Mr. and Mrs. Typical Flood Victim being restored to nearly whole, just across the city boundary a similar couple faces a $60,000 mortgage on a $30,000 house.

Inside that major part of the flood plain which is also in the urban renewal plan, there are a great many complex red tape problems which have arisen. After the flood zone was declared, some people were allowed to move back into the flood plain in repaired homes. Most, however, did not. The Relocation Act stipulates that homeowners must have lived in their unit for 180 days prior to the initiation of negotiations for relocation. For renters, it is 90 days. Since most flood victims could not move back into the flood plain, a waiver of the occupancy rule was needed. It was granted. Enter at least two problems: people who were non-flood victims who moved into the flood plain have become eligible for certain relocation benefits. The City Council of Rapid City recently petitioned its Congressional delegation for legislative relief. A copy of that petition is attached.

For the flood victims who moved back into the flood plain, another problem arises: due to eligibility criteria under the relocation act those persons who returned to reside in their dwelling units must stay in occupancy until the time negotiations are initiated before eligibility is established. Any commitment made prior to initiation of negotiations is not compensable under the relocation act. Since SBA has a one-year time limit for its borrowers to commit their funds, most people have commited themselves to new home financing, and thus they might become ineligible for the relocation assistance.

And then we have about a half dozen families who had purchased and mortgaged new homes in the flood zone but had not yet moved into them by June 9, 1972. They are not eligible for relocation benefits.

There are several dozen variations on these themes. This kind of problem accounts for perhaps a third of the present caseload in my office.

I am not familiar with what has been done in terms of long-range community development programs in other disaster areas, but it seems logical that many of them must have applied for some kind of non-disaster Federal grant-in-aid programs. One way, or the other, it would seem, the Federal government is commiting long-range money to some of these communities. Why go through all these contortions? Why not build long-range community re-development programs as an automatic component of disaster relief legislation in communities where there is substantial property damage? I see much more equity and flexibility arising from it, better projects resulting in the end, and much less red tape.

There is another strong argument for making long-range re-development programs a component of regular disaster legislation.

Whenever a community experiences a major disaster, its already limited resources are needed not only for the continuation of its governmental functions but also for repair or replacement of necessary facilities not entirely covered by Federal disaster aid. Moreover, the community may already have commitments for new and expensive facilities. In addition, the community must provide matching funds for many non-disaster Federal programs in which it participates.

The citizens and taxpayers of such a community are put to the task of providing revenue that is very possibly beyond their ability.

There are several avenues open to the Local Governing Body, namely:

1.) Curtail services to the community.
   (This is hardly acceptable when the services have been minimal.)
2.) Delay replacement of facilities destroyed. (Facilities are generally of a nature that such is not possible. Also, if Federal aid is to be obtained, the facilities must be restored in 24 months.)
3.) Do not enter into Federal programs where matching funds are required.

4.) Change the matching ratio. (Not the community's prerogative, plus the matching ratio is realistic in most instances.)

In the Rapid City situation, the City made commitments for several million dollars to be spent for supporting facilities, such as a library, an arena, and a convention center. These facilities will be constructed within the time limitation of its Urban Renewal program. Under the Urban Renewal guidelines, 25% of the cost of these structures may be used for non-cash grants-in-aid toward the $16,000,000 the City is to provide as its share in the Rapid City Urban Renewal program.

Short of a retroactive expansion of disaster relief legislation to include a broad program of community redevelopment this Committee can help us by getting that urban renewal language changed to allow Rapid City to count 100% of the cost of those facilities toward its local contribution of $16 million. It would not increase the Federal contribution above $48 million. It would only make it easier, to the tune of about $7 million easier, for the city to meet its urban renewal match requirement. Such a move would mitigate the possibility of the City's having to curtail other services in order to meet its match and it would allow the city to perhaps proceed with the construction of needed facilities in other areas of the City outside the urban renewal boundary.

In this Committee's hearings in Rapid City in March, we pretty well covered the suggestions that legal services and some sort of special entity to shepherd the disadvantaged through the bureaucracy be built into the Federal disaster response. Let me underscore the feelings I expressed then. Disasters do not single out the rich, the educated and the middle class—the people best able to cope with bureaucracy and its complex legalisms. It is safe to bet that the future holds thousands of disaster victims who because of age, poverty, illiteracy or lack of education are going to be swamped, befuddled, confused, frustrated, perhaps misled and often fearful of the bureaucratic process which will engulf them following a disaster. Special consideration needs to be made for those people.

In Rapid City, we were lucky. We were able to get legal services funding through OEO, and we had a local community action agency which just happens to be—in my opinion—one of the best in the country. It played an invaluable role in helping the disadvantaged suffer through the bureaucratic process.

So far in this testimony I have suggested things which ought to be component parts of the federal disaster response which we did manage to get, one way or the other, in Rapid City. There is another component, equally necessary, which we have not been able to provide as yet. That is expanded mental health care. It is absolutely essential if the goal is to make the disaster response as humane as possible.

There are terrible horror stories to tell in this area. To spare the families involved any further grief, I'll pass over them. Suffice it to say that people often suffer grueling trauma in a disaster and that sometimes that trauma leads to, or exacerbates, mental illness.

Presently the West River Mental Health Center is able to respond to only one-third of the requests for help. Since the flood there has been a 46% increase in its caseload. There has been a 39% increase in the number of families being referred to Lutheran Social Services and a dramatic increase in public intoxication arrests—as one symptom—as well as an increase in the number of people from that area admitted to the State Hospital in Yankton for treatment.

In October, 1972 the Black Hills Area-Wide Comprehensive Health Planning Council submitted a grant application for $248,162. That money was needed to help those people whose mental health had been disturbed by the losses which they had experienced and witnessed.

In January, 1973 the Director of the National Institute of Mental Health determined that the grant could not be awarded because of, "uncertainty regarding the level of funding which will be provided for National Institute Mental Health projects for Fiscal Year 1973." For the NIMH it was simply business as usual.

As a result of the reluctance of the NIMH to provide the resources needed to help the disaster victims and as a result of the testimony offered in Rapid City in March to this Subcommittee, during February, 1973 and again during April, 1973, Secretary Weinberger was asked to review the human consequences of the Rapid City flood and on the basis of that review direct the immediate authorization of the grant requested in October, 1972. In response, Secretary Weinberger noted that there is often a detrimental effect on the emotional well-being of people who experience a natural disaster some months after the disaster. Because of that possibility, which had already begun to occur, the Secretary asked representatives of the NIMH to visit with officials in Rapid City to assess the current situation and determine whether some short-term assistance could be funded.

In late May, 1973, the Department of Health, Education and Welfare indicated that, while the grant that had originally been requested could not be authorized, the Department intended to initiate a program, "in time to meet the anticipated June 9 and 10 anniversary reaction of mourning and grief affecting individuals as well as the community in its entirety." That program would train indigenous mental health outreach workers to identify those persons experiencing emotional trauma, to counsel them through their crisis, or to bring them to a clinic for appropriate care and treatment.

It is now September, 1973 and the Federal government has failed to provide the resources that are so desperately needed to train outreach workers and to provide clinical care and treatment. The question now is not, "when will the people of the Rapid City area get the assistance they need?", but, "will the people of Rapid City ever get the help they need?"

Inasmuch as mental health problems, like debris removal problems, seem to be an inevitable consequence of major disasters, provision ought to be made for them in the Federal disaster response.

If the disaster relief program is expanded to include built-in provisions for permanent housing replacement, community development programs, legal services, an ombudsman entity and a mental health component, it would be wise to do so with a keen attention to flexibility.

Each and every disaster has a distinct character, creating needs of varying proportions in the different areas. Our approach should be to anticipate every possible area of need, to make ready for it, and to issue resources to it in the proportion and kind dictated by the characteristics of a particular disaster. It is not impossible to do that in Federal Law. But to expect to do it through the states is simply expecting too much. The inevitable result of such an approach is less relief to those who need it most.

Thus I find that I cannot agree with the Administration's disaster bill. Don Barnett, the Mayor of Rapid City, wrote recently that he finds "every portion of this bill to be completely objectionable." He continued, "If Rapid City were to have a disaster such as the 1972 flood following the passage of this proposed law, our community would be in a terrible situation." He stated that the legislation would make disasters "much more painful to local units of government."

S. 1840 raised major policy questions.

First and foremost among them is whether states can or should be expected to assume primary responsibility for the management of disaster recovery. My argument is just the contrary, that states lack the resources, personnel, experience and disposition to do what needs to be done when a disaster of the scope of Rapid City or Agnes strikes. The bill's attempt to provide those managerial resources to the states is pitifully inadequate.

Emergency and long-range recovery can be most efficiently provided by the Federal government. Primary responsibility ought to remain at the Federal level, and ought to be expanded there. We learned in Rapid City that a heavy Federal responsibility does not automatically produce an objectionable heavy-handed Federal intervention in local affairs. We found the Federal people highly cooperative with the state and local people, very willing to go the extra mile and often able to bend where bending was needed. This was particularly true during the emergency phases. When we started getting long term recovery and reconstruction projects in place, the problems we encountered were not problems of cooperation; the opposite is true; the problems I have outlined on our long-range projects are the result of fund inadequacies, economics, statutes and regulations on programs designed primarily for non-disaster situation.

There are other problems with S. 1840.

The proposal to make purchase of reasonably-available disaster insurance an absolute condition of Federal disaster assistance is ill-considered. It would mean that many people, particularly the poor and elderly, simply will not receive—or take—Federal disaster benefits. Moreover, is it wise to require a man who is moving from the flood plain to a mountain top to buy flood insurance?

I have supported the consolidation of Federal disaster relief functions under a single roof. On the first case which has come up since this year's establishment of the Federal Disaster Assistance Administration, though, the cooperation we encountered was less than pleasing. It was a matter of seeking the release of 50 OEP trailers to ease the housing crunch in Rapid City. Something like 139 OEP-owned trailers which are unsuitable for long over-the-road hauls are stockpiled at Ellsworth Air Force Base near Rapid City. Since they are unfit for over-the-road hauls, they are unsuitable to remain in the temporary housing inventory; thus, we tried to free them to relieve a severe housing crunch between now and the time the subsidized housing becomes available. We have encountered severe hardening of the bureaucratic arteries and an inadequate Washington understanding of the true situation in Rapid City.

The Small Business Administration did a fair job with its loans, but there are problems which stem from taking a business-oriented concern and giving them a host of personal loans and a caseload more in the nature of social work. The Committee may be interested, by the way, in some correspondence I recently exchanged with SBA in regard to the number of personnel in their Rapid City office. They just plain don't have enough manpower there now. People used to call on our casework people to help negotiate a loan. Now it is often necessary for a call from my office just simply to get an appointment for borrowers to talk with someone in SBA about a problem.

As to Farmers Home, I have been arguing, on the housing front, that they, too, are under-staffed and under-funded administratively. You may recall from the March hearings that some Farmers Home loans in the Rapid City disaster had received only $2500 forgiveness because of an administrative bungle. I am happy to report that that has since been corrected, and that this Committee's hearings apparently had some impact on the situation, for which I am grateful.

On the whole, the question of consolidating the loan functions is a mixed bag. It seems logical, though, that where a person is located on the government organization charts is not as important as his special skills, dedication and having enough help to do the job right.

S. 1840's requirement that victims seek credit elsewhere first is bad news. Verily, it was the infusion of Federal credit which kept major local financial institutions from collapsing. There is enormous confusion following a disaster, and if the situation is somewhat localized as it was in Rapid City, there will be a mild form of panic in the financial community following a disaster. To send flood victims still reeling from the immediate trauma into such an uncertain financial community for assistance as a first resort is a formula for even more uncertainty and instability. Private interest rates will take such a high toll that total loan amounts will be considerably reduced, thus curtailing reinvestment and consumer purchases. And once again, the people who need the most will get the least. I have less objection to a guaranteed loan program, except that in that situation it, too, will lead to confusion. And if you subsidize interest, as I think you must, the problems become more severe. It is essential that credit going into a community must be delivered fairly, efficiently and uniformly—with rules that a layman can readily comprehend.

As to the proposal to charge the Treasury rate on whatever Federal loans are written, I'm opposed. Even more than the $5000 forgiveness, it was one per cent credit which prevented a high number of home mortgage and business loan defaults in the wake of the Rapid City flood. Widespread default and bankruptcy among the victimized population very possibly might have led to the collapse of local financial institutions. The idea should be to minimize the damage following a disaster, not multiply it.

The forgiveness features should not be limited to low-income families, unless you want to invite 16 varieties of local political bloodbath. The people one notch up on the income ladder are not going to enjoy watching their low-income neighbors get a $5000 grant while they have just been dealt a grievous setback and get nothing but an 18% loan from the local finance company.

As to putting the governors in charge of passing out Federal grants of up to $4000 to low-income families, I am most vehemently opposed.

The idea of limiting total funds provided to a state for temporary housing to a fixed amount per family is an invitation to chaos. Administrators of the temporary housing effort need to move quickly, boldly and aggressively. This proposal in and of itself ties their hands, and no doubt it would be followed by even more restrictive regulations to assure that the total amount spent is distributed somewhat equitably among the families. There are so many unknown factors entering into the cost picture on a crash push for temporary housing that the only real way to assure no exorbitantly expensive misadventures is to have the best possible personnel you can find. And this argues again for Federal expertise, for action plans made by people who have been under the fire of previous disaster experience.

The proposal to replace grants with loans to compensate disaster-stricken communities for revenue loss is a bad idea. A major disaster hits local government very hard in the pocket-book. The emergency outlays alone are killing, much less any long-term reconstruction financing which may be required. This proposal invites still another local political bloodbath: ultimately it would lead to increased property taxes, and not all local taxpayers will necessarily be disaster victims. Sooner or later they will resent regressive taxation to restore "somebody else." Sooner or later they will resent curtailed local spending on other things. The same disapproval goes for limiting grants for replacement of public facilities to 75% of estimated costs.

In conclusion, S. 1840 goes exactly the wrong direction. It is laden with opportunity for "systems breakdown" in the delivery of disaster recovery.

Only the Federal government has the resources and only the Federal government can be expected to assemble the needed experience and expertise, to deliver adequate disaster relief and long-range recovery and reconstruction. It is a legitimate responsibility of the Federal government. The Administration's proposal represents an incredible and appalling cheap attempt to withdraw from that responsibility.

C. HONORABLE HAROLD A. SWENSON,
MAYOR OF HARRISBURG, PENNSYLVANIA
National League of Cities,
United States Conference of Mayors
STATEMENT, SEPTEMBER 13, 1973.

STATEMENT OF
THE HONORABLE HAROLD A. SWENSON
MAYOR OF HARRISBURG, PENNSYLVANIA
on behalf of
THE NATIONAL LEAGUE OF CITIES
and
THE UNITED STATES CONFERENCE OF MAYORS
on
DISASTER PREPAREDNESS AND ASSISTANCE ACT
OF 1973
S. 1840
before the
SENATE PUBLIC WORKS SUBCOMMITTEE ON DISASTER RELIEF
September 13, 1973

Mr. Chairman, members of the Committee, my name is Harold
A. Swenson. I am the Mayor of Harrisburg, Pennsylvania. I am
here today speaking on behalf of the National League of Cities and
the United States Conference of Mayors. The National League of
Cities consists of, and is the national spokesman for, approximately
15,000 municipal governments in all fifty states and Puerto Rico.
The United States Conference of Mayors includes virtually all cities
with a population in excess of 30,000. Member cities are represented by their elected chief executives—the mayors.

We appreciate the opportunity to appear before the Senate
Public Works Subcommittee on Disaster Relief to present our views
on S. 1840, the "Disaster Preparedness and Assistance Act of
1973."

Mayors and city officials throughout the country are concerned about developing effective management and financing of disaster assistance. This, no doubt, was clear during the four field hearings (Biloxi, Miss., Rapid City, S. D., Wilkes-Barre, Pa. and Elmira-Corning, N. Y.) that your Subcommittee held this last spring to determine the adequacy, effectiveness and cost of the Federal disaster efforts.

Harrisburg was hard-hit by floodings in the wake of Agnes during the summer of 1972. And I am deliberate in the use of the plural "floodings", because part of the city was under water overflowing the Susquehanna River on our west, while another section, to the east, was inundated by the rampaging Paxton Creek. And then there were those areas hit by both Susquehanna River and Paxton Creek waters, first one and then the other.

In total, a third of the city was flooded; residential areas housing families ranging from high middle to low incomes; almost all our industrial, light industrial, and warehousing community; the Community College, the Governor's Mansion, the filtration plant—all these and many others were overrun by flood waters. Thousands of individuals and businesses were displaced, some only for days, others, including several hundred persons still housed in mobile homes, for well over a year with no permanent rehousing yet in sight. Damage mounted to the tens of millions of dollars; emergency operations and post-flood expenditures, in public and private funds, also can be calculated in millions upon millions of dollars.

It is no digression to point out that while property losses were high, fatalities were low for a disaster of this magnitude—the worst ever to come to my city. And this is due, in part, to our ability to anticipate the flooding and to alert and evacuate those in danger. Our capacity to carry out these and other emergency functions was facilitated, to put it modestly, by a modern public safety communications system which had recently been installed, thanks principally to Federal safe streets funds. I mention this to emphasize that on-going Federal programs which help local governments up-date and improve their equipment, facilities, and capacities have an invaluable impact when disaster strikes—and we in Harrisburg are grateful.

I will not detail all the events leading up to and immediately following the floods, other than to make several overall comments which, I believe, relate to the underlying theory and concept of the legislation you are considering.

Harrisburg's immediate recovery efforts were, I believe, effective and prompt, partly because the local government moved decisively and inclusively. We did not wait for the Federal government to come upon the scene; we got on with the work to be done in the expectation that Federal and State assistance would be available. We knew what had to be done and we set about doing it, without consulting manuals, guidelines, or regulations. Before the Susquehanna crested, we had started signing up every contractor in the area to aid in cleanup; when the Corps of Engineers came on board several days later, we merely assigned those contracts to them. But in the meantime, the work was underway.

When HUD told us mobile homes would be available, we began immediately on-site preparation, and in only five days had moved the first flood displaced family into temporary quarters—on the Fourth of July, appropriately enough.

The point of this is that local government can and must be in charge. State and Federal assistance is simply not able to mobilize to get on the job as fast and as massively as necessary.

Our relations with Federal officials generally ranged from good to outstanding. If I have any criticism, it relates to the turnover of Federal personnel, a kind of revolving door approach in which one official is moved out just when he begins to get a handle on the problem. Then we have to start all over again: decisions already made have to be reargued; conditions once understood have to be outlined and explained once again. All this, of course, is slowing and frustrating. We are still waiting for determinations on some flood expenditures made in Harrisburg almost 15 months ago, at least one of which was tentatively approved in August of 1972.

But even more depressing has been the failure to permit us to meet the community's rehousing needs. This is due not to any deficiency in the disaster assistance program, but rather to the HUD moratorium and restrictive guidelines. Secretary Lynn early this year promised relief; we are still waiting for it.

And a final observation:

A third of Harrisburg was flooded, as I said.

Two major areas of the city have been designated for flood assistance renewal, which was obviously needed. But the reuse of flooded lands is questionable, to put it mildly, in light of existing and proposed Federal restrictions. Unrealistic and unreasonable constraints on rebuilding can have a disastrous—and I use that word purposely—effect on the future of any urban area located on a floodable waterway.

We would not and could not suggest that there is no need for prudent precautions and conditions. But neither do we consider it sensible or realistic to make prime urban land fallow, which could be the result if some current thinking becomes dictum.

Flood protection devices, which Harrisburg wants and will fight for, obviously should afford a significant change in the flood plain, as it has in other areas. Let me just point out that if current thinking, as I understand it, had been past policy, Pittsburgh's Gateway Center, that city's economic heart, could never have been built.

Harrisburg and other communities affected by last year's floods do not, and cannot, accept a program, however well-intentioned, whose result would be to kill off their existence altogether—secure, but dead.

In turning to the provisions of S. 1840, it is our understanding that your Subcommittee did not plan to cover the insurance and interest rate aspects of S. 1840, as these aspects have been considered by the Senate Banking, Housing and Urban Affairs Subcommittee on Housing. For the record, I would like to point out that Mayor Carlos Romero-Barcelo of San Juan, Puerto Rico, did submit a statement to that Subcommittee, on behalf of the National League of Cities and U.S. Conference of Mayors.

Therefore, I will focus my remarks today on the adequacy of Federal financial assistance and the problems encountered at the local level in effectively and efficiently meeting disaster recovery needs. It is our understanding from discussions with local officials interviewed by the National League of Cities and U.S. Conference of Mayors staff last fall in Wilkes-Barre, Corning-Elmira and my city of Harrisburg, that the problems were not related to the Federal disaster benefits per se, but the way in which the assistance was provided—the attitudes of Federal representatives, the red tape and other obstacles which hampered local disaster operations. The final result was similar in all of these cities. Federal funds often were not provided quickly enough nor in sufficient amounts to meet the short-term needs, not to mention the failure to address long-term needs such as housing assistance.

It is our understanding that one of the purposes of this disaster legislation is to increase decision-making at the state and local level.

The main provisions of the bill, however, demonstrate little intent to back this shift with Federal financial support. Under this proposed legislation:

- Grants for city-disaster related expenses would be eliminated and replaced by loans at the Treasury rate,
- States would be given almost total administrative responsibility,
- Cities would be required to purchase disaster insurance as a prerequisite for Federal assistance,
- Local governments would be required to meet new "hazard mitigation standards,"
- The forgiveness provisions for loans to individuals and businesses would be eliminated, and
- Federal funding for restoration of public facilities and services would be reduced from the current level of 100 percent to a level of 75 percent, with total discretion as to use of funds left to the states.

In addition to these concerns, other specific provisions could have a serious and negative impact on a number of cities. For example, Title II, Section 205 provides a non-liability clause protecting Federal actions or failure to perform duties in carrying out the provisions of this Act. This clause applies not only to direct Federal disaster activities, but also to any effects of land use controls that may be mandated by Federal regulation to mitigate disaster hazards in local communities. The National League of Cities and U.S. Conference of Mayors believe that some form of redress should be made available to communities and individuals within those communities.

Title VIII, Section 801, would require State or local governments, as a condition of any loan or grant under the Act, to evaluate and take action to mitigate hazards in areas where loans and grants would be used. While no responsible local official would argue that action to limit or eliminate the possibility of disasters should not be taken, this provision could force cities to undertake expensive land use measures without having any opportunity to appeal Federal regulations or decisions and without having the opportunity to have their views known or considered. In addition to the possibility that such measures could require the relocation of parts of cities, they could also result in increased building costs, significant losses in property tax revenues and other indirect economic effects.

Another of our concerns is the provision, Title VI, Grants to States, that would give states discretion for restoring public facilities, debris removal, and temporary housing. We believe that these decisions must be made by the local governments involved. In fact, under this legislation, there is no guarantee that the state would be required to spend Federal assistance money to restore or rebuild existing facilities.

This section also would reduce the Federal share for repair and restoration of facilities and services, including debris removal, from a current level of 100 percent to a level of 75 percent. There is no provision, however, that would require the states to pay any of the remaining 25 percent, regardless of the possible inability of local governments to pay this share.

Finally, this section also discriminates against restoration of partially completed facilities. Such a grant would provide for restoration of a facility to its pre-disaster condition and would provide for increased costs to the extent that they are "attributable to changed physical conditions resulting from a major disaster." Increased labor and construction costs, however, would not be covered.

The Administration has justified the proposed disaster legislation primarily upon the basis that states, communities and individuals suffering disasters should bear the costs. Nothing in the proposed legislation, however, would require the state to pay one dime in disaster assistance. The legislation would simply transfer management of disaster assistance programs to the states, while reducing the Federal financial commitment to communities. We believe that a more reasonable division of responsibility would result from a program that gives specific assurances that the states will share the costs of recovery efforts and will provide a voice to local governments in program management and decision-making.

Local governments and local taxpayers can pay only a fraction of the costs of disaster recovery and reconstruction. Yet the proposed legislation would change from the present program of grants to local governments, based upon lost property taxes, which already has been recognized as inadequate, to a loan program that is not to exceed 10 percent of the city's operating budget. State-imposed debt limitations for local governments alone make this an unworkable alternative and clearly small cities that are hard hit by a disaster would find it difficult if not impossible to meet the financial needs of disaster recovery.

The local governments that most need financial assistance after a disaster are the ones that may be left out of this program altogether. They are the cities which are already financially hardpressed to carry out normal governmental functions, have exhausted this revenue source and are nearing debt limitations imposed at the state level. Borrowing is no answer for those communities. What is needed is a grant program that will enable them to perform governmental functions immediately following a disaster and a program that would provide additional grants not only to cover lost property tax revenues, but all revenue lost as a result of the disaster.

The provision that would allow a 75 percent grant to the state for restoration of public facilities and for debris removal, to be spent according to state discretion, will not necessarily permit more local decision-making about locally-determined needs. What it will permit is more state determination about local needs. The state also will decide what portion of the non-Federal share will be borne locally.

Finally, we believe that local governments should have the opportunity to participate in the selection of hazard mitigation and that an appeals procedure should be established in cases where the President or HUD finds that a city has not complied adequately with the provisions of this legislation.

We appreciate the opportunity to present our views on the disaster preparedness legislation.

D. DR. JOEL A. SNOW
NATIONAL SCIENCE FOUNDATION
STATEMENT, SEPTEMBER 12, 1973.

DR. JOEL A. SNOW
Deputy Assistant Director for Science and Technology
Research Applications National Science Foundation
before the
Subcommittee on Disaster Relief Committee on Public
Works
United States Senate

MR. CHAIRMAN AND MEMBERS OF THE SUBCOMMITTEE:

I would like to thank you for providing the National Science Foundation with the opportunity to describe how scientific research can be brought to bear on the important problem of disaster relief and on related legislation currently being considered by the Subcommittee. We at NSF share with you a deep concern for the need to mobilize the nation's resources to deal with disasters and to bring our best capabilities forward to deal with this problem. Operation of disaster relief assistance programs is not the responsibility of the Foundation. However, I endorse the strengthening of the authority of the President to undertake a broad Federal program of disaster preparedness, which, among other items, encourages disaster-related research and application of science and technology. I do hope to demonstrate how scientific research now in progress can aid in the formulation of future legislation and can contribute to the solution of this important national problem. In this sense, you gentlemen are the most important customers of the research on which we are working.

As you know, the NSF is charged with supporting basic and applied scientific research in the national interest, and in our Research Applications program we lay special stress upon bringing scientific knowledge to bear on important national issues. As I think my remarks will demonstrate, a broad and continuing range of scientific investigation is needed to produce the knowledge needed to deal with disasters. While much of the direct responsibilities lies with other federal, state, and local agencies the NSF provides an essential underpinning for their work. This occurs through the development of new basic understandings of how our social systems and individuals respond to disasters, how and why disasters occur and through the purposeful application of this knowledge in cooperation with the mission agencies.

The Problem

Disasters show us, forcefully and tragically, that nature is still preeminent over man and society. Compared to the immense uncontrolled power of earthquakes, hurricanes, and floods the forces which man controls are puny and our social systems are fragile. A major hurricane has the energy of about 220 days' power production of a large nuclear power plant, such as the Calvert Cliffs Facility. A major earthquake, such as that which occurred in Alaska in 1964, releases energy comparable to 63 years' output of a large nuclear power plant. A major flood can take thousands of lives and cause billions of dollars in property damage, to say nothing of the unmeasurable cost in disruption of transportation, communications, and the normal course of human activity. These problems strike people across the globe. Two weeks ago the headlines told of a massive earthquake in Mexico, taking hundreds of lives, and of mammoth floods in Pakistan. No agency or act of man can be expected to halt or fully control these enormous forces of nature. What research can do is to try to find ways to minimize the cost in life and property; to warn, predict, prepare for, and organize before disaster strikes and to provide effective, equitable relief and repair during and after a catastrophe.

Tasks for Research

There are four essential tasks which scientific research can undertake to enhance the nation's ability to deal with disasters. These are:

— *assessment of existing knowledge and practice:* how it is used, how present policies work, what insights can be gained from past

experience, what knowledge can be provided on the likely consequences of policy alternatives for disaster relief

   — *development of new socioeconomic and policy alternatives:* analysis
of the means society has at hand for reducing the human and
economic costs of disasters, including research on policy imple-
ments such as regulation, insurance, and planning to lessen the
impact of these catastrophes and allocate the costs equitably

   — *development of new technological approaches to disaster mitigation:*
including detection of impending disasters, measures for protection
of life and property, design of structures to resist disasters, and
possible technologies for disaster prevention

   — *development of a broader fundamental understanding:* how and
why disasters occur; the atmospheric physics behind hurricanes,
the hydrology of floods, the geophysics of earthquakes, and the
dynamics of fire.

These important tasks for research are essential elements of a
well-designed national program. They are the responsibility of
many federal, state, and local agencies. The range and scope of
national effort is well illustrated in the landmark study "A Federal
Plan for Natural Disaster Warning and Preparedness" which has
been developed under the leadership of the National Oceanic and
Atmospheric Administration. The NSF, with our strong orientation towards bringing science to bear on national problems, is now
making significant contributions to each of these major tasks.

Assessment of Existing Knowledge and Practice

   Getting the utmost benefit from existing knowledge is a primary
theme of the NSF/RANN program. As you may know, RANN was
established in order to focus scientific research on societal problems of national importance. RANN supports research in areas
which hold promise of technological, environmental or socioeconomic payoff through the application of scientific knowledge
derived from fundamental research. In order to make the best use
of what we already know for disaster protection and relief it is
essential to compile, analyze and assess this knowledge. In the areas
in which NSF/RANN has major technological thrusts—fire research and earthquake engineering—we have underway substantial efforts to assess the research base, to establish sharper research
priorities, and to transfer research results to those who can use this

information. A major effort in this last connection has been undertaken recently to transfer into the building codes the full range of knowledge developed in earthquake engineering research, including what we have learned from the San Fernando and Managua earthquakes.

But, there is a much broader task to be done. The research that is most directly relevant to disaster relief deals with human social factors. This research base has not been assessed systematically for many years. Thus, this knowledge has not been fully available to determine national disaster policy and operation procedures of agencies. To respond to this need we have undertaken a major study to assess the economic, social, organizational, and behavioral aspects of geophysical disasters. This assessment, under the direction of Professors Gilbert White and Eugene Haas of the University of Colorado is designed to apply modern social science theory, methods, and techniques to the analysis of fifteen major geophysical hazards and to develop, in collaboration with concerned public agencies, a statement of the immediate policy alternatives, their costs, and an agenda for new disaster research. This project will develop standard criteria for the production of social, economic, and human cost data for major natural hazards and assess the present and prospective economic and social costs from major natural hazards and alternative feasible ways of reducing these costs. This work is designed in collaboration with and for the benefit of several Federal agencies in the performance of their various disaster responsibilities and will also provide policy guidance in the further development of disaster reduction plans.

For several years, 50 or more Federal agencies and offices have had responsibility for providing a variety of services designed to prevent or lessen the effects of natural and manmade disasters. However, the nation, its regions, and states do not yet have reliable and valid data on the annual economic and social costs of disasters. Cost data which are available are based on a wide variety of criteria and collection systems. Under these circumstances responsible policy makers have not been able to develop satisfactory programs for minimizing the consequences of recurring disastrous events, or to assign priorities to needed disaster research.

The 15 geophysical hazards or disaster agents being analyzed are: avalanches, coastal erosion, droughts, earthquakes, floods, frost, hail, high winds, hurricanes, landslides, lightning, snow, tornadoes, tsunamis, and volcanoes.

The first major objective of this assessment is the production of good economic and social cost data on the 15 hazards.

The second major objective is to answer the following major policy questions in a rigorous way:

1. For each type of hazard what are the possible and most common modes of adjustment and what accounts for their use?

2. What do public agencies see as currently available alternative adjustments, including preventive strategies and post-impact counter measures, and what is known of the probable social and economic consequences of the various alternatives?

3. Are there other feasible alternatives which are not currently receiving serious consideration?

4. What are their probable consequences?

These questions are being answered by fitting the results of past and current research into a comprehensive conceptual model which relates variables concerning the physical characteristics of disaster to variables of population response. Population response is related, in turn, to alternative policies that are feasible. In performing the assessments, the Haas-White team has developed a series of simulation models of disaster occurrences, some of which have already been put to use by operating agencies.

The third objective is to present a summary report which identifies the major lines of additional research required for public policy purposes. This summary report will take the answers to the questions posed above, discuss the remaining uncertainties, and present productive lines of research for use by policy makers and the scholarly community. Although the Haas and White project was funded only last spring, some preliminary conclusions will soon be available from their activity and a major conference to consider these initial findings and future steps in the study will take place on October 15-19 in Estes Park, Colorado.

Development of New Socioeconomic and Policy Alternatives

Over the longer term the nation's decision-makers, particularly the Congress, need a greatly strengthened base of socioeconomic and policy analysis from which to formulate wise decisions. The sponsorship of research which can aid the public decision process is our central RANN objective.

One of the most important functions of assessments like the Haas-White work described earlier is to pinpoint which important policy issues need a full scale research thrust. A crucial matter that has been brought to the fore is that we have no fully consistent approach as a nation to the questions of who should pay the costs of disasters. The range of policy alternatives is broad: Federal vs. state vs. private insurance programs; zoning and land use control and so forth. NSF has selected a research team at the University of Pennsylvania under the direction of Professor Howard C. Kunreuther to probe deeply into such complex issues.

To aid the development of optimal Federal, state, and local policies for reducing future losses from selected natural hazards over the long range, a major policy question must be answered: Should the costs of repairing damages to residential property caused by disasters be treated primarily as a public or private responsibility? The significance of this question is underscored by the fact that in recent years the costs of disasters to the Federal Government have skyrocketed. This is primarily due to increasingly liberal Federal disaster relief provisions to aid the private sector in the form of forgiveness grants and low-interest loans. A principal reason for this development is the failure of individuals and businesses in hazard-prone regions to protect themselves adequately against potential damage from such catastrophic events. The response of Congress in the wake of major disaster events has been to authorize the Small Business Administration and the Farmers Home Administration through their disaster loan programs to provide relief for the victims. The total dollar value of all such loans has increased almost twelvefold in the last 10 years.

Policy makers need to assess the benefits and costs of alternative programs to reduce loss from natural hazards, particularly whether insurance programs should be made voluntary or compulsory. The evaluation of benefits and costs hinges on validating an appropriate model of the decision-making process of individuals in the pre- and post-disaster periods.

The Kunreuther project has the following principal objectives:

1. to evaluate the performance of alternative insurance and Federal assistance programs;
2. to determine what role insurance can play in reducing losses from future floods and earthquakes and its relationship to hazard

mitigation measures such as land-use controls as well as disaster assistance (e.g., What is the effect of alternative insurance programs, voluntary or compulsory coverage, on the economic development of hazard prone areas? What role should the private insurance industry and the Federal Government play with respect to private coverage?).

A survey instrument will be designed to test how individuals actually choose insurance. The survey will also give the proportions of the population using each form of model. These proportions in turn will be used in assessing the effects of voluntary versus compulsory insurance programs enacted or being considered at Federal, state, and local levels. Data will be developed through field surveys which will enable the research staff to evaluate the explanatory power of alternative models of choice under uncertainty in the pre-disaster period. The field survey data and SBA loan information on individuals suffering losses from floods and earthquakes will be utilized to develop a data base for analyzing how individuals recover financially from these disasters.

The following six types of areas will be sampled:

1. two areas in the Northeast subject to hurricane-type flooding
2. two areas subject to riverine flooding
3. two areas in California subject to earthquake damage.

In each of these three categories one of the areas will have recently suffered damage from a disaster while the other will not. Hence the survey will establish differences in behavior as a function of recent experience with the hazard. The six sites will be chosen in consultation with the Federal Insurance Administration, the Federal Disaster Assistance Administration, U.S. Water Resources Council, and private insurance industry executives.

In addition to the survey work, an experimental simulation model will be built of disaster effects upon particular communities. The disaster effects model will be joined with the survey data to create a simulation of individual response under varying effects and policies. In particular the pre- and post-disaster economic states of individuals will be tested under different policy assumptions.

The final socioeconomic project I shall discuss is also at the

University of Colorado under the direction of Dr. Eugene Haas, with a sub-contract to Clark University in Massachusetts under Dr. Robert Kates. This project addresses the following questions:

1. What are the range and frequency of significant community-related policy issues which follow a large-scale disaster?

2. With respect to each post-disaster issue, how do the timing, stability, irreversibility, and locational aspects of the related policy decision affect: a) social disruption and the economic cost of recovery; b) the speed of recovery, and c) the level of vulnerability to future hazards?

3. How does the pattern of urban reconstruction change the functional zonation, social stratification, and access to public urban amenities?

4. What are the critical constraints, influences, groups, and decisions which govern the reconstruction process?

The study will yield the kinds of empirical data that are needed for policy makers to be able to anticipate an answer to the major questions which arise in the wake of the natural disasters. It will focus on systematic data collection on two fairly recent disastrous events, the December 1972 earthquake in Managua, Nicaragua, and the June 1972 flood in Rapid City, South Dakota. Additionally, historical data on two more distant events, the 1964 earthquake in Anchorage, Alaska, and the 1906 San Francisco earthquake were analyzed. This study, too, is an outgrowth of the assessment project previously described.

The prime objective of this project is the accumulation and analysis of empirical data so that policy makers at local, state and Federal levels will have a set of guides for decision-making in the wake of future major disasters. The research plan focuses on the post-impact restoration period and the impacts of policy in that period will be seen through data collected on the events which affect families and decision makers. The impact of policy during the reconstruction period will be illuminated from the analysis of historical records which will reveal patterns of urban reconstruction, the process of decisions and choice, and future damage potential.

Approximately 1400 household survey interviews will be conducted; about 370 of these household surveys will be completed in

Rapid City and the remainder at Nicaragua. In addition to the household interviews, approximately 175 interviews with decision makers, political leaders, government officials, etc., will also be conducted in these two locations. About 20 of these will be done in Rapid City and the remainder in Nicaragua. It is expected that family interviews will be completed in 1973 or early 1974, and all field work will be completed by the end of the year.

The results of this research should make new and reliable information available to the many organizations and individuals involved in the disaster relief problem and should be of direct interest to the membership of the Subcommittee.

Development of New Technological Applications

I will not attempt to describe the technological developments underway in other Federal agencies but will restrict comment to the efforts underway in NSF. Bringing new tools to the task of disaster mitigation is a central element in the NSF effort. Much of this is undertaken in the Research Applied to National Needs Program. RANN serves to bridge the gap between the basic research programs long-supported by NSF and the mission-oriented research, development and operations programs of other agencies. Disaster-related research provides an excellent example of this flow. The three main efforts we have underway, Earthquake Engineering, Fire Research, and Weather Modification, began as NSF basic research activities.

The basic objectives of the *Earthquake Engineering* program are:

1. Develop economically feasible design and construction methods for building earthquake resistant structures;
2. Develop methods of analysis which integrate acceptable structural risk with the natural hazard potential of proposed construction sites for the purpose of improved structural design and land-use decisions; and
3. Develop an improved understanding of social and economic consequences of individual and community policy decisions on earthquake-related issues.

The accelerated research effort now underway places special emphasis on achieving the following specifics:

—The adoption of improved building design methods by local building officials and professional designers.

—The consolidation of best-knowledge design and analysis methods stemming from research performed and completed prior to FY 1974.

—The final design and preliminary subsystem research on a major experimental facility to improve our understanding of earthquake-induced soil and structural behavior.

—The development of improved socio-economic impact analyses of earthquakes. NSF has provided start-up support for the comprehensive Federal Program in Building Practices for Disaster Mitigation. This program will then enter the operational phase under the sponsorship of appropriate Federal mission agencies.

You should be aware of the results of one project in particular, a report on Building Practices for Disaster Mitigation. (Copies of the report have been made available to the Committee.) As part of the project, a workshop was held, concerned with earthquakes, extreme winds and similar dynamic hazards. The resulting recommendations have been made available to policy makers in government and industry as well as practitioners in engineering, architecture, land-use planning and the earth and meteorological sciences. These recommendations evaluate current building practices, define opportunities for improving current practice, and recommend research to fill gaps in knowledge. The workshop, resulting documentation, and various follow-on activities represent an attempt by NSF/RANN to close a long-evident gap between research results and actual building practices. Ten of the 71 recommendations involve the subject area of this Committee and I would urge you to review them as you proceed in your deliberations. One of the recommendations is that disaster assistance be modified to provide incentives to communities and individuals to take preparedness measures that would lessen the impact of disaster, as S1840 would do.

Earthquake-induced failure of underground conduits presents special problems. The rupture of a natural gas or petroleum products pipeline or storage facility can cause significant fire hazards as well as large monetary losses. The failure of sewer water distribution systems can cause serious health problems and delay economic recovery. A new research initiative is therefore underway to improve the design, analysis, and synthesis of information on earthquake-resistant underground conduits. This effort will include developing design specification procedures for such underground facilities.

Recently the responsibility for the Seismological Field Survey (SFS) was transferred from NOAA to the Earthquake Engineering activity of NSF. The SFS is responsible for work in strong motion seismology and instrumentation. It analyzes the resulting data and develops input information for design of specific types of structures, taking into account the geological foundations, soil condition, frequency responses, and other parameters. The current instrumentation network is placed throughout the United States. The SFS is the Earthquake Engineering Program's principal instrument placement and data collection agent, and it serves as the focal point for the development and maintenance of a Federal earthquake strong motion instrumentation network.

The research efforts of the RANN program on *Fire Research*, focus on understanding the process of combustion for various materials, the fire spread mechanism, and the methods for extinguishing fires. Attention is also given to the modeling of fire propagation, the effectiveness of fire-fighting systems, and the deleterious effects of smoke. Research to improve the detection and suppression of fires is also supported. The NSF effort complements the role of NBS through a closely-coupled cooperative arrangement. The NSF effort provides the university research base that is needed in many areas important to the National Bureau of Standards and the fire protection community.

Efforts will continue to emphasize the development of projects related to the direct needs of the fire services, including new and improved fire equipment technology.

The major goal of the *Weather Modification* program is to develop sufficient understanding of extreme weather phenomena to reduce their social, economic, and ecological impacts upon society through the scientific application of weather modification technology.

The primary objectives are to:

1. Develop sufficient understanding of the mechanism of hail formation in severe storms to determine if, when, and how the formation of damaging hail can be suppressed by cloud seeding techniques;

2. Develop sufficient understanding of the nucleation process in clouds that the concentration, type, and injection characteristics of artificial nuclei required to accomplish the desired modification effect can be accurately determined;

3. Develop sufficient understanding of the mechanisms by which human habitation may produce anomalies in the weather patterns that adverse effects may be forecast in advance and corrective action taken to minimize the impact;

4. Develop new and more accurate concepts of how, when and under what circumstances weather can be modified by artificial means;

5. Assess the impact of planned weather modification operations upon the social, economic, legal, and ecological aspects of the environment.

Our principal emphasis is on hail suppression and a major 5-year project, the National Hail Research Experiment, is underway to determine whether artificial seeding of storm clouds can reduce or eliminate hail damage.

New technologies with important national applications can arise directly from advances in fundamental science. Recognizing this, NSF's Technological Opportunities program provides a way to capitalize rapidly on opportunities opened up by fundamental research and bring the fruits of the most advanced scientific developments more rapidly into purposeful application. Thus, laser research at the University of Washington has led to development of a two-color laser system that can measure earth strains with high reliability and accuracy. The potential of such a device for use in earthquake prediction is so great that a prototype instrument has been constructed and is undergoing field tests by the U.S. Geological Survey at Hollister, California.

Development of Broader Fundamental Understanding

It is important to recognize that the nation's future ability to deal with disasters, in terms of prediction, warning, or possible control is very much dependent on making investments now to develop fundamental understanding of these phenomena. A considerable amount of fundamental research at NSF is related to national disasters. The Foundation has an extensive program of basic research in the atmospheric sciences, including such subjects related to disasters as hurricane mechanisms and the climatological effects of droughts. An extensive atmospheric modeling program also contributes to the understanding of weather mechanisms. Particular attention also is directed to modeling of convective storms, mesoscale structure of weather systems, and the nature and behavior of tornadoes. Related to these are projects studying the nature of lightning strokes and the physical processes that generate them. NSF has developed a wind engineering program that includes examining the fluid mechanics of cyclonic winds; their formation, development, movement, and interaction with topographic and physical structures. In hydrology and hydraulics NSF supports conceptual models for streamflow simulation and research on dynamic flood routing.

Fundamental research in geophysics has been making great strides in recent years toward understanding the nature of the earth's crust and the basic mechanisms that cause earthquakes. This work is carried out in close liaison with the USGS and may lead to new techniques for the possible prediction and control of earthquakes by the Geological Survey.

Summary

I hope, Mr. Chairman, that I have shown that scientific research is of vital importance to improving the nation's ability to cope with major disasters. The four main tasks—*assessment of existing knowledge and practice; development of new socioeconomic and policy alternatives; development of new technological approaches to disaster mitigation; and development of a broader fundamental understanding*—which I have described are difficult and challenging. They require a vigorous and long term commitment, both of ourselves, in the Federal community, and of the research community, where the work must be done. I believe that the necessary commitment is there, that good progress is being made, and that much will be accomplished in the years ahead to reduce the tragic toll that nature imposes upon man.

Appendix IV

The Modified Mercalli Scale of Earthquake Intensity

I. Not felt except by a very few who might live in an extremely undisturbed environment—no vibrations from passing cars, refrigerators, or other machinery.

II. Felt by only a few persons who are resting, especially on upper floors of buildings. Delicately suspended objects may swing.

III. Felt quite noticeably indoors, especially on upper floors of buildings, but many people do not recognize it as an earthquake. Standing automobiles may rock slightly. Vibrations are similar to those of a passing truck. It is possible to estimate the duration of the tremor.

IV. During the day felt indoors by many, outdoors by a few. At night some are awakened. Dishes, windows, and doors are disturbed. Walls make cracking sounds. Sensation similar to a heavy truck striking a building. Standing automobiles rock noticeably.

V. Felt by nearly everyone. Many are awakened at night. Some dishes, windows, and other glass objects are broken. In some places, there is broken plaster. Unstable objects are turned over. Trees, poles, and other tall objects are visibly disturbed. Pendulum clocks may stop.

VI. Felt by all. Many frightened and run outdoors. Some heavy furniture moved. Some instances of falling plaster and damaged chimneys. Other damage slight.

VII. Everyone runs outdoors. Damage is negligible in buildings of good design and construction, slight to moderate in well-constructed buildings, considerable in poorly built or badly designed structures. Some chimneys broken. People driving cars notice shaking.

VIII. Damage slight in specially designed structures; considerable in ordinary substantial buildings, with some suffering partial collapse; great in poorly built structures. Panel walls torn out of frame structures. Chimneys, factory stacks, columns, monuments, and walls fall. Heavy furniture is overturned. Underground sand and mud are ejected to the surface in small amounts. There are changes, in level and clarity, in well water. People driving automobiles are perturbed.

285

IX. Damage considerable in specially designed structures; well-designed frame structures thrown out of plumb; damage great in substantial buildings, with some suffering partial collapse. Buildings shifted off foundations. Ground is conspicuously cracked. Underground pipes are broken.

X. Some well-built wooden structures are destroyed. Most masonry and frame structures destroyed along with their foundations; ground badly cracked. Rails are bent. Numerous landslides around river banks and steep slopes. Sand and mud are shifted. Water is splashed over banks.

XI. Few, if any, masonry structures remain standing. Bridges are destroyed. Broad fissures open in the ground. Underground pipelines are put completely out of service. Earth slumps and land slips in soft ground. Rails are greatly bent.

XII. Damage total. Waves seen are reportedly moving across solid surfaces. Lines of sight and level are distorted. Objects are thrown upward in the air.

Appendix V

Curriculum Vitae of the Authors

PHILLIP HERMAN LISS

Born in Brooklyn, New York, November 23, 1939 at 2:20 P.M. Third child of Polish-Jewish (father White Russian) immigrants. Graduated from Stuyvesant High School. Queens College, BSc, 1961. Pianist in the Catskills for four summers. Woodrow Wilson Fellow. Graduate studies at McGill University, Montreal, with a PhD in physiological psychology, 1965. NIH Postdoctoral Fellow, 1965, at the Nencki Institute of Experimental Biology, Warsaw, Poland. Research associate and lecturer in the psychology department, Massachusetts Institute of Technology, 1966. Research Laboratory of the Electronics Information Processing Group, MIT, 1967. Center for Cognitive Studies, Harvard University, 1968. Assistant professor of psychology at City College, CUNY until 1971. Associate professor of psychology at the Institute for Cognitive Studies, Rutgers University, Newark, N.J., until 1974. Lives in Manhattan with wife, Barbara, and second child.

ALFRED LAMBREMONT WEBRE III

Born, Pensacola, Florida, May 24, 1942 at 8:42 P.M. First of nine children (eight boys, one girl) of Louisiana Creole father and Cuban-American mother. Reared in rural Cuba and southeastern U.S. Attended schools in Cuba, Florida, Louisiana, New Jersey, and Maryland. Graduate of Georgetown Preparatory School, Garrett Park, Maryland, in classics. Undergraduate in industrial administration honors at Yale University, 1964. Yale Catholics Abroad, Xalapa, Mexico, summer, 1964. Apprentice Ironworker, Summer 1965 and 1966. Graduate of Yale Law School in international trade, 1967. Assistant in instruction, economics department, Yale University, 1965–67. Fulbright Scholar, Montevideo, Uruguay, 1967–68. Practiced international law with Cleary, Gottlieb, Steen & Hamilton, New York City, 1968–70. General counsel and assistant administrator, New York City Environmental Protection Administration, 1971 through March, 1973. Consultant in environmental matters to the Ford Foundation, 1973–74. Lives in Manhattan with wife, Teresa, and one child.

References

INTRODUCTION

1. Professor P. J. Wyllie of the University of Chicago characterizes the dimension of the revolution in earth sciences as follows:

> J. Wilson Tuzo considers the revolution [in the earth sciences] to be similar to, and as significant as, that which changed the approach to chemistry about 1800, that which occurred in biology about a century ago with the introduction of Darwin's theory of evolution, and that which occurred in physics when classical views were replaced by modern. . . . The new global tectonics challenges all of the past tectonic theories based on fixist or stabilist concepts.

In *The Dynamic Earth* (New York: John Wylie & Sons, 1971)), p. 266. See also Bruce C. Heezen and Ian D. MacGregor, "Riddles Chalked on the Ocean Floor," *Saturday Review* (February 19, 1972), p. 58.

PART I

Epigraph

1. Philip Drew, *Third Generation—The Changing Meaning of Architecture* (New York: Praeger Publishers, 1972), p. 9.
2. Allen L. Hammond, "Earthquake Predictions: Breakthrough in Theoretical Insights?" *Science,* vol. 180 (May 25, 1973), p. 851.

Chapter 1

1. Heezen, *op. cit.,* p. 58. Wyllie, *op. cit.,* p. 345.
2. See National Academy of Sciences, *Seismology: Responsibilities and Requirements of a Growing Science,* 1969. D. P. McKenzie and J. G. Sclater cite the traditional opposition of land-trained geologists to the continental drift postulates of the oceanographers. This opposition has now largely ceased in the face of overwhelming dominance of plate tectonics. "The Evolution of the Indian Ocean," *Scientific American,* vol. 228 (May, 1973), p. 67.
3. The primitive continent—known as Gondwanaland—may have existed as recently as 150 million years ago, fitting these individual continents

together in a massive jigsaw puzzle. Eventually, with the breakup of this one land mass into five drifting continents, there came the collision with other continents, and the formation of mountain ranges and land bridges. The Himalayas, for example, are thought to be the result of the collision of India—then drifting northeastward on a single tectonic plate—with Asia. D. P. McKenzie, *et al.*, *op. cit.*, pp. 63 *et seq.*

4. D. P. McKenzie, *op. cit.*, p. 67.
5. United Nations. Report of the Secretary General entitled "Assistance in Cases of Natural Catastrophe," E/4994. May 13, 1971.
6. New York *Times* (February 15, 1974), p. 43.
7. *The Economist* (June 23, 1973), pp. 27–28.

CHAPTER 2

1. Executive Office of the President, Office of Emergency Preparedness. *Disaster Preparedness.* Report to the Congress, January, 1972. OEP Report, vol. III, p. 80, table I.
2. OEP Report, vol. 1, chapter 1.
3. U.S. Coast and Geodetic Survey. Earthquake History of the United States. U.S. Government Printing Office, 1956.
4. National Academy of Sciences, *op. cit.*
5. A. L. Hammond, *op. cit.*, p. 852 *et seq.*
6. Christopher H. Scholz, Lynn R. Sykes, and Yash P. Aggarwal, "The Physical Basis for Earthquake Prediction," *Science*, vol. 181, no. 4102 (August 31, 1973), p. 803.
7. OEP Report, *op. cit.*, vol. 1, p. 78.
8. Peter Briggs, *Will California Fall Into the Sea?* (New York: David McKay & Co., 1972).
9. *Nature*, vol. 241 (January 12, 1973), p. 85.
10. Scholz, *et al.*, *op. cit.*
11. Conversation with Christopher Scholz, Lamont Geological Laboratories, Columbia University, June, 1973.
12. OEP Report, vol. III, p. 75.
13. OEP Report, vol. III, p. 77.
14. New York *Times* (February 11, 1971), p. 32:2.
15. California Legislature Joint Committee on Seismic Safety. Earthquake Risk Conference, September, 1971, reported in OEP Report vol. 1, p. 74.
16. New York *Times* (February 14, 1971), p. 72:3.
17. OEP Report, vol. I; National Oceanic and Atmospheric Administration, *A Study of Earthquake Losses in the San Francisco Bay Area: Data and Analysis* (1972); National Oceanic and Atmospheric Administration, *A Study of Earthquake Losses in the Los Angeles, California Area* (1973).
18. OEP Report, vol. III, pp. 100 *et seq.*

19. OEP Report, vol. III, p. 103.
20. Seismic Risk Map of the Conterminous United States, after S. T. Algermissen, "Seismic Risk Studies in the United States," Proceedings of the Fourth World Conference on Earthquake Engineering (vol. 1, pp. 19–27), Santiago, Chile, 1969. In OEP Report, vol. III, p. 79.
21. Office of Science and Technology. Task Force on Earthquake Hazard Reduction. August, 1970.
22. Testimony of Dr. Clarence R. Allen, U.S. Senate, *Governmental Response to the California Earthquake Disaster of February, 1971*. Hearings before the Committee on Public Works, San Fernando, California. 92 Congress, 1st Session, 1971, pp. 562–563.
23. National Academy of Sciences, National Research Council. *The Great Alaska Earthquake of 1964*. 1970, p. 27.
24. Carl Kisslinger, *Geotimes*, vol. 18 (January, 1973), p. 30.
25. U.S. Coast and Geodetic Survey, *op. cit.*
26. New York *Post* (June 16, 1973), p.2.
27. U.S. Coast and Geodetic Survey, p. 12.
28. New York *Times* (November 21, 1971), p. 57:1.
29. New York *Times*, various editions, 1971 and 1972.
30. Most of the data cited here were derived from the Smithsonian Institution Center for Short-Lived Phenomena, *The Pulse of the Planet*. Harmony Books, 1972. A number were derived from the New York *Times* and from radio broadcast reports.
31. New York *Times* (June 19, 1972), p. 7:1, and (June 22, 1972), p. 19:8.
32. Robert W. Kates, *et al.*, "Human Impact of the Managua Earthquake," *Science*, vol. 182 (December 7, 1973), pp. 984–985.
33. *Reader's Digest* (May, 1973), pp. 128–131.
34. Kates, *et al.*, *op. cit.*, p. 989.

CHAPTER 3

1. Charles F. Richter, *Elementary Seismology* (San Francisco: W. H. Freeman & Co., 1958), p. 407.
2. Smithsonian Institution, *op. cit.*
3. OEP Report, vol. III, p. 119.
4. OEP Report, vol. III, p. 121.

CHAPTER 4

1. Tom Alexander, "Ominous Changes in the World's Weather." *Fortune* (vol. XXXIX, No. 2, February, 1974), p. 94.
2. *Ibid.*, p. 152.

3. *Ibid.*, p. 95.
4. *National Enquirer* (November 25, 1973).
5. New York *Times* (June 24, 1973), p. 32.
6. Smithsonian Institution, *op. cit.*
7. *The Economist* (June 23, 1973), p. 27.
8. Rhoades W. Fairbridge, "Climatology of a Glacial Cycle," *Quarternary Research,* vol. 2, no. 3 (November, 1972), p. 300.
9. *The Economist* (June 23, 1973), p. 28.
10. Alexander, *op. cit.*, p. 152.

CHAPTER 5

1. A. L. Hammond, "Earthquake Prediction (II): Prototype Instrumental Networs," *Science* (June 1, 1973), p. 938.
2. Personal communication from Roy S. Popkin, Assistant National Director, Disaster Services, The American National Red Cross, dated May 22, 1973. (A coordinated federal earthquake group has recently been formed under the U.S. Coast and Geodetic Survey, and will be headed by Robert Hamilton.)
3. OEP Report, vol. 1, p. 9.
4. OEP Report, vol. 1, p. 76.
5. *Report of the Los Angeles County Earthquake Commission, San Fernando Earthquake* (February 9, 1971), p. 21.
6. August H. Groeschel, "Study of the medical aspects of the Los Angeles Earthquake," memorandum to the director, OEP, February 22, 1971. OEP Report, vol. 1, p. 82.
7. National Academy of Sciences. *The Great Alaska Earthquake of 1964, op. cit., Human Ecology,* p. 14.

CHAPTER 6

1. Haroun Tazieff, *When the Earth Trembles* (New York: Harcourt, Brace & World, 1964), p. 4.
2. Alvin Toffler, *Future Shock* (New York: Random House, 1970), p. 308.
3. *Ibid.*, p. 307.
4. OEP Report, vol. I, p. 53.
5. Charles F. Richter, "Our Earthquake Risk—Facts and Non-facts," *California Institute of Technology Quarterly,* Winter 1963–64, vol. 5, no. 2, p. 2.

6. Peter Briggs, *op. cit.*
7. Executive Office of the President, Office of Emergency Preparedness. Report of OEP Conference on the Psychological Effects of Disasters (March 16, 1973).
8. *Wall Street Journal*, vol. CLXXXI, no. 112 (June 8, 1973), p. 1.
9. *Ibid.*, p. 20.
10. *Congressional Record* (April 19, 1973), p. E2531.
11. Report of OEP Conference on the Psychological Effects of Disasters. *op. cit.*, p. 3.

CHAPTER 7

1. OEP Report, vol. 1, p. 9.
2. OEP Report, vol. 1, p. 131.
3. "Prediction of Earthquakes," Earthquake Research Institute, University of Tokyo (January, 1962).

CHAPTER 8

1. OEP Report, vol. I, p. 9.
2. *Ibid.*, p. 84.

CHAPTER 9

1. C. F. Richter, "Earthquake Disasters—An International Problem," International Meeting on Earthquakes, San Francisco, May, 1971. NATO Committee on the Challenges of Modern Society.
2. OEP Report, vol. 1, p. 76.
3. *Building the American City,* Report of the National Commission on Urban Problems to the Congress and to the President. 91st Cong. 1st Sess. Document no. 91-34 (1938) p. 210.
4. Task Force on Earthquake Hazard Reduction, *op. cit.*, p. 21.
5. Gene Bryerton, *Nuclear Dilemma* (New York: Ballantine Books, 1970), p. 30.
6. New York *Times* (September 14, 1972), p. 21:1
7. *Ibid.*, April 6, 1972.
8. C. F. Richter, "Our Earthquake Risk—Facts and Non-facts."

9. Task Force on Land Use and Urban Growth. "Land Use and Urban Growth," synopsis of report (May, 1973), p. 3.
10. OEP Report, vol. I, p. 130.
11. New York *Times*(January 29, 1971).
12. *Ibid.*
13. *Ibid.*
14. C. F. Richter, "Earthquake Disasters."

CHAPTER 10

1. U.S. Department of Housing and Urban Development, "Summary and Recommendation of Studies in Seismicity and Earthquake Damage Statistics by ESSA," 1969, p. 53b.
2. *Ibid.*, p. 75.
3. Task Force on Earthquake Hazard Reduction, *op. cit.*, p. 43.

CHAPTER 11

1. Report on the United Nations Conference on the Human Environment. A/Conf. 48/14 (July 3, 1972).
2. United Nations. Report of the Secretary General, *op. cit.*

PART II

CHAPTER 1

1. C. F. Richter, "Our Earthquake Risk," p. 3.
2. Arthur Koestler, *The Roots of Coincidence* (New York: Random House, 1972), p. 43 *et seq.*
3. *Ibid.*, p. 14.
4. Gertrude R. Schmeidler and R. A. McConnell, *ESP and Personality Patterns* (New Haven: Yale University Press, 1958). Also personal communication on recent findings, 1971 and 1972.
5. Personal communication, December, 1972.
6. Arthur Koestler, *op. cit.*, p. 21.

Chapter 2

1. Alan Vaughan, *Patterns of Prophecy* (New York, Hawthorn, 1973).
2. Hal Lindsey, *The Late, Great Planet Earth* (New York, Bantam, 1973).

Chapter 3

1. Hugh Lynn Cayce, *Venture Inward* (New York, Paperback Library, 1964).
2. Thomas Sugrue, *There is a River* (New York, Dell, 1942).
3. Anonymous, *Earth Changes* (Virginia Beach, A.R.E. Press, 1959), reprinted 1971 with addendum dated March 26, 1968.
4. Immanuel Velikovsky, *Earth in Upheaval* (New York, Dell, 1955), p. 16.
5. *Ibid.*, p. 17.
6. The following references are to catalogued readings by Edgar Cayce. They are referenced according to their index number in the collection at the Association for Research and Enlightenment, Virginia Beach, Virginia. 377–8.
7. Cayce, *op. cit.*, 3976–15.
8. *Ibid.*, 3976–15.
9. *Ibid.*, 1152–11.
10. *Ibid.*, 294–185.
11. *Ibid.*, 270–30 (February, 1933).
12. *Earth Changes, op. cit.*, p. 35.
13. Cayce, *op. cit.*, 364–3.
14. *Id.*
15. Cayce, *op. cit.*, 958–3.
16. *Earth Changes, op. cit.*, p. 74.
17. Robert Ferro and Michael Grumley, *Autobiography of a Search* (New York: Doubleday, 1970).
18. *Ibid.*, p. 165.
19. *Ibid.*, p. 161.
20. *Ibid.*, p. 151.
21. *Ibid..*, p. 163.
22. Personal communication, June, 1973. Robert Ferro and Michael Grumley.
23. Cayce, *op. cit.*, 270–35.
24. *Earth Changes, op. cit.*, p. 39.
25. *Geotimes, op. cit.*, p. 32.

26. Cayce, *op. cit.*, 826–8.
27. *Ibid.*, 3976–15.
28. *Earth Changes, op. cit.*, p. 45.
29. Arthur Koestler, *op. cit.*, p. 135.
30. Immanuel Velikovsky, *op. cit.*, p. 140.
31. *Ibid.*, p. 142.
32. *Ibid.*, p. 111.
33. *Ibid.*, p. 110.
34. *Ibid.*, p. 17.
35. *Ibid.*, p. 223.
36. Cayce, *op. cit.*, 254–57.
37. *Ibid.*, 3620–1.
38. *Ibid.*, 416–17.
39. *Ibid.*, 3976–19.
40. Mary Ellen Carter, *Edgar Cayce on Prophecy* (New York: Paperback Library, 1968), p. 78.
41. *Ibid.*, p. 79.
42. C. P. Idyll, "The Anchovy Crisis," *Scientific American* (June, 1973), vol. 228, no. 6, p. 28.
43. *Ibid.*, p. 29.

PART III

CHAPTER 1

1. Lynton K. Caldwell, *In Defense of the Earth* (Bloomington: Indiana University Press, 1972), p. 3.
2. Richard A. Falk, *This Endangered Planet* (New York: Random House, 1971), p. 353.
3. *Ibid.*, p. 292.

CHAPTER 2

1. John McHale, *World Facts and Trends* (New York: Macmillan, 1972).
2. *Ibid.*, p. 29.

3. U.N. Conference on the Human Environment. Human Settlements for Environmental Quality. A/Conf. 48/6.
4. John McHale, *op. cit.*, p. 10.
5. Josué de Castro, *The Black Book of Hunger* (Boston: Beacon Press, 1967), p. 7.
6. Georg Borgstrom, *The Hungry Planet* (New York: Macmillan & Co., 1967), p. 53.
7. Josué de Castro, *op. cit.*, p. 8.
8. Georg Borgstrom, *op. cit.*, p. 51.
9. Colin Clark, *Starvation or Plenty?* (New York: Taplinger Publishing Co., 1970), p. 154.
10. John McHale, p. 39.
11. John G. Fuller, *Incident at Exeter* (New York: Putnam), p. 236.
12. *Ibid.*

Chapter 3

1. John McHale, p. 43.
2. *Ibid.*, p. 69.
3. *Ibid.*, p. 44.
4. *Ibid.* p. 49.
5. Calvin Kentfield, "The River Did Not Stay Away," *The New York Times Magazine* (July 15, 1973), p. 14.
6. Richard A. Falk, *op. cit.*, p. 286.
7. *Ibid.*, p. 285.

Chapter 4

1. Friedrich A. Hayek, *The Constitution of Liberty* (Chicago: Henry Regnery Company, 1960), pp. 20 and 21.
2. *Ibid.*, p. 31.

Chapter 5

1. John McHale, *op. cit.*, p. 82.
2. *Ibid.*, p. 83.

Chapter 7

1. U.N. Report on the Human Environment, *op. cit.*, Principle No. 6.

Epilogue

Chapter 3

1. New York *Times* (February 3, 1974), p. 38.
2. U.S. Department of Commerce, *Statistical Abstract of the United States*, 1972, p. 372, No. 595.

Index

299

301